Best-Selling Chapters

MIDDLE LEVEL

Chapters from 10 Books for Young
Adults—With Lessons for Teaching
the Basic Elements of Literature

Raymond Harris

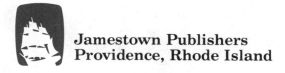

Jamestown Publishers
Providence, Rhode Island

Best-Selling Chapters, Middle Level

Chapters from 10 Books for Young Adults—With Lessons for Teaching the Basic Elements of Literature

Catalog No. 790

Copyright ©1982 by Jamestown Publishers, Inc.

Cover and text design by Deborah Hulsey Christie
Illustrations by Howard B. Lewis, Jr.

Printed in the United States

DO 82 83 84 85 7 6 5 4 3 2

ISBN: 0-89061-248-X

Contents

look
at

summarize
these idea
on a list of
things to think
about while
reading the
bounty.

Acknowledgments

Acknowledgment is gratefully made to the following publishers and authors for permission to reprint excerpts from these works:

Julie of the Wolves. Text excerpt from *Julie of the Wolves* by Jean Craighead George. Text copyright © 1972 by Jean Craighead George. By permission of Harper & Row, Publishers, Inc.

Summer of My German Soldier. Excerpted from the book *Summer of My German Soldier* by Bette Greene. Copyright © 1973 by Bette Greene. Reprinted by permission of The Dial Press.

A Day No Pigs Would Die. Text excerpt from *A Day No Pigs Would Die* by Robert Newton Peck. Copyright © 1972 by Robert Newton Peck. Reprinted by permission of Alfred A. Knopf, Inc.

To Kill a Mockingbird. Text excerpt from *To Kill a Mockingbird* by Harper Lee (J.B. Lippincott Company). Copyright © 1960 by Harper Lee. Reprinted by permission of Harper & Row, Publishers, Inc.

Of Mice and Men. Text excerpt from *Of Mice and Men* by John Steinbeck. Copyright © 1937, renewed 1965 by John Steinbeck. Reprinted by permission of Viking Penguin, Inc.

Mom, the Wolf Man and Me. Text excerpt from *Mom, the Wolf Man and Me* by Norma Klein. Copyright © 1972 by Norma Klein. Reprinted by permission of Pantheon Books, a division of Random House, Inc.

A Separate Peace. Text excerpt from *A Separate Peace* by John Knowles. Copyright © 1959 by John Knowles. Published by Macmillan Publishing Company. Reprinted by permission of Curtis Brown, Ltd.

Anne Frank: The Diary of a Young Girl. Excerpts from *Anne Frank: The Diary of a Young Girl* by Anne Frank. Copyright © 1952 by Otto H. Frank. Reprinted by permission of Doubleday & Company, Inc. Canadian rights by permission of Vallentine, Mitchell & Co., Ltd.

Johnny Tremain. Text excerpt from *Johnny Tremain* by Esther Forbes. Copyright © 1943 by Esther Forbes Hoskins; copyright © renewed 1971 by Linwood M. Erskine, Jr., Executor of Estate. Reprinted by permission of Houghton Mifflin Company.

The Hobbit. Text excerpts from *The Hobbit* by J.R.R. Tolkien. Copyright © 1966 by J.R.R. Tolkien. Reprinted by permission of Houghton Mifflin Company. Canadian rights by permission of George Allen & Unwin Publishers, Ltd.

Gratitude and thanks are also due the teachers and librarians who contributed suggestions and generously shared their knowledge of what young readers like, especially Roger Genest, Barbara Menard, Ben Nicholson, Lucinda Ray, Pam Shoemaker and Peg Vohr.

Finally, Christine Powers Harris has been the sustaining force of the entire effort. Her insights and talents are reflected in all the lessons, and especially in the unit on fantasy.

To the Teacher

Introduction

Ever since the appearance of *Best-Selling Chapters* there have been requests from teachers in the middle school and junior high grades for a comparable book at a lower reading level for their students. *Best-Selling Chapters, Middle Level* is the response to these requests.

We have assembled chapters from books that have proven themselves favorites among young readers, and we have designed lessons around them with just enough challenge to demonstrate the obvious pleasures of familiarity with basic elements of literature. In addition, accompanying exercises allow students to prove to themselves that they can read with insight and understanding.

The selections are all contemporary. Four were chosen from among the best of recent "young adult" novels: *Julie of the Wolves, Summer of My German Soldier, A Day No Pigs Would Die* and *Mom, the Wolf Man and Me*. Three other chapters are from contemporary classics which were not written for any special age group, but which have been taken to heart by middle school and junior high readers as enduring favorites: *Of Mice and Men, A Separate Peace* and *To Kill a Mockingbird*.

For the last three selections we thought it appropriate to offer popular reading that would introduce students to the idea of genre. *The Hobbit* is a delightful book for teaching fantasy. *Anne Frank: The Diary of a Young Girl* is an important document for our times and is so popular among young teens and pre-teens that it seems a good choice for introducing students to the genres of autobiography and biography. Esther Forbes's brilliant concept of showing a boy experiencing the American Revolution with some of its great heroes makes *Johnny Tremain* one of the best ways of introducing the special thrills of historical novels.

The Contents of a Unit

Here is what you will find in each unit:

1. An Illustration with Questions for Discussion. Each unit opens with an illustration which is accompanied by questions for discussion on the following page. The illustration and questions are designed to play an important role in the students' experience of both the reading selection and the lesson. The illustration shows a key scene from the story in order to spark the students' interest, thereby generating questions and expectations that will make the students more actively involved in the reading they will do. The questions for discussion focus attention on aspects of the illustration's detail and composition that correspond to the literary element being taught in the lesson. Discussion of the illustration, then, will accomplish several important things. It will preview the reading selection in a way that will excite interest and create an audience that participates. Perhaps more importantly, it will give the students experience in looking critically at something, encouraging them to see that their responses, whether it be to writing or drawing, are the result of details and patterns carefully planned out and executed by the artist, and are not "just opinions." Finally, they will gain valuable experience in expressing, developing and supporting their ideas orally.

2. The Reading Selection. With a few exceptions, the reading selections are unabridged, unadapted originals taken from the books. The chapter from *The Hobbit* has been judiciously shortened since it was too long, when accompanied by a lesson, for students to handle comfortably. Representative selections were taken from *Anne Frank: The Diary of a Young Girl.* Students of average reading ability in grades 6–9 will be able to complete their reading of a selection in a sitting or two.

3. The Literary Lesson. Each lesson explains a literary concept in a general way. Then four major elements of the concept are discussed one at a time in connection with passages from the selection. Students are then given other passages to work with to demonstrate their new knowledge and ability.

4. Skill-Oriented Comprehension Questions. The fifteen Comprehension Questions provide a quick check on five major reading skills. Each question is labeled with the skill it tests. A Comprehension Skills Profile is provided at the back of the book so that you can keep track of the kinds of questions students miss most often. A Comprehension Scores Graph helps you keep track of overall progress in reading comprehension.

5. Discussion Guides. Nine discussion questions with each unit are divided into three categories: discussing the literary element of the lesson, discussing the story, and discussing the author's work. Answering these questions will encourage students to a thoughtful review of their reading and give them practice in discussing pieces of literature.

6. The Writing Exercise. Practice in reading is not quite complete without some parallel practice in writing. The writing exercise in each unit is directly related to what has been learned in the lesson.

The best follow-up to a lesson and chapter, of course, is to have students read the whole book. Where there is a larger body of work by the same author, encourage students to find and read these books as well. Like adult readers, students latch on to authors they know and like.

How to Use This Book

This text, used creatively, can be an effective tool for teaching students basic literary concepts. Here are some suggestions for using this text successfully:

1. Discuss the Illustration Using the Accompanying Questions. Ask students to look carefully at the illustration which begins each unit. While they are studying the illustration, begin the discussion by reading aloud the first question connected with the illustration and suggesting that the class as a group should arrive at an answer for it as a conclusion to the discussion. Then ask the other suggested questions about the illustration to lead up to the conclusion. Emphasize the importance of the students' supporting or clarifying what they say by pointing out details in the picture. When you feel that the students see how the illustration works to make a particular impression on them, return to the first question. Have the class work together to summarize what's been said so that this first question can be answered.

2. Emphasize the Questions to Consider While Reading. Read aloud together the four questions at the end of each Introduction. Discuss what the students should look for in the reading selection in order to be able to answer the questions. The questions are designed to guide the students' reading of the selection towards an awareness of the literary concept that will be discussed in the lesson; this preview discussion will help the students to keep the questions in mind while they read.

3. Have Students Read the Selection. Tell students to read the selection carefully and to think about the introductory questions while they read. Have them take note of places in the selection that might help them to answer those questions. Remind them that they will have to answer Comprehension Questions about what they read.

4. Explain the Exercises. Each lesson is divided into four sections with an exercise following each section. Explain that the exercises should be completed as the students come to them. Using the Answer Key which starts on page 433, students should check their answers when they finish each exercise. Emphasize the importance of their understanding wrong answers before they go any further in the lesson.

5. Have Students Answer the Comprehension Questions. Without looking back at the reading selection, students should go on to answer the Comprehension Questions which focus on five important reading skills:

      a. Recognizing Words in Context

      b. Recalling Facts

      c. Keeping Events in Order

      d. Making Inferences

      e. Understanding Main Ideas

6. Have Students Correct Their Answers. Using the Answer Key which starts on page 433, students can check their responses to the Comprehension Questions. It is important for students to see what the correct response is when they have made an error. Have students count the number of each kind of Comprehension Question they got wrong and record those numbers in the spaces provided at the end of the Comprehension Questions.

7. Have Students Record Their Progress. Students should graph the number of correct answers for each set of Comprehension Questions on the Comprehension Scores Graph at the back of the book. Using the numbers they have recorded at the end of each set of Comprehension Questions, they should keep track of the kinds of questions they get wrong by filling in the Comprehension Skills Profile.

    Students enjoy keeping track of their progress. The graph and profile show in a very concrete and easily understandable way the student's progress or lack of it. Seeing a clear representation of rising scores gives the student incentive to strive for improvement.

8. Go Over Discussion Guides and Writing Exercises. Use the Discussion Guides and Writing Exercises to guide students through a more thoughtful review of their reading. The questions and exercises will reinforce what students have learned from the lesson and will encourage them to use that knowledge in talking and writing.

9. Check Graphs and Profiles Regularly. Establish a routine for reviewing each student's progress. Discuss what you are looking for with each student and the kind of progress you expect. Establish guidelines and warning signals so that students will know when to approach the teacher for counseling and advice.

To the Student

This textbook can help you to become a better reader. Its goal is not to make you memorize facts or details. Instead, its goal is to help you enjoy and understand your reading. It teaches you how to become more involved in what you read. Once you do that, books will have more meaning for you.

The reading selections in this book have been chosen because they have proved to be favorites among young people. There is a selection from each of ten different books that you will probably enjoy. Each selection has an introduction that provides hints about what the rest of the book is like so that you will see how exciting and interesting it is. Be sure to read the introductions. They are important for understanding the reading selection.

Each reading selection is followed by a lesson. In the lesson, you will learn about how a story is written. Writing a story takes certain skills—the author's "tricks of the trade," so to speak. The lessons point out some of these skills and how they work in the stories. You will read descriptions of things like plot, character and setting. You will begin to see how authors use language and how they tell you their ideas. Exercises that go with the lessons allow you to practice and "show off" what you have learned. Comprehension Questions, Discussion Guides and a Writing Exercise which come after the lesson let you check to see how well you understand the lesson as a whole.

Lessons and skills that you learn here will serve you well even beyond your school career. In the future, you will read with a sharper eye. You will be alert to details and ideas that you may have missed before.

You can also use some of what you learn here in your life outside school. Skills that you learn in order to read well can also be used in talking or thinking about people. Understanding more about characters in novels can help you to understand more about people that you know. Grasping ideas is another skill you learn in reading that you can apply in your life. You will also learn about detecting changes in tone and putting your finger on the source of conflict.

Whatever effort you put into using this text will reward you with increased abilities. You will read with better judgment and more enjoyment. And you will learn to be more alert to what goes on in your life and the world around you.

Unit 1   Setting

Julie of the Wolves
BY JEAN CRAIGHEAD GEORGE

About the Illustration

How do you think the girl in this drawing feels? What might she be thinking about? Point out some details in the drawing to support your response.

Here are some questions to help you think:

☐ How would you describe this beach? How does it make you feel? What details make you feel that way?

☐ Would you like to change places with this girl? Why or why not?

Unit 1

Introduction   What the Novel Is About/What the Lesson Is About

Selection   **Julie of the Wolves**

Lesson   **Setting**

Activities   Comprehension Questions/Discussion Guides/Writing Exercise

Introduction

What the Novel Is About

Julie is a thirteen-year-old Alaskan girl. Her Eskimo name is Miyax, and this is what she is called throughout most of *Julie of the Wolves*. She is Julie only in the white settlements and among Eskimos who have adopted the "new" ways.

As *Julie of the Wolves* opens, Miyax is running away from an arranged marriage to a boy, Daniel, whom she finds hateful. She intends to cross the Arctic plains (the tundra) on foot to Point Hope. There she will catch a steamer to San Francisco where she has a pen pal, Amy. But things don't work out quite as she has planned. She becomes lost in the grassy wilderness, realizes she is walking in circles and finds herself in danger of starving to death.

Luckily, she had spent a great deal of time watching and listening to her father, Kapugen, when she was growing up. Kapugen was an expert hunter and taught Miyax many of the old Eskimo skills necessary for survival in the harsh northern climate. One thing he had told her was that wolves could be useful in helping to find food. "Wolves are brotherly," he had said. "They love each other, and if you learn to speak to them, they will love you too." The fear that wolves eat people— "That's *gussak* talk. Wolves are brothers," Kapugen had insisted.

Miyax finds herself camped near a den of wolves—several adults and a few pups. She gives them all names, calling the leader Amaroq, and sets about figuring out how to "talk" to them. She wants to show them that she is hungry and needs food. She hopes that somehow she can get the wolves to bring her food as they do for their pups.

By watching with great patience, Miyax learns the meaning of signs and actions the wolves make among themselves and she copies them. She learns their "body language." She finds she can communicate with them in this way. What happens finally is that a bond of love and respect develops between Miyax and the wolves.

From there the story tells of the adventures of Miyax and her wolf friends during the time that she makes her way to a coastal settlement and civilization. Things go quite well for Miyax as long as she is in the wilderness living close to the land. The most disturbing and heart-stopping moments come as she begins to get close to civilization. And that conflict with civilization provides a lot of food for thought.

Anyone who likes stories of wilderness adventure will find *Julie of the Wolves* one of the finest of this kind.

In this unit we pick up the story at a point where the wolves have left Miyax to go their own way for awhile. Miyax thinks they have abandoned her. This causes her to think back to the time when she was small and living in a seal-hunting camp with her father, Kapugen. Her mother had died when Miyax was four, so she had been raised by Kapugen. He took her everywhere with him: to feasts, to seal hunts, and on long walks along the beaches or across the tundra. Her father was both teacher and companion for her and she adored him. Now she thinks he is dead and she recalls the years she spent with him as the happiest of her life.

What the Lesson Is About

The lesson that follows the reading selection is about setting.

The setting of a novel consists of many things. It is where the action of the story takes place and it is also the time when the story takes place. Setting is made up of sights and sounds and smells and feelings. It also includes people and the way they dress and act. It is scenery and animals and vehicles and anything else that helps readers understand where they are and what is going on in the story.

The questions below will help you to focus on setting in the chapter from *Julie of the Wolves*. Read the chapter carefully and try to answer these questions as you go along:

1 At the beginning of the selection, you will read about the day when Miyax's mother died. How do the descriptions of the setting make you feel at this point?

2 A little further along in the selection, the author describes Kapugen's house at seal camp. How does the author make you "really see" the setting?

3 There is a scene where a whale is caught. What does this scene make you think about Eskimos and the way they feel about animals and the outdoors?

4 Near the end of the reading selection, Miyax's Aunt Martha arrives at seal camp. How does the setting seem to change when she arrives?

Julie of the Wolves

Jean Craighead George

The wind, the empty sky, the deserted earth—Miyax had felt the bleakness of being left behind once before.

She could not remember her mother very well, for Miyax was scarcely four when she died, but she did remember the day of her death. The wind was screaming wild high notes and hurling ice-filled waves against the beach. Kapugen was holding her hand and they were walking. When she stumbled he put her on his shoulders, and high above the beach she saw thousands of birds diving toward the sea. The jaegers screamed and the sandpipers cried. The feathered horns of the comical puffins drooped low, and Kapugen told her they seemed to be grieving with him.

She saw this, but she was not sad. She was divinely happy going somewhere alone with Kapugen. Occasionally he climbed the cliffs and brought her eggs to eat; occasionally he took her in his arms and leaned against a rock. She slept at times in the warmth of his big sealskin parka. Then they walked on. She did not know how far.

Later, Kapugen's Aunt Martha told her that he had lost his mind the day her mother died. He had grabbed Miyax up and walked out of his fine house in Mekoryuk. He had left his important job as manager of the reindeer herd, and he had left all his possessions.

"He walked you all the way to seal camp," Martha told her. "And he never did anything good after that."

To Miyax the years at seal camp were infinitely good. The scenes and events were beautiful color spots in her memory. There was Kapugen's little house of driftwood, not far from the beach. It was rosy-gray on the outside. Inside it was gold-brown. Walrus tusks gleamed and drums, harpoons, and man's knives decorated the walls. The sealskin kayak beside the door glowed as if the moon had been stretched across it and its graceful ribs shone black. Dark gold and soft brown were the old men who sat around Kapugen's camp stove and talked to him by day and night.

The ocean was green and white, and was rimmed by fur, for she saw it through Kapugen's hood as she rode to sea with him on his back inside the parka. Through this frame she saw the soft eyes of the seals on the ice. Kapugen's back would grow taut as he lifted his arms and fired his gun. Then the ice would turn red.

The celebration of the Bladder Feast was many colors— black, blue, purple, fire-red; but Kapugen's hand around hers was rose-colored and that was the color of her memory of the Feast. A shaman, an old priestess whom everyone called "the bent woman," danced. Her face was streaked with black soot. When she finally bowed, a fiery spirit came out of the dark wearing a huge mask that jingled and terri- fied Miyax. Once, in sheer bravery, she peeked up under a mask and saw that the dancer was not a spirit at all but Naka, Kapugen's serious partner. She whispered his name and he laughed, took off his mask, and sat down beside Kapugen. They talked and the old men joined them. Later that day Kapugen blew up seal bladders and he and the old men carried them out on the ice. There they dropped them into the sea, while Miyax watched and listened to their songs. When she came back to camp the bent woman told her that the men had returned the bladders to the seals.

"Bladders hold the spirits of the animals," she said. "Now the spirits can enter the bodies of the newborn seals and keep them safe until we harvest them again." That night the bent woman seemed all violet-colored as she tied a piece of seal fur and blubber to Miyax's belt. "It's an *i'noGo tied,*" she said. "It's a nice little spirit for you."

Another memory was flickering-yellow—it was of the old men beating their drums around Kapugen's stove. She saw them through a scarf of tiny crystals that was her breath on the cold night air inside the house.

Naka and Kapugen were on their hands and knees, prancing lightly, moving swiftly. When Naka tapped Kapugen's chin with his head, Kapugen rose to his knees. He threw back his head, then rocked back on his heels. Naka sat up and together they sang the song of the wolves. When the dance was over the old men cheered and beat their paddle-like drums.

"You are wolves, you are real wolves," they had cried.

After that Kapugen told her about the wolves he had known on the mainland when he went to high school in Nome. He and his joking partner would hunt the wilderness for months, calling to the wolves, speaking their language to ask where the game was. When they were successful, they returned to Nome with sled-loads of caribou.

"Wolves are brotherly," he said. "They love each other, and if you learn to speak to them, they will love you too."

He told her that the birds and animals all had languages and if you listened and watched them you could learn about their enemies, where their food lay and when big storms were coming.

A silver memory was the day when the sun came over the horizon for the first time in winter. She was at the beach, close to Kapugen, helping him haul in a huge gleaming net. In it was a beautiful white whale. Out of sight on the other side of the whale, she could hear the old men as they cheered this gift from the sea.

The whale was a mountain so high she could not see the cliffs beyond, only the sunlit clouds. Kapugen's huge, black, frostbitten hand seemed small as it touched the great body of the whale.

Not far away the bent woman was dancing and gathering invisible things from the air. Miyax was frightened but Kapugen explained that she was putting the spirit of the whale in her i'noGo tied.

"She will return it to the sea and the whales," he said.

Walking the tundra with Kapugen was all laughter and fun. He would hail the blue sky and shout out his praise for the grasses and bushes. On these trips they ate salmon berries, then lay in the sun watching the birds. Sometimes Kapugen would whistle sandpiper songs and the birds would dip down to see which of their members had gotten lost in the grass. When they saw him and darted away, Kapugen would laugh.

Fishing with Kapugen was murky-tan in her memory, for they would wade out into the river mouth where the stone weirs were built and drive the fish into nets between the walls. Kapugen would spear them or grab them in his hand and throw them to the men in the wooden boats. Occasionally he skimmed after the biggest cod and halibut in his kayak and he would whoop with joy when he caught one and would hold it above his head. It gleamed as it twisted in the sun.

Summers at seal camp were not as beautiful to Miyax as the autumns and winters, for during this season many families from Mekoryuk came to Nash Harbor to hunt and fish and Kapugen was busy. Sometimes he helped people set nets; somtimes he scouted the ocean in his kayak as he searched for seal colonies.

During these hours Miyax was left with the other children on the beach. She played tag and grass ball with them and she pried prickly sea urchins off the rocks, to eat the sweet meat inside. Often she dug for clams and when

Julie of the Wolves

Kapugen returned he would crack them open and smack his lips as he swallowed them whole.

The Eskimos from Mekoryuk spoke English almost all the time. They called her father Charlie Edwards and Miyax was Julie, for they all had two names, Eskimo and English. Her mother had also called her Julie, so she did not mind her summer name until one day when Kapugen called her that. She stomped her foot and told him her name was Miyax. "I am Eskimo, not a gussak!" she had said, and he had tossed her into the air and hugged her to him.

"Yes, you are Eskimo," he had said. "And never forget it. We live as no other people can, for we truly understand the earth."

But winters always returned. Blizzards came and the temperatures dropped to thirty and forty below zero, and those who stayed at hunting camp spoke only in Eskimo and did only Eskimo things. They scraped hides, mended boots, made boats, and carved walrus tusks. In the evenings Kapugen sang and danced with the old men, and all of their songs and dances were about the sea and the land and the creatures that dwelled there.

One year, probably in September, for the canvas tents were down and the campground almost empty, Kapugen came into the house with a sealskin. It was a harbor seal, but had so few spots that it was a rare prize.

"We must make you a new coat," he had said. "You are getting big. Since your mother is not here to help us, I will do her work. Now watch and learn."

The skin was metallic silver-gold and so beautiful that even the velveteen parkas of the children from Mekoryuk paled by comparison. Miyax stroked it lovingly as Kapugen lay her old coat upon it and began to cut a larger one. As he worked he hummed, and she made up words about the seal who wanted to be a coat. Presently they became aware of the distant throb of a motorboat. The sound grew louder, then shut off at the beach. Footsteps crunched, the cold air rushed in the door, and there was Martha, Kapugen's aunt. She was thin and her face was pinched. Miyax disliked her immediately, but was spared the necessity of speaking nicely to her, for Martha had words only for Kapugen.

She talked swiftly in English, which Miyax barely understood, and she was angry and upset. Martha shook her finger at Kapugen and glanced at Miyax from time to time. The two were arguing very loudly when Martha pulled a sheet of paper from her pocket and showed it to Kapugen.

"No!" he shouted.

"We'll see!" Martha screamed, turned around, and went toward the boat where a white man waited. Kapugen followed her and stood by the boat, talking to the man for a long time.

The next morning Miyax was awakened as Kapugen lifted her up in his arms and held her close. Gently he pushed the hair out of her eyes and, speaking softly in Eskimo, told her she was going to live with Aunt Martha.

"There's a law that says you must go to school . . . and I guess you should. You are nine years old. And I must go to war. The government is fighting somewhere."

Miyax grabbed him around the neck, but did not protest. It never occurred to her that anything that Kapugen decided was not absolutely perfect. She whimpered however.

"Listen closely," he said. "If anything happens to me, and if you are unhappy, when you are thirteen you can leave Aunt Martha by marrying Daniel, Naka's son. Naka is going to Barrow on the Arctic Ocean. I shall make arrangements with him. He is like me, an old-time Eskimo who likes our traditions. He will agree."

Miyax listened carefully, then he put her down and hastily packed her bladder-bag, wrapped her in an oilskin against the wild spray of the sea, and carried her to the boat. She sat down beside Martha and stared bravely at Kapugen. The motor started and Kapugen looked at her until the boat moved, then he turned his back and walked quickly away. The launch sped up a huge wave, slammed down into a foaming trough, and Kapugen was no longer visible.

With that Miyax became Julie. She was given a cot near the door in Martha's little house and was soon walking to school in the darkness. She liked to learn the printed English words in books, and so a month passed rather happily.

One morning when the air was cold and the puddles around the house were solid ice, an old man from seal camp arrived at the door. He spoke softly to Martha, then pulled his hood tightly around his face and went away. Martha came to Miyax's bed.

"Your father," she said, "went seal hunting in that ridiculous kayak. He has been gone a month this day. He will not be back. Bits of his kayak washed up on the shore." Martha stumped to the fire and turned her back.

Julie ran out of the house into the dark morning. She darted past the store, the reindeer-packing house, the church. She did not stop until she came to the beach. There she crouched among the oil drums and looked out on the sea.

The wind blew across the water, shattering the tips of the waves and shooting ice-sparklets north with the storm. "Kapugen!" she called. No one answered. Kapugen was gone. The earth was empty and bleak.

Setting

Everyone is familiar with the cry of the director who is about to shoot a scene for a new movie: "Quiet on the set!" is the command. When all is ready, the next order is "Action!" Then the actors begin to play their roles in the setting that has been made for them.

Before they have gotten this far, however, great pains have been taken to set the scene just the way the director wants it. The reason such care is taken to set a scene is that the setting must do a great deal for the viewers when the movie is completed.

Think for a moment about a movie or television show you have seen recently. As soon as the show begins, you get some very distinct impressions. From the way people dress, the way they live, and the vehicles they ride in, you know at once where you are and if the story takes place in the present or in the the past. If it's a bright, sunny day in a park, you will tend to feel bright and sunny yourself. But if clouds are lowering darkly over a cemetery, you will probably scrunch down and get set for a good scare. If you are shown a mansion in Texas, you will begin to think about what it's like to be rich. If the setting is a city slum, you will begin to think about the problems of the poor.

So the setting does a number of things. It prepares a scene that allows you to believe you are really viewing a certain place at a certain time. The setting prepares you for the action that will take place. And because it makes you feel a certain way, the setting helps put you in the proper mood to appreciate that action. Setting also starts you thinking about important ideas that are presented through the movie.

Setting in a novel must do all of these same things. As a matter of fact, when you stop to think about it, every movie, TV show, or stage play must first be set down as a written story. The director must read the story and translate the settings into something you can hear and see. The difference when you read rather than view a story is that the sounds and settings must be projected on your mind rather than on a screen.

Setting is very important in understanding *Julie of the Wolves*. Julie's world is vastly different from anything most of us are used to. And before we can appreciate what is going on there, we must somehow be brought into that world. Author Jean George uses setting very skillfully to do just that.

In this lesson, we will look at how the author uses setting in four different ways:

1 Setting is used to make you feel a certain way about Julie's world.

2 Setting is used to make you imagine you are really on the scene.

3 Setting is used to present ideas that are important in the story.

4 Setting can help you understand and share in the action that takes place.

Settings can affect your feelings, and your feelings can affect the way you view a setting. It works both ways. For example, you might look at a lake ringed by pine trees and say, "I just love the peaceful beauty of this place!"

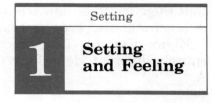

Setting

1 Setting and Feeling

But what if you had just seen someone drown in the lake? Then your feelings would likely create a totally different view of the setting: "The somber pine trees stared down on the murky waters where my friend died."

In *Julie of the Wolves*, Miyax (Julie's Eskimo name) often feels differently about the Arctic wilderness when she is alone from when she has loving companionship. In the following passages, Miyax is recalling the time when her mother died and she and her father, Kapugen, were left alone. Notice how the settings are used to emphasize the feelings expressed. And notice how Kapugen's feelings affect your view of the Arctic setting.

> The wind, the empty sky, the deserted earth—Miyax had felt the bleakness of being left behind once before.
>
> She could not remember her mother very well, for Miyax was scarcely four when she died, but she did remember the day of her death. The wind was screaming wild high notes and hurling ice-filled waves against the beach. Kapugen was holding her hand and they were walking. When she stumbled he put her on his shoulders, and high above the beach she saw thousands of birds diving toward the sea. The jaegers screamed and the sandpipers cried. The feathered horns of the comical puffins drooped low, and Kapugen told her they seemed to be grieving with him.

How lonely this setting makes you feel: "The wind, the empty sky, the deserted earth." It is a barren scene. And the barrenness matches the barrenness felt by Kapugen when his wife died.

Notice that sounds are a part of the setting too. The wind is screaming; the birds are screaming and crying. Kapugen felt that they were grieving with him, and we feel that way too.

As you become more aware of setting in your reading, you will see that there is more than scenery in a good setting. People can be part of a setting, and even smells and clothing are important.

Miyax was only four when her mother died. Her feelings give an entirely different view of the Arctic setting in the passage in Exercise A.

Exercise A

The passage below is from the selection you have read. Answer the questions about this passage using what you have learned in this part of the lesson. Choose the best answer for each question. Put an x in the correct box or fill in the appropriate words.

She [Miyax] saw this, but she was not sad. She was divinely happy going somewhere alone with Kapugen. Occasionally he climbed the cliffs and brought her eggs to eat; occasionally he took her in his arms and leaned against a rock. She slept at times in the warmth of his big sealskin parka. Then they walked on. She did not know how far.

1. How does Miyax feel in this setting?
   ☐ a. Cold and miserable
   ☐ b. Warm and happy
   ☐ c. Lonely and sad
   ☐ d. Giddy and foolish

2. a. What features of the landscape are part of the setting here?

   _____

b. What article of clothing is part of the setting?

_____

Now check your answers using the Answer Key on page 433. Correct any wrong answer and review this part of the lesson if you don't understand why your answer was wrong.

	Setting
2	**Setting and the Sense of Really Being There**

In a novel, just as in a movie, you must be able to "see" the place where the action occurs. It makes no difference that one time you see with your eyes and another time you see with your "mind's eye." The important thing is that you get the sense, the feeling, of really being where the action is.

Setting helps to do this for you. An author often describes sights and sounds, smells and textures in great detail. As the details pile up, you get a better and better picture, or feeling for where you are. Then, if the vision becomes strong enough in your mind, the author succeeds in placing you in the very midst of things. This is one mark of a good story.

In the preceding passages we were made to stand on a cold Arctic seashore. Now we will visit Kapugen's house and then attend a feast with him and Miyax. Notice how many details are provided to give you a sense of really being there.

> To Miyax the years at seal camp were infinitely good. The scenes and events were beautiful color spots in her memory. There was Kapugen's little house of driftwood, not far from the beach. It was rosy-gray on the outside. Inside, it was gold-brown. Walrus tusks gleamed and drums, harpoons, and man's knives decorated the walls. The sealskin kayak beside the door glowed as if the moon had been stretched across it and its graceful ribs shone back. Dark gold and soft brown were the old men who sat around Kapugen's camp stove and talked to him by day and night.

This is a description in technicolor: rosy-gray, dark gold, soft brown. In a way it gives a better feeling of "really being there" than you could get from seeing Kapugen's house in a movie. A camera might just "pan" or sweep across the scene very quickly. Here we are made to linger and see the details through Miyax's memory. And as in the other passages before this, we begin to feel as well as see the setting from the description.

Notice how people become a part of the setting. It is not important who the old men are. But for Miyax, and for us, they supply the golds and browns in the setting.

People and colors become even more important in placing readers at the scene in the passage in Exercise B.

Exercise B

The passage below is from the selection you have read. Answer the questions about this passage using what you have learned in this part of the lesson. Choose the best answer for each question. Put an x in the correct box or fill in the appropriate words.

The celebration of the Bladder Feast was many colors— black, blue, purple, fire-red; but Kapugen's hand around hers was rose-colored and that was the color of her memory of the Feast. A shaman, an old priestess whom everyone called "the bent woman," danced. Her face was streaked with black soot. When she finally bowed, a fiery spirit came out of the dark wearing a huge mask that jingled and terrified Miyax. Once, in sheer bravery, she peeked up under a mask and saw that the dancer was not a spirit at all but Naka, Kapugen's serious partner. She whispered his name and he laughed. . . .

1. If you were attending the Bladder Feast, which one of these things would you see there?

☐ a. The shaman coloring herself fire-red

☐ b. Miyax looking in from outside

☐ c. Miyax sitting and holding Kapugen's hand

☐ d. Everyone being extremely serious

2. Which two people included in the description help you to know that this is a religious feast?

_____

_____

_____

Now check your answers using the Answer Key on page 433. Correct any wrong answer and review this part of the lesson if you don't understand why your answer was wrong.

When you ask someone why they liked a novel, they will probably say it was exciting, or sad, or funny, or romantic, or a great adventure. But if a story is interesting, it is usually because of the ideas it presents.

An author introduces ideas into a story in many ways. A character in a story may speak to another character and express an idea that way. The way people act in a story may give readers ideas to think about. Or, the author may even pause in telling a story to present an idea directly to the readers. Setting is also used to express ideas.

An important idea in *Julie of the Wolves* is the way the Eskimos had of living close to nature. Nature and its creatures are described so often in the story that you can't help stopping to think about how important they are.

Here the idea of the Eskimos' closeness to nature appears in a description of a fishing scene.

> A silver memory was the day when the sun came over the horizon for the first time in winter. She [Miyax] was at the beach, close to Kapugen, helping him haul in a huge gleaming net. In it was a beautiful white whale. Out of sight on the other side of the whale, she could hear the old men as they cheered this gift from the sea.
>
> The whale was a mountain so high she could not see the cliffs beyond, only the sunlit clouds. Kapugen's huge, black, frostbitten hand seemed small as it touched the great body of the whale.

Two very welcome things are described—the sun and the whale. Remember that the sun doesn't shine for months on end during an Arctic winter. So the sun peeking over the horizon was a welcome sight indeed.

Capturing a whale was a real stroke of luck. It would provide food, clothing, heat and light for an entire village. It is described as "this gift from the sea." Generally we think of hunting as taking things from nature. The Eskimos are hunting too, but they think of their catch as a gift from a higher being.

Notice in the second paragraph how the author, Jean Craighead George, shows us the clouds, Kapugen's hand, and the whale, all together. She seems to being saying that all are a part of one nature. There is an attitude of respect in the way that Eskimos look at this relationship with nature that others would do well to copy.

A lighter side of the same idea is presented in the passage in Exercise C.

Exercise C

The passage below is from the selection you have read. Answer the questions about this passage using what you have learned in this part of the lesson. Choose the best answer for each question. Put an *x* in the correct box or fill in the appropriate words.

Walking the tundra [Arctic plains] with Kapugen was all laughter and fun. He would hail the blue sky and shout out his praise for the grasses and bushes. On these trips they ate salmon berries, then lay in the sun watching the birds. Sometimes Kapugen would whistle sandpiper songs and the birds would dip down to see which of their members had gotten lost in the grass. When they saw him and darted away, Kapugen would laugh.

1. Which part of the scene gives readers the idea that Kapugen can communicate with nature?

   ☐ a. Playing with the birds
   ☐ b. Walking the tundra
   ☐ c. Eating berries
   ☐ d. Kapugen's laughing

2. What sentence in the passage says best that Kapugen
   was thankful for the beauty of nature? Write the sentence here.

   _____

   _____

   _____

Now check your answers using the Answer Key on page 433.
Correct any wrong answer and review this part of the lesson if you
don't understand why your answer was wrong.

	Setting
4	**Setting and Action**

An author takes great care to see that what is happening in a story fits the setting where that action takes place. This is easily seen in some cases. You would not expect action set on the Arctic tundra, for example, to include a cops-and-robbers car chase. Miyax's adventures are much more appropriate for this setting.

But there are also small details of setting that an author must choose to go with some particular action. And these details often add to the action to make readers more clearly aware of what is going on. One thing an author can do with a detail or two in the setting is tip you off that something new is about to happen. The change in setting indicates a change in the action. A happy scene may turn suddenly tense. A calm scene can turn into one of confusion or great excitement.

Think of a group of happy people having a picnic beside a lake. The sun is shining and the birds are singing. Then the sky grows dark. There is a rumbling followed by a low growl. The gaiety turns to fear and panic as the water on the lake churns and froths and a monster rises from the deep.

In the following passage, the change in setting is a change of sounds. See if you can spot the place where the setting and the action change together.

One year, probably in September, for the canvas tents were down and the campground almost empty, Kapugen came into the house with a sealskin. . . .

"We must make you a new coat," he had said. . . .

The skin was metallic silver-gold and so beautiful that even the velveteen parkas of children for Mekoryuk paled by comparison. Miyax stroked it lovingly as Kapugen lay her old coat upon it and began to cut a larger one. As he worked he hummed, and she made up words about the seal who wanted to be a coat. Presently they became aware of the distant throb of a motorboat. The sound grew louder, then shut off at the beach. Footsteps crunched, the cold air rushed in the door, and there was Martha, Kapugen's aunt. She was thin and her face was pinched. Miyax disliked her immediately, but was spared the necessity of speaking nicely to her. For Martha had words only for Kapugen.

Julie of the Wolves

The scene begins as a happy one. Kapugen is making Miyax a new coat. She is delighted and strokes the fur lovingly. Kapugen hums a tune and Miyax makes up a song to it. This is a happy sound that matches the happy action.

But then there is the distant throb of a motorboat. A detail of setting has changed and the action is about to change. Notice also that there is a change from things Eskimo—the seal catch and the homemade coat—to things from the white people's world—the motorboat. The sound grows louder, then stops. We wait to see what will happen next. Thus, the detail of setting is helping to move the action.

What happens is unpleasant, exactly what the author has prepared us for by changing small details of setting. And there is a larger change going on that will come later in the story. With the intrusion of the motorboat and its foreign sound, and of Aunt Martha with her foreign ways, Julie is about to begin a new part of her life, living in white society.

You should be able to match action and setting in the passage in Exercise D. As you read, remember that Julie and Miyax are the same person.

Exercise D

The passage below is from the selection you have read. Answer the questions about this passage using what you have learned in this part of the lesson. Choose the best answer for each question. Put an x in the correct box or fill in the appropriate words.

Martha came to Miyax's bed.

"Your father," she said, "went seal hunting in that ridiculous kayak. He has been gone a month this day. He will not be back. Bits of his kayak washed up on the shore." Martha stumped to the fire and turned her back.

Julie ran out of the house into the dark morning. She darted past the store, the reindeer-packing house, the church. She did not stop until she came to the beach. There she crouched among the oil drums and looked out to sea.

The wind blew across the water, shattering the tips of the waves and shooting ice-sparklets north with the storm. "Kapugen!" she called. No one answered. Kapugen was gone. The earth was empty and bleak.

1. The action and the setting here closely match the action and the setting of the first passage quoted in this lesson. In both cases the action and setting combine to show that

   ☐ a. the beach is fun to explore with people you love.

   ☐ b. life in the sea continues, even after a human death.

   ☐ c. the beach is a dangerous place for children to be by themselves.

   ☐ d. the world seems lonely after a relative's death.

2. Julie (Miyax) runs from the world of white people back to the world she shared with Kapugen. In the passage above, from where to where does she run?

   _____

   _____

   _____

Use the Answer Key on page 433 to check your answers. Correct any wrong answer and review this part of the lesson if you don't understand why your answer was wrong. Now go on to do the Comprehension Questions.

Comprehension Questions

Answer these questions without looking back at the selection. Choose the best answer to each question and put an *x* in the box beside it.

Recalling
Facts

1. When her mother died, Miyax was

   ☐ a. about four years old.

   ☐ b. a young teen-ager.

   ☐ c. an infant not yet two.

   ☐ d. a grown woman.

Recognizing
Words in
Context

2. "The *jaegers* screamed and the *sandpipers* cried. The feathered horns of the comical *puffins* drooped low. . . ." *Jaegers, sandpipers* and *puffins* are names of

   ☐ a. spirits.

   ☐ b. Eskimo tribes.

   ☐ c. birds.

   ☐ d. animals.

Keeping
Events in
Order

3. Immediately after her mother died, Miyax

   ☐ a. spent some years at a seal camp.

   ☐ b. went to live with Aunt Martha.

   ☐ c. went off to school.

   ☐ d. ran away to marry Daniel.

4. What kind of a father was Kapugen?

☐ a. Loving but severe

☐ b. Loving and gentle

☐ c. Strict and demanding

☐ d. Rough and uncaring

5. Kapugen had a good job managing a reindeer herd

☐ a. while he was at seal camp.

☐ b. when Miyax went to school.

☐ c. all the time Miyax was growing up.

☐ d. before his wife died.

6. From *Julie of the Wolves* we can learn

☐ a. how to forecast weather.

☐ b. some of the old ways of the Eskimos.

☐ c. how Alaska came to be part of the United States.

☐ d. what whales do in winter.

7. The seal camp was very crude. Still, Miyax enjoyed the years spent there. Why?

☐ a. She felt she was safe from Aunt Martha.

☐ b. She knew someday she would be a seal hunter.

☐ c. She loved Kapugen and the things he did.

☐ d. She was always warm there and had lots to eat.

8. Who was "the bent woman"?

☐ a. A shaman or priestess

☐ b. Kapugen's sister

☐ c. An old witch

☐ d. A fire spirit

9. The Eskimos were hunters and fishers. Judging from what you have read, what would you say is a good word to describe their attitude toward animals?

☐ a. Fearful

☐ b. Cruel

☐ c. Soft-hearted

☐ d. Respectful

10. "Occasionally he [Kapugen] *skimmed* after the biggest cod or halibut in his kayak . . . ." The word *skimmed* means

☐ a. jogged.

☐ b. drifted.

☐ c. glided.

☐ d. crawled.

11. Miyax became angry when Kapugen called her Julie. She said: "I am Eskimo, not a *gussak*!" A *gussak* is probably

☐ a. a white person.

☐ b. any Alaskan.

☐ c. a whale.

☐ d. an evil spirit.

12. Miyax attended the Bladder Feast

    ☐ a. when she heard of the death of her father.

    ☐ b. after the seal hunt.

    ☐ c. while the whale still lay on the beach.

    ☐ d. before the seal hunt.

13. Which of these quotations tells a main idea of the novel?

    ☐ a. "Often she dug for clams . . . and he would crack them open."

    ☐ b. " 'We must make you a new coat,' he said."

    ☐ c. " 'We live as no other people can, for we truly understand the earth!' "

    ☐ d. " 'We'll see!' Martha screamed, turned around and went toward the boat."

14. Why did Julie go to live with Aunt Martha?

    ☐ a. Kapugen no longer wanted her.

    ☐ b. The seal camp was closed.

    ☐ c. Julie needed to learn the old ways.

    ☐ d. Julie had to be sent to school.

15. Miyax and Kapugen are also called Julie and Charlie Edwards. What do these changes in their names represent?

    ☐ a. Their lives as children and their lives as adults

    ☐ b. Eskimo old ways and Eskimo new ways

    ☐ c. Their first names and their last names

    ☐ d. Life on the coast and life on the plains

Now check your answers using the Answer Key on page 433. Correct any wrong answers you have by putting a check (✓) in the box next to the right answer. Count the number of questions you answered correctly and plot the total on the Comprehension Scores graph on page 444.

Next, look at the questions you answered incorrectly. What types of questions were they? Count the number of each type and enter the numbers in the spaces below:

Recognizing Words in Context   _____

Recalling Facts   _____

Keeping Events in Order   _____

Making Inferences   _____

Understanding Main Ideas   _____

Now use these numbers to fill in the Comprehension Skills Profile on page 445.

Julie of the Wolves

Discussion Guides

The questions below will help you to think about the selection and the lesson you have just read. If you don't discuss these questions in class, try to think about them or discuss them with your classmates.

Discussing Setting

1. "The wind, the empty sky, the deserted earth. . . ."
   How are these things important in the story?

2. There are three dance scenes in the reading selection: one at the Bladder Feast, one at the death of the whale and one at night at Kapugen's house. What purposes do the dance scenes serve in the story?

3. When Julie heard Kapugen was missing and thought to be dead, she ran to the beach, crouched among oil drums there, and looked out to sea. What meanings would the beach, the oil drums and the sea have for Julie at a time like this?

Discussing the Story

4. How would you describe Aunt Martha? Is she entirely good or evil? Give reasons for your answer.

5. Are the old ways of the Eskimos better than the new ways, or just the opposite? Give reasons for your opinion.

6. Miyax seemed to admire Kapugen and everything he did. Give examples of how this happens sometimes in your family or among your friends. Compare your examples with the way Miyax acted in the story.

Discussing the Author's Work

7. The author uses colors a great deal in her descriptions. Find a place in the story where a color is used in a description. Read the passage aloud. Then tell how the color affects your feelings about that scene.

8. The name of the book is *Julie of the Wolves*. Why do you think the author used "Julie" in the title rather than "Miyax"?

9. Jean George dedicated the book this way: "To Luke George who loves wolves and the Eskimos of Alaska." Why is this an appropriate way to dedicate *Julie of the Wolves*?

Writing Exercise

Author Jean George describes memories of scenes and events as "beautiful color spots." Here are examples of some of them.

Kapugen's driftwood house: "It was rosy-gray on the out side. Inside it was golden-brown."

The Bladder Feast: "The celebration of the Feast was many colors—black, blue, purple, fire-red; but Kapugen's hand around hers was rose-colored and that was the color of her memory of the Feast."

The sun in winter: "A silver memory was the day when the sun came over the horizon for the first time in winter."

Write a color description like these for at least two of the things listed below. Use at least two or three sentences in your description.

An animal you love	A person you dislike
A person you like	Your home
Work or a hobby you enjoy	Eating a favorite meal
An event that frightened you	Doing something outdoors
Relaxing on a lazy day	A favorite possession

Unit 2 Character

Summer of My German Soldier
BY BETTE GREENE

About the Illustration

What can you tell about what each of these people is like? Describe each one separately. Point out details in the drawing to support your response.

Here are some questions to help you think:

☐ How would you describe the expression on the woman's face? Why do you think she is touching the girl in this way?

☐ How would you describe the expression on the girl's face? What does the way she is sitting tell you about her feelings?

Unit 2

Introduction	What the Novel Is About/What the Lesson Is About
Selection	**Summer of My German Soldier**
Lesson	Character
Activities	Comprehension Questions/Discussion Guides/Writing Exercise

Introduction

What the Novel Is About

Patty Bergen, age twelve, is the oldest daughter in the only Jewish family in a small Southern town, Jenkinsville, Arkansas. For some reason, her parents don't seem to like her. When her father, Harry Bergen, isn't annoyed with her, he is angry at her. When he is angry enough, he beats her. Patty's mother, Pearl Bergen, doesn't find much to like about her daughter either. She goes out of her way to be insulting to Patty about her appearance and her manners.

Patty has few acquaintances and no real friends among her schoolmates. As you may well imagine, then, she feels lonely, ugly and unloved. The one friend and protector Patty has is Ruth, the Bergen's housekeeper. It is Ruth who provides the only mothering that Patty has ever had.

Summer of My German Soldier takes place in 1944 when Hitler's Germany is on its way to defeat in World War II. German prisoners of war are arriving in the United States in growing numbers. A prisoner-of-war camp is opened outside of Jenkensville and the first German prisoners arrive. They are put to work picking cotton in nearby fields.

A group of prisoners is brought to Harry Bergen's store to buy field hats for their work in the sun. Among them is a young German named Anton Reiker who speaks English and translates for the others. Patty sells him some pencils and other small articles and they chat. They like one another instantly, and after their brief meeting, Patty hopes she can see him again.

Anton, of course, is considered a dangerous enemy of the United States by the townspeople. And if he felt the same way about Jews as Hitler, his friendship with a Jewish girl would be very strange indeed. But Anton, though German, doesn't feel as Hitler did. Anton is educated, sensitive and loving, and he thinks Hitler is a madman.

Patty doesn't see Anton again until he escapes from the prison camp and she accidentally finds him by the railroad tracks. She takes him home and hides him in some empty rooms over an unused garage. She and Anton become good friends. He seems to understand Patty and he genuinely likes her.

This is an extremely dangerous situation for Patty to be in. Anton is a fugitive who could be shot on sight. To shelter him in wartime is treason. For a Jewish girl to befriend and protect a German soldier is unbelievable and unthinkable. She risks the anger of the law and her father's wrath.

Just before the chapter you will read, Anton sees Patty's father beating her for a small disobedience. She has been caught with a neighbor boy she was forbidden to talk to. Anton rushes from his hiding place to help her. But Patty waves him away before he is discovered. Anton can only watch while Harry Bergen beats Patty unmercifully with his belt.

Ruth is watching, too, and she sees Anton rush out. She faces Patty with her discovery. Later, Patty and Anton discuss the beating and they try to think about why Patty's father behaves as he does.

What happens after this chapter is first suspenseful and then painful. Patty's story is not a happy one.

Like Patty, author Bette Greene grew up in a small town in Arkansas. To a large extent, *Summer of My German Soldier* is based on her personal experiences. The novel has won many awards and was made into a movie for television, starring Kristy McNichol.

After reading the complete novel, you will want to read its sequel, *Morning Is a Long Time Coming*. This picks up the story of Patty Bergen when she is graduating from high school and facing the question of what to do with her life.

Other books by Bette Greene include *Philip Hall Likes Me, I Reckon Maybe* and *Get On Out Of Here, Philip Hall*.

What the Lesson Is About

The lesson following the reading selection is about character.

It is an author's job to create characters that seem real and believable. If the job is done well, readers come to think of the characters as they would of people in real life. An author does this through characterization.

The lesson will point out some of the ways authors create characters and it will show how good characterization helps to make a novel more enjoyable.

The questions below will help you to focus on character in the chapter from *Summer of My German Soldier*. Read the chapter carefully and try to answer these questions as you go along:

1 Where does Patty speak to readers about her father? About Freddy?

2 In a conversation over breakfast, Patty tells Ruth that she is hiding Anton. How would you describe Patty in this conversation? What does Ruth seem like?

3 How does Patty feel after she tells Ruth about Anton? How does the author try to get you to share those feelings?

4 Throughout most of the selection, Harry Bergen seems to be a mean person. How does the author get you to understand him a little?

Summer of My German Soldier

Bette Greene

"She has to be taking it home with her; I can't think of any other explanation. That kosher salami cost one dollar and ten cents." My mother repeated the price a second time for added emphasis.

I pulled the top sheet over my head to block out the early morning sounds from the kitchen and rolled over a now very warm ice bag and remembered. In another few minutes they would be leaving for the store. Only then would I get out of bed. Just as soon as my mother downs her second cup of coffee and my father finishes his corn flakes. As long as I can remember it has been corn flakes and nothing but corn flakes. He's got the same loyalty towards cars. "I'll buy any kinda car as long as it's a Chevrolet." And cigarettes too. He's never had a cigarette in his mouth that wasn't a Lucky Strike.

"So you'd better talk to her, Harry."

"Talk to who?"

"To Ruth!" Her voice hit a shrill note. "I want to know what's happening to the salami and chicken and all the other food that's been disappearing around here lately."

"Well, how do you know she's taking it home? I don't know what you're talking about. But she'll be coming any minute now, and if you want to fire her it's fine with me. Something about that woman I never liked."

I didn't speak to them, but I didn't want them to suspect either. I yelled out, "I'm sorry about the salami 'cause I ate most of it myself. And about the leftover chicken, Sharon and Sue Ellen ate the last of it."

"Now you see that!" he told her. "Don't ever talk to me again about missing food."

I'll have to say this for him, he's always generous about food, even when we eat in restaurants. Like that Sunday in Memphis not too long ago when we ate at Britlings' and I ordered the chopped sirloin steak and he said, "That's nothing but a hamburger. Wouldn't you like to have a real steak?" My mother didn't like the idea of ordering "an expensive steak that will just go to waste." But my father told her to mind her own business, and that as long as he lived I could eat anything I wanted.

The phrase, "as long as he lived" sounded like a vague prophecy, and I became sorrowful that he might die now that he was being good to me. I became so sorrowful, in fact, that it was Mother's prediction that was soon fulfilled. An expensive steak went to waste.

The familiar sounds of a spiritual—Ruth was passing below my window on her way to the back door. "Morning, folks," she called. "Well, I heard the weatherman say we're gonna get us a little rain by afternoon, enough to cool things off." My mother agreed that a little shower would be very nice. "Is that piece of toast all you've had to eat?" asked Ruth. "That's no kinda breakfast, Miz Bergen. I could make you some hurry-up griddle cakes."

"Griddle cakes are fattening. Besides I have to leave now."

A couple of minutes later the car backed out of the garage, the motor gunned for the two-block trip, and they were gone.

Ruth came into my room, bent over and picked up the flowery chenille bedspread that had fallen to the floor, and asked, "Are you feeling all right?"

I remembered who had brought me the ice bag and aspirins for my head and the ointment for my legs. "I don't know. I guess I am."

From the other twin bed came a long, low, early morning

sound as Sharon flopped over to a better dreaming position.

"Come on into the kitchen," whispered Ruth as she tip-toed out of the room.

The marshmallow slowly began to bleed its whiteness over the steaming cup of chocolate. On the shelf of the breakfast room's built-in cabinet our one surviving gold-fish, Goldilocks, began her vigorous after-breakfast swim.

"How come that fish got sense enough to eat her breakfast and you don't?" asked Ruth as she sat down at the table.

I ignored the buttered toast and scrambled egg, but took a long drink of the now lukewarm chocolate. "Don't know except maybe Goldilocks has a better cook than I do."

"Must be the truth," Ruth smiled, showing her left-of-center, solid-gold tooth. "You know what you needs, Honey? One of them fancy Frenchmen who cooks up a fine dinner and jest 'fore serving it, he sets it all afire."

We sat for a while in silence, Ruth taking small now-and-then sips of coffee while I sat stirring my chocolate and watching Goldilocks. Ruth's spoon made an attention getting noise and I saw that those brown eyes were upon me.

"I want you to tell Ruth the truth about something. You hear me talking, girl?" I nodded Yes.

"You tell me who is the man."

"Man?"

"Honey Babe, you can tell Ruth. The man that ran out from the garage. The man that wanted to save you from your daddy."

"That man—the man—the—" My voice was still in some kind of working order even if my brain did just up and die.

How can those eyes that rest so lightly see so deeply? And from them there is nothing in this world to fear. "The man is my friend," I said at last.

"You got him hid up in them rooms over the garage?"

"Yes."

Ruth sighed like she sometimes does before tackling a really big job. "He's not the one the law's after? Not the one from the prison camp?"

"Yes."

Her forehead crinkled up like a washboard. "You telling me, Yes, he's not the one?"

"No, Ruth, I'm telling you Yes. Yes, he's the one."

Ruth's head moved back and forth in a No direction. "Oh, Lord, why are you sending us more, Lord? Don't this child and me have burden enough?"

I stood up and felt this sensation of lightness, near weightlessness, like somebody had just bent down, picked up, and carried away all my trouble. My arm fell across Ruth's shoulder. "Everything'll be all right, honest it will." Beneath my arm, there was no movement, no feeling of life. I squeezed Ruth's shoulder and a hearable breath rushed through her nostrils. "You know how you're all the time helping me because you're my friend? Well, Anton's my friend and I have to help him, you know? Don't you know?"

"I don't know what it is I know," she said in a weighted voice.

In the pantry there was plenty of peanut butter, but the jar of strawberry jam was only fingernail high. I turned on the gas burner under the aluminum percolator. I began to worry that maybe prison camp food was better than this, but at least the loaf of white bread was yesterday fresh.

Ruth followed me into the kitchen. "Honey, them peanut butter and jelly sandwiches ain't no kinda breakfast for no kinda man." She looked up at the kitchen clock. "After I bring Sharon down to Sue Ellen's I'll fix up some hot griddle cakes with maple syrup and a fresh pot of coffee."

I threw my arms as far around Ruth's waist as they would go and tried to lift her up by the pure strength of my will.

"Oh, Ruth, you're good, good, good!"

"Now, girl, don't go 'specting no amount of praise to turn my mind about 'cause my mind ain't come to no clear thought yet. All I knows for sure is that I'm gonna fix up a proper breakfast for you and the man."

"O.K., thanks, but would you mind not calling him the man, 'cause he's my friend, Anton. Mr. Frederick Anton Reiker. You may not know this, but you and Anton are all the friends I've got."

Ruth nodded slowly. "I understands that, Honey."

That understanding made me want to tell her everything all at once. "Ruth, he talks to me and he tells me things because I'm his friend. Ruth, he likes me. He really and truly likes me."

"I knows that too."

My heart swelled up for if Ruth knows it, it must be the truth. "How do you know that? Tell me how you know!"

She gave my arm a couple of short pats before finding my eyes. "That man come a-rushing out from the safety of his hiding 'cause he couldn't stand your pain and anguish no better'n me. That man listens to the love in his heart. Like the Bible tell us, when a man will lay down his life for a friend, well, then there ain't no greater love in this here world than that."

Before I reached the landing I heard his footsteps, and then the door opened. I felt certain he was smiling a welcome, although I was looking past him into the familiar interior of the room much as I would look past the brilliance of the sun.

"How are you?" he asked, making it sound more like an inquiry than a greeting.

"Fine." Cowardliness kept me from looking at him. "Did you sleep O.K.? Were you too hot?" I asked.

"No."

The shortness of his answer frightened me. Maybe it's disgust for what he saw yesterday. My eyes shut in a feeble try at pushing away the memories.

"Sure you're all right?" His eyes were on the red raw stripes that crisscrossed my legs.

I moved quickly to the opposite side of the desk. "Oh, yes, thanks."

"About yesterday—"

"It's O.K."

"No," he said with a force I had never heard him use before. "It's not O.K.! Listen to me, P.B. What happened yesterday bothers me. Tell me if I was in any way responsible." Between his eyebrows there was a deep crease, a mark of concern—for me.

All that painful dabbing of layer after layer of face powder that I subjected my legs to may have been a mistake. Concern might be a little like love.

"It wasn't you," I said. "You weren't responsible."

"Then what? Please tell me what you did to deserve such a beating?"

How could I say in words what I couldn't really understand myself? Sometimes I think it's because I'm bad that my father wants to do the right thing by beating it out of me. And at other times I think he's beating out from my body all his own bad. My head began its confused revolutions.

"Come over to the window," I said finally, pointing toward the tracks. "See over there? The shack with the tin roof? There's a boy who lives there who my father told me

A/ I'm not to have anything to do with. Yesterday he saw Freddy sitting next to me on our front steps." I told Anton about sleepy Freddy who cuts grass in his spare time so he can make enough money to sleep during the Saturday matinee. Scholarly Freddy who has been in Miss Bailey's fourth grade for two years because he's finally found, "The one teacher I likes." Fearless Freddy, brave hunter of crawdads. And generous Freddy who once bought me the gift of not quite half of a melted mess of a Hershey bar.

C/ "He sounds perfectly delightful," said Anton with a smile. "But why is your father so opposed to him?"

"Maybe it's because he's so poor, but I'm not sure."

He looked a little perplexed. "Why don't you inquire?"

"I can't inquire." My words had a harshness that I didn't intend. "In my father's vocabulary to ask why is to contradict him."

"I don't like him!" The words seemed to dash out. Then Anton caught my eyes as though asking permission.

"Oh, that's O.K.," I said pleased that Anton was taking my side. "I'll tell you something I've never told anyone before. If he weren't my father, I wouldn't even like him."

"But because he is, you do?"

"Oh, well, I guess I—" Then the image came. The image of his thin, rabid face. "I guess I don't too much. No, I don't like him." That was the first time I had even thought anything like that myself. Funny, but Edna Louise once told me, "Your daddy is so sweet." Probably because every time he sees her he says, "Edna Louise, you sure do look pretty today." To Edna Louise he has to say nice things as if she weren't conceited enough.

"Do you have any idea where your father went—what he did immediately following the beating he gave you?"

"Not exactly, I could guess. He probably went into the house, smoked a Lucky Strike cigarette, washed his hands, and ate a perfectly enormous supper while he listened to the evening news."

"Not true. He stood watching the housekeeper help you into the house. Then he came into the garage and talked to himself. Over and over he kept repeating, 'Nobody loves me. In my whole life nobody has ever loved me.' "

"Anton, it must have been somebody else. That doesn't sound like my father."

"It *was* your father."

"I don't understand. Why? How could he be so mean and then worry that he isn't loved? It doesn't make sense."

Anton shook his head. "I met your father once; I interpreted for some of the prisoners who came into the store."

"I remember! You said the prisoners needed hats to protect themselves from our formidable Arkansas sun."

Anton smiled, and the smile made him look very young, more like a boy my age than a man. "How could you possibly remember that?"

"Easy. Nobody from around here says things like that. I also remember that he didn't think your remark was very amusing."

"I can believe that because—" Anton paused like he was trying to put some new thoughts into good running order before continuing—"because it seems to me that a man who is incapable of humor is capable of cruelty. If Hitler, for example, had had the ability—the detachment—to observe the absurdity of his own behavior he would have laughed, and today there might not be a madman named Adolph Hitler."

Was he making a comparison between Hitler and my father? "Do you think my father is like that? Like Hitler?"

Anton looked thoughtful. "Cruelty is after all cruelty, and the difference between the two men may have more to do with their degrees of power than their degrees of cruelty.

One man is able to affect millions and the other only a few. Would your father's cruelty cause him to crush weak neighboring states? Or would the *Führer's* cruelty cause him to beat his own daughter? Doesn't it seem to you that they both need to inflict pain?"

"I don't know."

Anton smiled. "I don't know either. But you see, the only questions I like to raise are those that are unanswerable. Trying to calculate the different degrees of cruelty is a lot like trying to calculate the different degrees of death."

I laughed, but I knew that tonight while our house slept I would stay awake trying to understand his words. "I'm so glad you're talking to me, teaching me." I heard my enthusiasm running over. "I want you to teach me everything you've learned."

Anton stood, executing a princely bow. "I'm at your service."

"I think I want to be intelligent even more than I want to be pretty."

"You're already intelligent and pretty."

"Me?"

"You. I come from a line of men who have a sure instinct for a woman's beauty. So, P.B., I speak as an expert when I tell you you're going to have it all."

"Well, why hasn't anyone else seen it? That I'm going to have—what you say?"

"They will. Because you are no common garden flower—you are unique."

"Oh."

"I think I'm going to enjoy being your teacher if you'll keep in mind that life produces no maestros, only students of varying degrees of ineptitude. Wait!" said Anton. He jumped from his chair to go rummaging through a GI regulation duffel bag. "Here it is!" He waved a book with a bruised, blue cover. "I checked it out of the prison library the same day I checked myself out. R.W. Emerson. Are you familiar with his work?"

I admitted that I wasn't while I wondered if escaping with a book could be called anything besides stealing. My father would never do anything like that.

Anton asked, "Is something wrong?"

"Uhhh, no. Well, I was wondering how you are going to return the book."

"Oh," he said thoughtfully. "You want to know if I am a thief?"

"Oh, no! I know you're not!"

"In this classroom we call things by their rightful name. I became a thief when I took that book. I couldn't very well pay for it, and I didn't want my brain to starve if I had to go into hiding."

I felt close to laughing. "You're very honest. I mean you don't lie, do you?"

Anton shook his head. "I try never to lie to myself, and I dislike lying to friends." He took a yellow pencil from his hip pocket and made two small check marks in R.W. Emerson's Table of Contents. "Read these essays," he said, like he felt pleased to be making a contribution to my education. "And tomorrow we can start mining the gold."

Then a voice from below us called up, "Come on folks! It's ready." Anton's face was caught in a moment of fear.

"It's all right," I whispered. "That's only Ruth, our housekeeper. She's made griddle cakes for us."

He looked at me. "Why did you—tell?"

He believed—he actually believed—that I would. "But I didn't! Honest! Ruth saw you run out of the garage last night; she saw how you wanted to protect me from my father."

Anton's hand rushed to his forehead. "I came running

out of hiding to—My God, I did, didn't I?" His hand dropped to his side, and I could see he was smiling his wonderful glad-to-be-living smile. "After almost two years of being as inconspicuous a coward as possible I had no idea that I would voluntarily risk my life for anyone." He shook his head in disbelief. "But I'm glad I could. I'm glad I still could."

Character

Most people will agree that there is nothing more important to creating a good story than creating interesting and believable characters. The better the characters, the better the story. That's why authors take great care to make their characters believable. In a way, the best characters seem to come alive for readers. By the time you have finished reading a good book, the characters are more than words on a page. The author has turned them into real-life acquaintances for you.

Some characters are so believable that they take on a life of their own outside their stories. Tom Sawyer, for instance, will always be *the* example of a boy growing up in Middle America. To many, Sherlock Holmes is a real, living detective. And for years to come, all sorts of robots will be compared to the "living" characters R2-D2 and C-3PO of *Star Wars*.

It is easy to forget that all of these familiar figures came from someone's imagination. But they were, of course, given life by an author. The process by which this is done is called *characterization*.

Authors use the same techniques to create characters that people use to get to know one another in real life. For example, you get to know some people by hearing about them from others. Someone says, "Let me tell you about George," and a lively conversation follows in which George is described in great detail. In a story, too, description is an important part of developing a character.

Another way you get to know people in real life is by listening to what they say and watching what they do. Once again, authors use a similar method to get you to know their characters. In a story, what characters say and what they do adds to the characterization.

You don't really know people, however, until you come to understand them. Understanding people can be very difficult. One of the most common expressions you hear from people who disagree is, "Oh, I'll never understand you!" What that means is, "I don't understand how you feel, and I don't understand why you act the way you do."

Here an author of a story has a great advantage. An author can make you understand how a character feels. An author can also make you think about the reasons behind a character's actions.

In this lesson we will look at four ways in which author Bette Greene creates characters and helps you to understand them:

1 Characters are presented by description.

2 Characters are revealed through dramatic action.

3 Characters are revealed through their feelings.

4 Analyzing characters will help you understand them better.

The simplest way for an author to create a character is to come right out and tell readers what a character is like. Height, weight, eye color, likes and dislikes are all part of a character description. You may be told about a character's disposition. Is the charac-

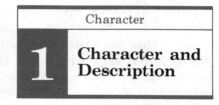

Character

1 Character and Description

ter brave or timid? Generous or spiteful? These are the same things you want to find out when you get to know someone.

An author gives these descriptions in a number of ways. Sometimes the author speaks directly to readers. This is called a *third-person narration*. Other times, the author has a character give the description, as Patty does in *Summer of My German Soldier*. This is called a *first-person narration*. The author speaks to readers through the character.

When Ruth first appeared in the story in an earlier chapter, Patty described her to readers this way:

> She is the color of hot chocolate before the marshmallow bleeds in. Sometimes I hear my mother telling her to lose weight. . . . But she isn't actually fat; it's just that she has to wear large sizes. I mean it wouldn't be Ruth if she were like my mother. And another thing, a little extra weight keeps a person warm inside.

The author has Patty come right out and tell readers what Ruth is like. Ruth is chocolate brown, large (maybe on the fat side), and she is a warm person. This first impression of Ruth is confirmed by what we see of her as the story goes along.

In Chapter 11, Patty describes her father for you:

> As long as I can remember it has been corn flakes and nothing but corn flakes. He's got the same loyalty towards cars. "I'll buy any kinda car as long as it's a Chevrolet." And cigarettes too. He's never had a cigarette in his mouth that wasn't a Lucky Strike.

This is not a description of what Harry Bergen looks like. It is a description of the kind of man he is. He is a creature of habit. Patty suggests that he'll never change. Other passages which show his character make it plain that he is unreasonably stubborn.

One other way that an author describes a character is by showing you a conversation in which the character is discussed. Here, Ruth is talking to Patty about Anton. Ruth describes something important about Anton's character for Patty and for readers.

> She gave my arm a couple of pats before finding my eyes. "That man come a-rushing out from the safety of his hiding 'cause he couldn't stand your pain and anguish no better'n me. That man listens to the love in his heart."

In this short passage, Ruth tells us an important fact about Anton's character. In doing so, she also reveals something about herself. Anton, Ruth says, is the kind of man who listens to the love in his heart. He can't bear to stand by and watch Patty's pain and anguish. "No better'n me," Ruth says. We learn from this that Ruth, like Anton, is a person who is filled with love.

Exercise A

The passage below is from the selection you have read. Answer the questions about this passage using what you have learned in this part of the lesson. Choose the best answer for each question. Put an *x* in the correct box or fill in the appropriate words.

I told Anton about sleepy Freddy who cuts grass in his spare time so he can make enough money to sleep during the Saturday matinee. Scholarly Freddy who has been in Miss Bailey's fourth grade for two years because he's finally found, "The one teacher I likes." Fearless Freddy, brave hunter of crawdads. And generous Freddy who once brought me the gift of not quite half of a melted mess of a Hershey bar.

1. Patty's description makes Freddy seem like a

☐ a. dangerous enemy.

☐ b. lovable blunderer.

☐ c. community leader.

☐ d. loyal movie fan.

2. In one short sentence, Patty makes fun of Freddy's courage. Write that sentence here.

_____

_____

_____

Now check your answers using the Answer Key on page 434. Correct any wrong answer and review this part of the lesson if you don't understand why your answer was wrong.

	Character
2	**Character and Dramatic Action**

Dramatic action is the kind of action you see in a play or a movie. The action may be as exciting as a daring rescue. It may be as quiet as a friendly conversation. Sometimes the "action" may simply be a character thinking out loud. Dramatic action is any action or talk that shows something about what characters in the play or movie are like.

You learn about people in real life in the same way—by watching what they do and listening to what they say. And in the same way, you learn about characters in stories. Here, for example, is a dramatic action involving Patty and Ruth. You can learn a great deal about these characters from this conversation.

"I want you to tell Ruth the truth about something. You hear me talking, girl?" I nodded Yes.

"You tell me who is the man."

"Man?"

"Honey Babe, you can tell Ruth. The man that ran out from the garage. The man that wanted to save you from your daddy."

"That man—the man—the—" My voice was still in some kind of working order even if my brain did just up and die. . . .

"The man is my friend," I said at last.

"You got him hid up in them rooms over the garage?"

"Yes."

Ruth sighed like she sometimes does before tackling a really big job. He's not the one the law's after? Not the one from the prison camp?"

"Yes."

Her forehead crinkled up like a washboard. "You telling me, Yes, he's not the one?"

"No, Ruth, I'm telling you Yes. Yes, he's the one."

Ruth's head moved back and forth in a No direction. "Oh, Lord, why are you sending us more, Lord? Don't this child and me have burden enough?"

I stood up and felt this sensation of lightness, near weightlessness, like somebody had just bent down, picked up, and carried away all my trouble.

Summer of My German Soldier

For good reason, Patty is weighted down with fears. She fears her mother's next insulting remark. She fears the next beating she may get from her father. Now she is burdened by the worst fear of all. She may be caught hiding a prisoner. Ruth has seen Anton and makes Patty confess. With that, Patty feels "like somebody had just bent down, picked up, and carried away" her troubles.

What does this dramatic action tell readers about Patty and Ruth? It emphasizes the fear that Patty feels all the time. And it shows that in spite of her fear, Patty persists in doing what she feels she must do. In this case she feels she must protect Anton, and she does.

We are also shown something about Ruth. She understands Patty's need and she will do what she can to help. She is shown here as being understanding, loving and courageous. She is also deeply religious and has a thought for her God as she takes up this new burden.

Exercise B

The passage below is from the selection you have read. Answer the questions about this passage using what you have learned in this part of the lesson. Choose the best answer for each question. Put an x in the correct box or fill in the appropriate words.

"You may not know this, but you and Anton are all the friends I've got."

Ruth nodded slowly. "I understands that, Honey."

That understanding made me want to tell her everything all at once. "Ruth, he talks to me and he tells me things because I'm his friend, Ruth, he likes me. He really and truly likes me."

"I knows that too."

1. What does this dramatic action tell you about Ruth?

   ☐ a. She is impatient with Patty now.

   ☐ b. She gets quite angry at times.

   ☐ c. She is sometimes a know-it-all.

   ☐ d. She is an understanding person.

2. What does Patty say that shows she has been a lonely girl? Write the sentence here.

_____

_____

_____

Now check your answers using the Answer Key on page 434. Correct any wrong answer and review this part of the lesson if you don't understand why your answer was wrong.

Authors deliberately set out to make you feel differently about each character. You are expected to like Patty and Ruth, for instance. And you are expected to work up a healthy dislike for Harry Bergen, Patty's father.

	Character
3	**Character and Feeling**

Something happens between readers and characters in a well-written story. As the story goes along, readers begin to understand the characters' deepest feelings. You come to sympathize with the main characters and you begin to feel as they do. It is said that you *identify* with certain characters. Because you identify with them, you become more involved in the story.

When Patty's secret is discovered, you know exactly how she feels. You have probably been in such a situation yourself. Even if you haven't, the author makes you understand what the feeling is like.

> "That man—the man—the—" My voice was still in some
> kind of working order even if my brain did just up and die.

How many times have you said: "When they found out, I thought I'd drop dead on the spot!" Because you share Patty's feeling of shock, you understand her situation better. You may also recognize the feeling that Patty has after confessing to Ruth. And you probably understand Ruth's feeling as she takes on this new burden.

> I stood up and felt this sensation of lightness, near weightlessness, like somebody had just bent down, picked up, and carried away all my trouble. . . . I squeezed Ruth's shoulder and a hearable breath rushed through her nostrils. "You know how you're all the time helping me because you're my friend? Well, Anton's my friend and I have to help him, you know? Don't you know?"
>
> "I don't know what it is I know," she said in a weighted voice.

Bette Greene has made you feel Patty's sense of relief. She makes you feel the weight flowing from Patty's shoulders. The last sentence lets you know where the burden has gone. It has been transferred to Ruth. Her voice is "weighted" and heavy with concern. You probably know just how she feels.

Exercise C

The passage below is from the selection you have read. Answer the questions about this passage using what you have learned in this part of the lesson. Choose the best answer for each question. Put an *x* in the correct box or fill in the appropriate words.

[Anton and Patty are talking about Mr. Bergen's dislike of Freddy.]

"But why is your father so opposed to him?"

"Maybe it's because he's so poor, but I'm not sure."

He looked a little perplexed. "Why don't you inquire?"

"I can't inquire." My words had a harshness that I didn't intend. "In my father's vocabulary to ask why is to contradict him."

"I don't like him!" The words seemed to dash out. Then Anton caught my eyes as though asking permission.

"Oh, that's O.K.," I said pleased that Anton was taking my side. "I'll tell you something I've never told anyone before. If he weren't my father, I wouldn't even like him."

"But because he is, you do?"

"Oh, well, I guess I—" Then the image came. The image of his thin, rabid face. "I guess I don't too much. No, I don't like him." That was the first time I had even thought anything like that myself.

1. What is the strongest feeling that these two characters share here?

   ☐ a. Amusement

   ☐ b. Loneliness

   ☐ c. Wonder

   ☐ d. Dislike

2. There is one sentence that describes the way Anton speaks which shows that Anton can't help telling Patty that he dislikes her father. Write that sentence here.

_____

_____

_____

Now check your answers using the Answer Key on page 434. Correct any wrong answer and review this part of the lesson if you don't understand why your answer was wrong.

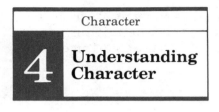

Character

4 Understanding Character

We all must learn to live with other people. For this reason, it is important to be able to understand others. You can come to understand another person through *character analysis*. Character analysis is what you have been doing in the first three parts of this lesson.

People form a first impression of others from appearances. That's why you are careful of how you dress and act when you want to impress someone. Or, you may form an early opinion of a person based on what others have told you. In a novel, first impressions usually come from the author's description of a character. You saw how this works in the first part of the lesson.

Your opinions take shape when you see the way characters act and when you listen to the way they talk. Finally, when you come to understand how the characters feel, you are able to understand why they act and speak as they do.

This is what character analysis is. It is a process of putting facts and feelings together in order to make a judgment about a person. It is an effort at understanding.

Harry Bergen, Patty's father, is one of the most complicated characters in the story. He is the hardest to understand. Though you meet him only briefly in Chapter 11, he is the subject of much of the conversation. He has been described for you, and you have heard about some of his vicious actions. Why does he act the way he does? See if you can make a judgment based on the following passage and on what you already know about the man. Anton is telling Patty how her father acted after he beat her.

> "Do you have any idea where your father went—what he did immediately following the beating he gave you?"
>
> "Not exactly, I could guess. He probably went into the house, smoked a Lucky Strike cigarette, washed his hands, and ate a perfectly enormous supper while he listened to the evening news."
>
> "Not true. He stood watching the housekeeper help you into the house. Then he came into the garage and talked to

himself. Over and over he kept repeating, 'Nobody loves me. In my whole life nobody has ever loved me.' "

"Anton, it must have been somebody else. That doesn't sound like my father."

"It *was* your father."

"I don't understand. Why? How could he be so mean and then worry that he isn't loved? It doesn't make sense."

This new information challenges you to think about Harry Bergen. You are just as puzzled as Patty. In an effort to understand her father, you try to put the pieces of the puzzle together. You don't like Harry Bergen because of the way he treats Patty. But after listening to Anton in this passage, you probably also feel a little sorry for Harry Bergen. Little by little, you try to put the whole picture together.

Harry Bergen is a bitter man. Rightly or wrongly, he feels that no one loves him. For some reason, he doesn't realize that it is his own fault. Perhaps others have been cruel to him. Being cruel may be his way of getting back at the world.

There are many Harry Bergens in the world. Often they are sweet and charming in society and ogres in their own homes. They are badly disturbed people. Feeling unloved, they strike out at those closest to them. When you learn to analyze and to understand such a character in a novel, you will be better able to understand the same kind of person in real life.

Exercise D

The passage below is from the selection you have read. Answer the questions about this passage using what you have learned in this part of the lesson. Choose the best answer for each question. Put an *x* in the correct box or fill in the appropriate words.

[Anton is talking to Patty about her father.]

". . . it seems to me that a man who is incapable of humor is capable of cruelty. If Hitler, for example, had had the ability—the detachment—to observe the absurdity of his own behavior he would have laughed, and today there might not be a madman named Adolph Hitler." . . . .

Anton looked thoughtful. "Cruelty is after all cruelty, and the difference between the two men may have more to do with their degrees of power than their degrees of cruelty. One man is able to affect millions and the other only a few. Would your father's cruelty cause him to crush weak neighboring states? Or would the *Führer's* cruelty cause him to beat his own daughter? Doesn't it seem to you that they both need to inflict pain?"

1. What do you understand about Harry Bergen that you probably didn't before?

   ☐ a. He has no sense of humor.

   ☐ b. He tends to laugh at the wrong time.

   ☐ c. He uses Hitler as his example in life.

   ☐ d. He would like to rule the world.

2. What one word in the passage describes Harry Bergen's worst fault? The word appears six times in the passage. Write the word here.

Use the Answer Key on page 434 to check your answers. Correct any wrong answer and review this part of the lesson if you don't understand why your answer was wrong. Now go on to do the Comprehension Questions.

Comprehension Questions

Keeping
Events in
Order

1. When did Mrs. Bergen complain about the missing food?

   ☐ a. While Patty was lying in bed

   ☐ b. Just after Ruth arrived for the day's work

   ☐ c. As Anton was eating his breakfast

   ☐ d. Just before the family went to the Britlings' restaurant

Recalling
Facts

2. There was one thing Harry Bergen was generous with. That was

   ☐ a. food.

   ☐ b. himself.

   ☐ c. money.

   ☐ d. his car.

Recognizing
Words in
Context

3. "The phrase, 'as long as he lived' sounded like a *vague prophecy*" to Patty. This means the phrase sounded

   ☐ a. almost like a threat to Patty's safety.

   ☐ b. somewhat like a prediction of the future.

   ☐ c. fuzzy, as if the words hadn't been said.

   ☐ d. something like a voice from the past.

4. Patty says that Ruth has eyes that "see so deeply."
   What does this mean?

   ☐ a. Ruth has very sharp eyesight.

   ☐ b. Ruth sees things she shouldn't see.

   ☐ c. Ruth is probably well educated.

   ☐ d. Ruth is a very understanding person.

5. Ruth and Patty had a long talk. When did this
   occur?

   ☐ a. Before Patty ever met Anton

   ☐ b. During Mr. and Mrs. Bergen's breakfast

   ☐ c. Shortly after Mr. and Mrs. Bergen drove away

   ☐ d. After Anton handed Patty the book of essays

6. How were Patty's troubles made lighter?

   ☐ a. By talking to Anton

   ☐ b. By confessing to Ruth

   ☐ c. By besting her father

   ☐ d. By praying

7. What seemed to be Patty's greatest need in life?

   ☐ a. To have a friend

   ☐ b. To rescue a prisoner

   ☐ c. To love her father

   ☐ d. To love Ruth better

8. What was wrong with Patty's legs?

☐ a. They were not as pretty as she wanted them to be.

☐ b. She had put on powder to hide a sunburn.

☐ c. There was nothing wrong except what she imagined.

☐ d. They had red marks from her beating.

9. Who is Freddy?

☐ a. Freddy is Harry Bergen's friend.

☐ b. Freddy is Anton's nickname.

☐ c. Freddy is a bright neighborhood boy Patty loves.

☐ d. Freddy is a boy Patty is forbidden to play with.

10. According to Anton, Patty's father went into the garage and talked to himself. When did this happen?

☐ a. While Patty and Anton were together

☐ b. After Mr. Bergen had beaten Patty

☐ c. Before Anton bought hats for the prisoners

☐ d. During Patty's confession to Ruth

11. There may be one character trait that both Patty and her father have. What is it?

☐ a. An urge to be mean to people

☐ b. An uncontrollable urge to eat a lot of food

☐ c. A feeling that most people don't like them

☐ d. A need to be intelligent and attractive

12. The German prisoners needed hats to protect themselves from the *"formidable* Arkansas sun." The sun was

☐ a. fearfully strong.

☐ b. splendidly bright.

☐ c. pleasantly warm.

☐ d. formless but hot.

13. Harry Bergen is *"incapable* of humor." This means he

☐ a. doesn't know what the word means.

☐ b. reacts violently when someone makes a joke.

☐ c. hasn't the ability to understand humor.

☐ d. is inwardly humorous but won't admit it.

14. Anton said Patty's father and Hitler had something in common. What was it?

☐ a. They have a hatred for Jews.

☐ b. They feel a need to rule nations.

☐ c. They need to inflict pain.

☐ d. They are fearful of the future.

15. Anton told Patty that she was "no common garden flower." To him, she seemed "unique." What did he mean?

☐ a. He felt Patty might become a wallflower.

☐ b. He was only trying to flatter her.

☐ c. He thought Patty was a wild, free spirit.

☐ d. He thought Patty had special talents and beauty.

Now check your answers using the Answer Key on page 434. Correct any wrong answers you have by putting a check (√) in the box next to the right answer. Count the number of questions you answered correctly and plot the total on the Comprehension Scores graph on page 444.

Next, look at the questions you answered incorrectly. What types of questions were they? Count the number of each type and enter the numbers in the spaces below:

Recognizing Words in Context   _____

Recalling Facts   _____

Keeping Events in Order   _____

Making Inferences   _____

Understanding Main Ideas   _____

Now use these numbers to fill in the Comprehension Skills Profile on page 445.

Discussion Guides

The questions below will help you to think about the selection and the lesson you have just read. If you don't discuss these questions in class, try to think about them or discuss them with your classmates.

Discussing Characterization

1. One way authors make characters seem real is by describing small details about their personalities. What small details do you know about the characters in this chapter?

2. Small, unimportant actions help to make characters seem real. Point out some of these small actions in the chapter. (For example, at the beginning of the chapter Patty pulls the sheet over her head.)

3. If characterization is well done, you can imagine what the characters sound like when they speak. Try to act out one of the conversations in the story: between Mr. and Mrs. Bergen; Ruth and Patty; Patty and Anton. Read both parts aloud yourself. Allow others to say whether or not your performance has been convincing.

Discussing the Story

4. You have read Anton's analysis of Harry Bergen. What is your own analysis?

5. Patty loves Ruth and Anton, and they love her. Considering the time and place of the story, what problems do you foresee in these relationships?

6. Patty says, "If he weren't my father, I wouldn't even like him." How do you feel toward Patty when she says this? Does she seem like a hateful person to you? Why or why not?

Discussing the Author's Work

7. Author Bette Greene says the story is based on a true personal experience. What do you think is true in this chapter? What might be made up? Give reasons for your opinion.

8. Sometimes an author will idealize a character. That is, the character is made to seem better than he or she should be. Does Bette Greene do this?

9. When she wrote her book, Bette Greene had almost surely read *Anne Frank: The Diary of a Young Girl* (Unit 8). What similarities and differences do you notice between Anne and Patty?

Writing Exercise

Try one of the following exercises:

1. Write a conversation between two people. They are discussing the character of a third person they both know. That person is not present. To get started, reread the portion of the chapter where Patty and Anton are discussing Patty's father.

2. Describe someone you like, or someone you don't like. Emphasize character traits rather than the person's appearance.

Unit 3   How Authors Use Language

A Day No Pigs Would Die
BY ROBERT NEWTON PECK

About the Illustration

How would you describe this boy's feelings about the man sitting beside his bed? Point out some details in the drawing to support your response.

Here are some questions to help you think:

☐ Are the man and boy related to each other? How do you know?

☐ How do you think the man feels?

☐ What do you think is going on in this scene?

Unit 3

Introduction	What the Novel Is About/What the Lesson Is About
Selection	A Day No Pigs Would Die
Lesson	How Authors Use Language
Activities	Comprehension Questions/Discussion Guides/Writing Exercise

Introduction

What the Novel Is About

A well-kept farm is beautiful to see and pleasant to visit. But growing up on a farm is not all fun and frolic and petting cute animals as we are often led to believe. There is endless hard work. And frequently, the work is dirty and distasteful. The reality of farm life is filled with doing tasks that must be done.

When the farm and the farmer are poor, the problems are greater, the work is harder, the rewards fewer. In *A Day No Pigs Would Die,* Robert Peck is a very poor farm boy, age twelve, growing up on a Vermont farm in the early part of this century. His father has to struggle mightily to make a bare living, so he adds to his small income by butchering pigs for other farmers. The father, or Papa as he is called in the story, has two goals in life. He wants to finish paying the bank the money he owes on his farm, and he wants to see his son Robert educated. Haven Peck, Papa, can neither read nor write his own name.

The family belongs to a Shaker community church. An offshoot of the Quakers, Shakers were a strict sect that included hard work and no-frills living in its creed. They called themselves the United Society of Believers in Christ's Second Coming, or just the Millenial Church. The popular name, Shakers, came from the way some members moved in moments of religious ecstasy at church meetings. The sect grew very rapidly, especially in New England, but it began to decline about the time of the Civil War. There are not many Shakers today.

The story begins with the birth of a calf. It is not a pretty storybook birth where a lovable little creature suddenly appears. The mother cow is in a field, in agony, with the calf stuck in the birth canal. To complicate matters, the cow has a goiter blocking her breathing. A goiter is an enlarged gland in the neck. Without help, cow and calf will die. There is no one else around but Robert, so he sets about doing what must be done. Unfortunately, he is badly mauled by the frantic animal.

The book pulls no punches. People are shown with both strengths and weaknesses; the story includes living and dying, happiness and hurting. And there is a lot of love mixed in, which is the one thing that seems to make the whole terrible struggle worthwhile.

A Day No Pigs Would Die is what is called an *autobiographical novel.* It is a novel, a story made up in the author's imagination, but it is based on the life and real experiences of the author. Robert Newton Peck was born on a Vermont farm like the one he describes. He says the story is 85 percent true. The real Robert Peck was born about fifteen or twenty years later than Robert in the story. Robert in the story grows up in the 1920s. The author grew up in the thirties and forties. And his family was not as staunchly Shaker as the Pecks in the book.

But the story is a real story of the year a boy came to manhood. The author calls it his *bar mitzvah* book: at twelve a boy, at thirteen a man. In the Jewish faith, a boy is made a man in a religious ceremony on his thirteenth birthday, his *bar mitzvah.* The twelve-year-old boy we meet at the beginning of the book grows to be a man in charge of his family at the end.

A Day No Pigs Would Die is one of the books most in demand today in school libraries. And those who read one of Robert Newton Peck's books usually go on to read his others. If you have already read the novel, you will enjoy looking at it again in relation to the lesson. If you have not yet read it, you will surely add the title to your must-read list after seeing the chapters presented here.

What the Lesson Is About

The lesson following the reading selection deals with some of the ways authors use language to make their books more interesting and more enjoyable.

Within your own experience you have surely met people you enjoy listening to. And there are others who bore you, or even annoy you, with the way they speak. Mostly, it's the words they choose and the way they put them together that make the difference. This happens in your reading, too, as you must have noticed. Some things are a pleasure to read. Others are dull as dust. The good writer and the bad writer can use the same language but somehow it doesn't come out the same. How a writer *uses* language makes the difference.

In this lesson we will talk about some of the tricks of the writing business. We can't cover them all, of course; we'll look at just a few that are prominent in the first two chapters of *A Day No Pigs Would Die*. Others may come up in class discussions. What's important is that you become aware that there are very definite techniques authors think about and use when they are writing.

The questions below will help you to focus on the use of language in the chapters from *A Day No Pigs Would Die*. Read the chapters carefully and try to answer these questions as you go along:

1. The characters have an unusual way of speaking. They use expressions different from any you may have heard. This is their *dialect*. How does the use of dialect add to your interest in the story? How does it help you enjoy the story more?

2. In the story, Robert has a way of describing things that is almost like "coloring" or drawing pictures. Which passages would you call vivid or colorful, and why?

3. Good writers use interesting and entertaining comparisons in their writing. One comparison in the story describes a cow's tongue lashing to and fro "like the tail of a clock." What are some of the other comparisons you can find in the story?

4. Sometimes, to emphasize a point, people say things in a round-about way. When rain spoils your plans for a picnic, you might look out the window and say: "Some great day for a picnic!" Or perhaps, "It looks like a flood out there." Neither statement is true, but everyone understands your feelings better than if you had just said, "It's raining out." What are some other "round-about" expressions you can find in your reading?

A Day No Pigs Would Die

Robert Newton Peck

Chapter 1

I should of been in school that April day.

But instead I was up on the ridge near the old spar mine above our farm, whipping the gray trunk of a rock maple with a dead stick, and hating Edward Thatcher. During recess, he'd pointed at my clothes and made sport of them. Instead of tying into him, I'd turned tail and run off. And when Miss Malcolm rang the bell to call us back inside, I was halfway home.

Picking up a stone, I threw it into some bracken ferns, hard as I could. Someday that was how hard I was going to light into Edward Thatcher, and make him bleed like a stuck pig. I'd kick him from one end of Vermont to the other, and sorry him good. I'd teach him not to make fun of Shaker ways. He'd never show his face in the town of Learning, ever again. No, sir.

A painful noise made me whip my head around and jump at the same time. When I saw her, I knew she was in bad trouble.

It was the big Holstein cow, one of many, that belonged to our near neighbor, Mr. Tanner. This one he called "Apron" because she was mostly black, except for the white along her belly which went up her front and around her neck like a big clean apron. She was his biggest cow, Mr. Tanner told Papa, and his best milker. And he was fixing up to take her to Rutland Fair, come summer.

As I ran toward her, she made her dreadful noise again. I got close up and saw why. Her big body was pumping up and down, trying to have her calf. She'd fell down and there was blood on her foreleg, and her mouth was all thick and foamy with yellow-green spit. I tried to reach my hand out and pat her head; but she was wild-eyed mean, and making this breezy noise almost every breath.

Turning away from me, she showed me her swollen rump. Her tail was up and arched high, whipping through the air with every heave of her back. Sticking out of her was the head and one hoof of her calf. His head was so covered with blood and birthsop that I had no way telling he was alive or dead. Until I heard him bawl.

Apron went crashing through the puckerbush, me right behind. I'd never caught up. But because she had to stop and strain, I got to the calf's head and got a purchase on him.

He was so covered with slime, and Apron was so wandering, there was no holding to it. Besides, being just twelve years old, I weighed a bit over a hundred pounds. Apron was comfortable over a thousand, and it wasn't much of a tug for her. As I went down, losing my grip on the calf's neck, her hoof caught my shinbone and it really smarted. The only thing that made me get up and give the whole idea another go was when he bawled again.

I'd just wound up running away from Edward Thatcher and running away from the schoolhouse. I was feathered if I was going to run away from one darn more thing.

I needed a rope. But there wasn't any, so I had to make one. It didn't have to be long, just strong.

Chasing old Apron through the next patch of prickers sure took some fun out of the whole business. I made my mistake of trying to take my trousers off as I ran. No good. So I sat down in the prickers, yanked 'em off over my boots, and caught up to Apron. After a few bad tries, I got one pantleg around her calf's head and knotted it snug.

"Calf," I said to him, "you stay up your ma's hindside and you're about to choke. So you might as well choke getting yourself born."

A Day No Pigs Would Die

Whatever old Apron decided that I was doing to her back yonder, she didn't take kindly to it. So she started off again with me in the rear, hanging on to wait Christmas, and my own bare butt and privates catching a thorn with every step. And that calf never coming one inch closer to coming out. But when Apron stopped to heave again I got the other pantleg around a dogwood tree that was about thick as a fencepost.

Now only three things could happen: My trousers would rip. Apron would just uproot the tree. The calf would slide out.

But nothing happened. Apron just stood shaking and heaving and straining and never moved forward a step. I got the other pantleg knotted about the dogwood; and like Apron, I didn't know what to do next.

Her calf bawled once more, making a weaker noise than before. But all old Apron did was heave in that one place.

"You old bitch," I yelled at her, grabbing a dead black-berry cane that was as long as a bullwhip and big around as a broom handle, "you move that big black smelly ass, you hear?"

I never hit anybody, boy or beast, as I hit that cow. I beat her so hard I was crying. Where I held the big cane, the thorns were chewing up my hands real bad. But it only got me madder.

I kicked her. And stoned her. I kicked her again one last time, so hard in the udder that I thought I heard her grunt. Both her hind quarters sort of hunkered down in the brush. Then she started forward, my trousers went tight, I heard a rip and a calf bawl. And a big hunk of hot stinking stuff went all over me. Some of it was calf, some of it wasn't.

As I went down under the force and weight of it, I figured something either got dead or got born.

All I knew was that I was snarled up in a passel of wet stuff, and there was a strong cord holding me against something that was very hot and kicked a lot. I brushed some of the slop away from my eyes and looked up. And there was Apron, her big black head and her big black mouth licking first me and then her calf.

But she was far from whole. Her mouth was open and she was gasping for air. She stumbled once. I thought for sure I was going to wind up being under a very big cow. The noise in her throat came at me again, and her tongue lashed to and fro like the tail of a clock. It looked to me as if there was something in her mouth. She would start to breathe and then, like a cork in a bottle, some darn thing in there would cut if off.

Her big body swayed like she was dizzy or sick. As the front of her fell to her knees, her head hit my chest as I lay on the ground, her nose almost touching my chin. She had stopped breathing!

Her jaw was locked open so I put my hand into her mouth, but felt only her swollen tongue. I stretched my fingers up into her throat—and there it was! A hard ball, about apple-size. It was stuck in her windpipe, or her gullet. I didn't know which and didn't care. So I shut my eyes, grabbed it, and yanked.

Somebody told me once that a cow won't bite. That somebody is as wrong as sin on Sunday. I thought my arm had got sawed off part way between elbow and shoulder. She bit and bit and never let go. She got to her feet and kept on biting. That devil cow ran down off that ridge with my arm in her mouth, and dragging me half-naked with her. What she didn't do to me with her teeth, she did with her front hoofs.

It should have been broad daylight, but it was night. Black night. As black and as bloody and as bad as getting hurt again and again could ever be.

It just went on and on. It didn't quit.

Chapter 2

"Haven Peck."

Somebody was yelling out Papa's name, but I couldn't see anything. And it was real strange, because my eyes were open. They sort of stinged. So I blinked, but the fog was still there.

There was a wool blanket around me. I could feel the wool rub against the raw place on my arm, but the hurt of it seemed to keep me awake. And keep me alive.

There were more voices now. I heard Papa answer, and the man who was carrying me asked him, "Is this your boy? There's so much blood and dirt and Satan on him, I can't tell for sure. Besides, he's near naked."

"Yes," said Papa. "That's our Robert."

And then I heard Mama's voice, soft and sweet like music; and I could feel her hands on my head and my hair. Aunt Carrie was there, too. She was Mama's oldest sister, who lived with us.

Strong hands were touching my legs now, and then my ribs. I tried to say something about not being in school. Somebody had some warm water and washed my face with it. The water had lilac in it, and smelled right restful.

"We're beholding to you, Benjamin Tanner," said Papa, "for fetching him home. Whatever he done, I'll make right."

"Better look to his arm. It got tore up worse than proper. May be broke."

"Haven," I heard Mama say, "the boy's holding something in his hand. Can't make it out."

I felt them taking something from my right hand. I didn't want to render it up, but they took it.

"I never see the like of it," Mama said. "Like it's near to be alive."

I could hear Mr. Tanner's rough voice over the others. "I know what that is. It's a goiter."

"Goiter?"

"Where'd he get it?"

"It's an evil thing. But for now let's tend his arm. Mr. Tanner, we may got to cut away part of your blanket."

"Ain't mine. Belongs to my horse. So cut all you're a mind to."

I felt Papa pulling the blanket down off my right shoulder, until it got caught in the clotted blood. I heard his jackknife click open, and cut away part of the wool.

"I tied my bandana on his arm," said Mr. Tanner, "so he wouldn't bleed dry." When Papa loosened it up, Mr. Tanner said, "He'll bleed again with it loose, Haven."

"He will," said Papa, "and that'll be a good thing for his arm. Let it open up and holler out all the dirt. Only way to treat a wound is to bleed it, 'til it's clean as a cat's mouth."

"True."

"Lucy," Papa spoke soft to Mama, "better get a needle threaded. He'll want sewing."

He picked me up in his arms, carried me into the house and to the kitchen. He laid me flat on the long lammis table, face up. Mama put something soft under my head, and Aunt Carrie kept washing me off with the lilac water while Papa cut off my shirt and took off my boots.

"The poor lamb," said Mama.

Somebody put a hand on my forehead to see if I was cool. It was followed by a cold wet cloth, and it felt real good. Funny, but it was the only thing on my entire body that I could feel. Then I felt the first of Mama's stitches going into the meat of my arm. I wanted to yell out, but didn't have the will for it. Instead I just lay there on my back on that old

A Day No Pigs Would Die

kitchen table and let Mama sew me back together. It hurt. My eyes filled up with crying and the water ran in rivers to my ears, but I never let out a whimper.

When I had took all the sewing to be took (and by this time I must of been more thread than boy) Papa burdened me upstairs to my room. I could smell Mama, crisp and starched, plumping my pillow, and the cool muslin pillowcase touched both my ears as the back of my head sank into all those feathers.

"Tell Mr. Tanner," I said.

Mama rushed to where my head was, and Papa and Aunt Carrie were at bed foot.

"Tell Mr. Tanner," I said again, "that were he to look up on the ridge, he'll find a calf. I helped get it born. Afterward, old Apron was still choking so I had to rip the ball out of her throat. And I didn't mean to skip school."

"I'll be," said Papa.

"Where are your trousers, Rob?" said Aunt Carrie, who took quite a stock in appearances.

"Up on the ridge. When I tied 'em round a tree they got busted some. I'm sorry, Mama. You'll just have to cut me out another pair."

Mama put her face right down close to mine, and I could smell her goodness.

"I'm preferenced to mend busted pants than a busted boy."

"I . . . I can't feel nothing in my right hand."

"That's 'cause it's resting," said Mama. "It wants to get well, and so do you. So right about now your Pa and Carrie and I are going to tiptoe out of here and let you get some rest. You earned it."

They left. And I closed my eyes and went right off. Later I woke up when Mama brought me a dish of hot succotash and a warm glass of milking, fresh from the evening pail.

The bubbles were still on it.

"That's real good," I said.

At bedtime, Papa came upstairs with his big shoes kicking one of the risers, and brought me one of the last of the winter apples from the cellar. He pulled up a chair close to my bed and looked at me for a long time while I ate the apple with my left hand.

"You mending?"

"Yes, Papa."

"I ought to lick you proper for leaving the schoolhouse."

"Yes, Papa. You ought."

"Someday you want to walk into the bank in Learning and write down your name, don't you?"

"Yes, sir."

"I don't cotton to raise a fool."

"No, Papa."

I tried to move my right arm, but it made me wince up. I couldn't help but make a noise about it.

"She bit you up fair, that cow. Clear to bone."

"Sure did. I always thought cows don't bite."

"Anything'll bite, be it provoked."

"I guess I provoked old Apron. Boy, she sure did some provoking on me."

"You put a hand in her mouth?"

"Yes."

"You rip out that . . . goiter?"

"Yes, sir."

"Was that 'fore or after the calfing?"

"I disremember. All I recall is that Apron was choking something fearful with a piece of stuff in her throat that she wanted me to fetch out."

"So you tore out that goiter."

"Yes, sir. Her calf was hung up, too. So I tore him out. Tore my pants and tore myself. Between me and the calf and Apron, we tore up a good part of Vermont as well as each other."

"How do you feel?"

"Like if I die, at least I'll stop hurting."

"Best you don't complain, a boy who skips school and don't get no stick put on him."

"No, sir. I won't complain. Except when I move it sharp and sudden, my arm is real numb. It's the rest of me that's in misery."

"Where?"

"My backside and my privates. I'm stuck so full of prickers, it makes me smart just to think on it. Every damn—"

"What'd I hear?"

"Every darn pricker in Vermont must be in me, working their way through, and coming out the yonder side. It's enough to sell your soul."

"Well, if your soul looks as poorly as your carcass, I don't guess it'll bring much."

"I don't guess it will."

Papa fished around in his pocket.

"Here's two beads of spruce gum. One's for me. But I don't mention you'd want one."

"Yes, I sure would. Please."

"Here, then. Might help you forget where those prickers are nested."

"It's helping already. Thanks, Papa."

The spruce gum was hard and grainy at first. Then the heat of your mouth begins to melt it down so that it's worth the chewing. The bit that Papa gave me was rich and full of sappy juices. Except that every so often you have to spat out a flick of the bark.

"I saw sumac today, boy."

"Is it ripe yet?"

Out of his pocket, Papa pulled a twig of sumac that was finger-thick and four-inch long.

"How's that look?"

"Papa, that looks real good. Got your knife?"

Papa cracked out his knife, ringed the bark, and set a good notch at one end. All there was left to do now was to bucket soak it overnight, just enough to slip the bark sleeve. And boil it to kill the poison.

"That'll be some whistle, Robert."

"Sure will."

"A boy with a whistle as fine as this won't have no earthy reason to skip school. You of a mind to agree?"

"I agree, Papa."

He stood up, big and tall with his head not quite bumping the roof of my bedroom.

"Don't be going to sleep with spruce gum in your mouth."

"I won't, Papa."

He bent down and pulled the crazy quilt up around my throat. I could tell by the smell of his hand that he'd killed pigs today. There was a strong smell to it, like stale death. That smell was almost always on him, morning and night. Until Saturday, when he'd strip down to the white and stand in the kitchen washtub, up to his shins in hot soapy water, and wash himself clean of the pigs and the killing.

He smelled the best on Sunday morning, when I sat next to him at Shaker Meeting. He smelled just like the big brown bar of soap that he used, and sometimes there was some store-bought pomade on his hair. But when you kill pigs for a living, you can't always smell like Sunday morning.

You just smell like hard work.

How Authors Use Language

Someone once suggested that poets be sent along with astronauts on space missions. Why? Because the view is said to be so beautiful that only a poet could describe it properly. A poet would make you see the scene in your mind's eye and make you feel how it is to be in space looking down on Earth.

Most people would express their feelings more like this: "Gosh, it sure is beautiful." Hearing this, you wouldn't know *how* it is beautiful, and there is no way to understand how the speaker really feels. A writer, on the other hand, thinks long and hard before describing beauty.

Trained writers know they can project pictures, ideas and feelings with the right choice of words. They can make readers see and feel what they want them to see and feel. So a description of Earth might begin like this: "The Earth hung in the blackness of space, a brilliant and perfect sphere, a swirl of many colors, blues, greens and browns, with wisps of white floating delicately on its surface. It seemed a Garden of Eden at the very gates of Heaven."

Now you have not only a picture of the Earth in your mind, you have a feeling for its beauty, and knowledge of how the author feels about it.

When writing a story, an author is careful to choose words that are appropriate to the situation at hand. The language must do the job the author wants it to do. In a mystery the author might want to frighten you, and so uses words with a slinky, slimy sound: "The monster was lurking in the murky mire. And an unearthly moan floated eerily through the gloom." Notice the long vowel sounds and how the sentences drag.

But a sports story will have fast, crisp words: "The sharp crack of bat on ball signalled a base hit. Pete Anders drove for home in a cloud of red dust, and the roar from the stands became thunder as the crowd went wild."

In writing *A Day No Pigs Would Die*, author Robert Newton Peck had to convey to readers the feeling of what it was like to be a poor Vermont farm boy in years gone by. He had to make readers see the situations and experience them as much as possible, without having lived the life he had. He had one thing to do it with—words.

In this lesson, we will look at four things author Robert Peck does with words:

1 The author uses dialect, the local speech of the people.

2 The author uses colorful language and unusual expressions in his descriptions.

3 The author uses comparisons to be sure that readers understand what he is saying.

4 The author uses roundabout expressions for emphasis.

Groups of people in certain places at certain times have special ways of speaking. These special ways are their dialects. Dialect consists mainly of two things: distinctive sounds in the way words are spoken, and special expressions that have grown up over the years in one particular place.

Some Canadians and some Scots, for example, say *hoose* or *hohse* for the place they live in. In the southern United States you might hear *hay-owse*. In some places people "act up" when they are being silly. In other places they "play the fool." You may "make fun" of a person, while others "make sport," as young Robert says in *A Day No Pigs Would Die.*

Dialect is one of the first things you notice in this story. The author doesn't try to spell out Robert's New England pronunciations. This would be too clumsy and difficult to read. But there are many expressions native to rural Vermont early in the century that the author uses to give you an idea of where you are and among what kind of people.

"I should of been in school . . ." is the way the story opens. It turns out that Robert is upset because Edward Thatcher has "made sport" of his clothing. We immediately get a feeling for what it must have been like to be very poor and from a family where mother makes all the clothing, and not very good clothing at that.

In a sense, listening to Robert talk, you can imagine yourself in his shoes wishing you could "light into" Edward Thatcher and "sorry him good." Thus, by using dialect, the author takes you on a trip into a world that only he knows, that you can never know except through the words that spring out of his memory and his imagination.

In the following passage you will notice several examples of Robert's way of speaking, his dialect.

> Apron went crashing through the puckerbush, me right behind. I'd never caught up. But because she had to stop and strain, I got to the calf's head and got a purchase on him.
>
> He was so covered with slime, and Apron was so wandering, there was no holding to it. Besides, being just twelve years old, I weighed a bit over a hundred pounds. Apron was comfortable over a thousand. . . .

Dialect is always interesting because it is a new sound to the ear. Visitors to England are fascinated by the various speech patterns they hear. And visitors from England take great delight in listening to Americanisms. In the same way, dialect makes for a different kind of reading experience when it is used well.

And dialect is often a very expressive way of speaking. Local expressions are apt to put an idea very precisely in just a few words. Saying that Apron was "so wandering," for example, describes in only two words exactly what the poor cow was doing.

Exercise A

The passage below is from the selection you have read. Answer the questions about this passage using what you have learned in this part of the lesson. Choose the best answer for each question. Put an *x* in the correct box or fill in the appropriate words.

"You mending?"

"Yes, Papa."

"I ought to lick you proper for leaving the schoolhouse."

"Yes, Papa. You ought."

"Someday you want to walk into the bank in Learning and write down your name, don't you?"

"Yes, sir."

"I don't cotton to raise a fool."

"No, Papa."

I tried to move my right arm, but it made me wince up. I couldn't help but make a noise about it.

1. Which of the following expressions is *not* an example of local dialect?

☐ a. "You mending?"

☐ b. "I ought to lick you proper. . . ."

☐ c. "Someday you want to walk into the bank. . . ."

☐ d. ". . . it made me wince up."

2. Robert's father is uneducated. He can neither read nor write. He does not want his son to grow up uneducated. Find the expression that puts this idea in just a few words. Write it in the space provided.

_____

_____

_____

Now check your answers using the Answer Key on page 435. Correct any wrong answer and review this part of the lesson if you don't understand why your answer was wrong.

2 Using Colorful Language

No one likes to be bored. Everyone likes new experiences, even surprises. So it is that people enjoy listening to someone who has a fresh and different way of speaking. The best teachers have a talent for this. They have a way of speaking that catches your attention and holds it. They know how to find ways of explaining ideas so that the ideas are understood and remembered. Some public speakers also have this talent. It is often referred to as a colorful way of speaking. It is like the colors, the shadings, the lights and the darks that make a picture interesting and meaningful.

The best writers, too, are colorful. They take great pains to make their writing fresh, different and attractive. They color and shade with their words and sentences to make their work interesting and meaningful.

Calling Apron, the cow, "wild-eyed mean," for example, lets you know exactly how Apron looked at the moment, how she felt, and how Robert must have felt looking back at her. Robert's saying the lilac water smelled "restful," and that he could smell his mother's goodness, are other examples of colorful language.

You can't always point to color, however, as coming from this word or that. Most of the time, color comes just from the way the author puts words together. And just as you see a whole picture as pleasing, the whole effect of the story is pleasing. It has a sound and clarity to it that hold your interest, and it makes you understand exactly what is going on and exactly how the characters feel. See how it works here where Robert describes the end of his ordeal of being sewn back together by his mother.

> When I had took all the sewing to be took (and by this time I must of been more thread than boy) Papa burdened me upstairs to my room. I could smell Mama, crisp and starched, plumping my pillow, and the cool muslin pillowcase touched both my ears as the back of my head sank into all those feathers.

If you have ever gone to bed sick or tired or both, you know how good it feels to sink your head into a soft pillow. The author reminds you of that and makes you feel it here. After all the dirt and pain, here is Mama "crisp and starched," and the cool pillowcase that "touched both my ears." How peaceful and relaxed it is. How secure Robert feels among his family after all the trouble he has had both with the cow and at school. The author has "arranged" his picture and has colored it exactly right so that you know just what Robert is feeling and what the story is about.

Exercise B

The passage below is from the selection you have read. Answer the questions about this passage using what you have learned in this part of the lesson. Choose the best answer for each question. Put an x in the correct box or fill in the appropriate words.

He [Papa] bent down and pulled the crazy quilt up around my throat. I could tell by the smell of his hand that he'd killed pigs today. There was a strong smell to it, like stale death. That smell was almost always on him, morning and night. Until Saturday, when he'd strip down to the white and stand in the kitchen wash-tub, up to his shins in hot soapy water, and wash himself clean of the pigs and the killing.

He smelled the best on Sunday morning. . . . He smelled just like the big brown bar of soap that he used. . . . But when you kill pigs for a living, you can't always smell like Sunday morning.

You just smell like hard work.

1. The author describes smells to make you realize that

　□ a. Robert hates his father and his work.

　□ b. Robert understands his father and his work.

　□ c. Robert dislikes having his father tuck him into bed.

　□ d. Robert wishes that every day were like Sunday.

2. There are four colorful descriptions of smells in this passage. One describes a smell "like Sunday morning." Write down at least two of the other descriptions of smells.

_____

_____

_____

Now check your answers using the Answer Key on page 435. Correct any wrong answer and review this part of the lesson if you don't understand why your answer was wrong.

There are many things that are best described by comparing them to something else. "How was poor old Jim when you saw him?" someone asks. "He looked like death warmed over," you might say. Or, "He was as frisky as a young goat."

Such comparisons, which begin with *like* or *as*, are called *similes* (sim'-ih-lees). A simile is one of many turns of language that are known as "figures of speech." Often it is difficult or impossible to describe something or express an idea without using a simile. Other times the description is clearer and more colorful when a simile is used.

You can't describe the color red, for example, without comparing it to something: red as a cherry, like a fire engine, as a rose. It is more dramatic, and perhaps more exact, to say you slept like a log than just to say you slept well. When Robert said that his father smelled like Sunday, he was using a simile to describe the smell and express a feeling at the same time.

Another figure of speech used to make comparisons, and thus describe something more clearly, is the *metaphor* (met'-a-for). This comparison omits the words *like* or *as*. A metaphor refers directly to one thing as if it were something else. "The black cat night sneaks about on silent paws" is a metaphor. Here night is called a black cat. Without the words *like* or *as* you are left to understand for yourself that this is a comparison. "One by one the withered leaves of age fall from the tree of life." In this metaphor, aging is compared to falling leaves and life is compared to a tree.

When Mr. Tanner finds Robert and brings him home, he uses a metaphor: "There's so much blood and dirt and Satan on him. . . ." Robert is covered with evil-smelling glop that is worse than simple dirt; the only way Mr. Tanner can describe it is to use a metaphor. He compares the stuff to what Satan might have on him should he ever appear.

Notice that all of the following comparisons from the story are similes. They are introduced with *like* or *as*.

> Someday that was how hard I was going to light into Edward Thatcher, and make him bleed like a stuck pig.

> . . . her tongue lashed to and fro like the tail of a clock.

> "Only way to treat a wound is to bleed it, 'til it's clean as a cat's mouth."

Exercise C

Mama put something soft under my head, and Aunt Carrie kept washing me off with the lilac water while Papa cut off my shirt and took off my boots.

"The poor lamb," said Mama.

1. "The poor lamb" is a metaphor that Mama uses because

   ☐ a. she wants everyone to know that she likes lambs.

   ☐ b. she thinks Robert is acting like a lamb.

   ☐ c. she wants to compare Robert to a poor sick lamb.

   ☐ d. she thinks it is a pretty thing to say.

2. Pick out three similes from among the following sentences and write them on the lines provided.

   "I'm stuck so full of prickers, it makes me smart just to think on it."

   "That'll be some whistle, Robert."

   . . . she was mostly black, except for the white along her belly which went up her front...like a big clean apron.

   She would start to breathe and then, like a cork in a bottle, some darn thing in there would cut it off.

That somebody is as wrong as sin on Sunday.

It just went on and on. It didn't quit.

_____

_____

_____

Now check your answers using the Answer Key on page 435. Correct any wrong answer and review this part of the lesson if you don't understand why your answer was wrong.

4 Using Roundabout Expressions

In everyday speech, people often stress what they are saying by saying something different from what they really mean. Strange? Not at all. Here are some expressions you hear all the time:

Leaving a boring class on a beautiful spring day you might say: "What a great way to spend a day like this." You mean exactly the opposite, of course. It was a terrible way to spend the day. You are being *ironic*. The figure of speech you are using is called *irony*. It is the opposite of what you mean. If a friend carries the irony further so that it becomes sharp or biting—"Don't you just love the way they pile on the work in nice weather?"—the irony may be called *sarcasm*. The remark is *sarcastic*.

In the same situation you could say: "I was sitting in there so long that I got calluses on my backside." You didn't really get calluses; you are exaggerating or overstating your discomfort. This figure of speech is called *exaggeration*.

Still another way to stress or call attention to your boredom would be to say: "Things went a little slow in there today, didn't they!" You really mean that things went extremely slow. In fact you thought the clock had stopped! This figure of speech is called *understatement*.

Just as you find these figures of speech in conversation, you will find them in most of your reading. In *A Day No Pigs Would Die*, when Robert thinks about Edward Thatcher he says: "I'd kick him from one end of Vermont to the other." This is clearly an overstatement. It is exaggeration.

Chasing the cow and getting scratched and kicked for his pains, Robert says: "Chasing old Apron through the next patch of prickers sure took some fun out of the whole business." This is irony. Robert means the opposite of what he says. There was no fun to start with in dealing with the cow, and now things were getting worse.

Then Robert says of the cow's attitude: "Whatever old Apron decided that I was doing to her back yonder, she didn't take kindly to it." This is understatement. Not only didn't Apron take kindly to what Robert was doing, she objected violently.

Sometimes these roundabout twists of expression are funny. Sometimes they are dramatic, angry, sad or just thought-provoking. They are always used for emphasis, to call attention to something being said.

Exercise D

The passage below is from the selection you have read. Answer the questions about this passage using what you have learned in this part of the lesson. Choose the best answer for each question. Put an *x* in the correct box or fill in the appropriate words.

I brushed some of the slop away from my eyes and looked up. And there was Apron, her big black head and her big black mouth licking first me then her calf.

1. Robert might have added an ironic statement to this. Which one of the following expressions could be considered an ironic addition to the passage?

   ☐ a. That's just what I needed, to be slop-licked by a cow.

   ☐ b. I could smell her breath and it was awful.

   ☐ c. Her tongue was as rough as sandpaper.

   ☐ d. I felt like I was being hit by a wet towel.

"Yes sir. Her calf was hung up, too. So I tore him out. Tore my pants and tore myself. Between me and the calf and Apron, we tore up a good part of Vermont as well as each other."

2. In the space provided, write the expression that can be called exaggeration.

   _____

   _____

Use the Answer Key on page 435 to check your answers. Correct
any wrong answer and review this part of the lesson if you don't
understand why your answer was wrong. Now go on to do the
Comprehension Questions.

Comprehension Questions

Answer these questions without looking back at the selection. Choose the best answer to each question and put an *x* in the box beside it.

Making
Inferences

1. Robert ran away from school when Edward Thatcher made fun of his clothes. This suggests that Robert was

   ☐ a. afraid of Edward Thatcher.

   ☐ b. embarrassed about being different.

   ☐ c. afraid his father would find out.

   ☐ d. too timid to face his teacher.

Recalling
Facts

2. Why was Apron in trouble?

   ☐ a. She hadn't been milked for days.

   ☐ b. She was caught in a bunch of brambles.

   ☐ c. She was having trouble giving birth to her calf.

   ☐ d. She couldn't get away from Robert.

Keeping
Events in
Order

3. Which of these statements is true?

   ☐ a. After her calf was born, Robert helped Apron to breathe.

   ☐ b. The calf was born while Robert was dragged by the arm.

   ☐ c. Apron bit Robert as she was having her calf.

   ☐ d. Robert didn't know the calf was born; he had passed out.

4. Apron "sort of *hunkered down* in the brush" when she was having her calf. This probably means she

   ☐ a. ran with her head down.

   ☐ b. backed out of the brush.

   ☐ c. kicked and bit.

   ☐ d. squatted or crouched.

5. Which one of these statements is true?

   ☐ a. Robert just didn't use his head in helping Apron.

   ☐ b. Robert had no idea what was bothering Apron.

   ☐ c. Robert must have known a good deal about animals.

   ☐ d. Robert was stupid to stick his hand in a cow's mouth.

6. Who brought Robert home?

   ☐ a. Mr. Tanner, a neighbor

   ☐ b. Miss Malcolm, the teacher

   ☐ c. Aunt Carrie, Mama's sister

   ☐ d. Haven Peck, Robert's father

7. Robert's father said: "We're *beholding* to you . . . for fetching him home." What is another way to say the same thing?

   ☐ a. We see you had found him.

   ☐ b. We're in your debt for bringing him home.

   ☐ c. We're glad you drove him home.

   ☐ d. We see how you meddle with our home.

8. Robert was

☐ a. put to bed before he was sewn up by Mama.

☐ b. patched up by a neighbor before he was brought home.

☐ c. laid on the table and then sewn up by Mama.

☐ d. taken upstairs as soon as he was brought home.

9. When Robert was being sewn up, he "never let out a *whimper.*" A *whimper* is

☐ a. a small cry.

☐ b. a drop of blood.

☐ c. a secret.

☐ d. soft talking.

10. What was Robert's attitude toward his father?

☐ a. Fear

☐ b. Respect

☐ c. Suspicion

☐ d. Shame

11. When did Robert's father have a talk alone with him?

☐ a. At bedtime

☐ b. The next morning

☐ c. When Robert came home

☐ d. On Saturday after washing

12. What can you gather from the talk between Robert
and his father?

☐ a. They hated each other.

☐ b. Papa was visiting because it was his duty.

☐ c. Robert and Papa loved one another.

☐ d. Robert was terribly afraid of his father.

13. Papa said to Robert: "I don't cotton to raise
a fool." This and other talk about school means
that Papa

☐ a. thinks Robert is a foolish boy.

☐ b. finds Robert's schooling not good
enough.

☐ c. intends that Robert will be educated.

☐ d. refuses to raise Robert if he is foolish.

14. When Papa pulled the quilt around Robert's neck,
what did Robert smell?

☐ a. Butchered pigs

☐ b. The earth of the garden

☐ c. Lilac water

☐ d. Tobacco and whiskey

15. Robert ends Chapter 2 saying: "When you kill pigs
for a living, you can't always smell like Sunday
morning. You just smell like hard work." This
suggests that

☐ a. Robert despises his father's work.

☐ b. Robert doesn't like hard work.

☐ c. Robert accepts what his father has to do.

☐ d. Robert feels sorry for the pigs that die.

Now check your answers using the Answer Key on page 435. Correct any wrong answers you have by putting a check (✓) in the box next to the right answer. Count the number of questions you answered correctly and plot the total on the Comprehension Scores graph on page 444.

Next, look at the questions you answered incorrectly. What types of questions were they? Count the number of each type and enter the numbers in the spaces below:

Recognizing Words in Context   _____

Recalling Facts   _____

Keeping Events in Order   _____

Making Inferences   _____

Understanding Main Ideas   _____

Now use these numbers to fill in the Comprehension Skills Profile on page 445.

Discussion Guides

The questions below will help you to think about the selection and the lesson you have just read. If you don't discuss these questions in class, try to think about them or discuss them with your classmates.

Discussing Use of Language

1. A good writer can make you understand how a character feels. Find a passage in the reading selection that makes you understand how Robert feels at some point. How does the language used help you understand Robert's feelings?

2. In the following passage from the story, the author describes Robert's pain and loss of consciousness. It was probably very difficult for the author to write just the way he wanted it. Why do you think it may have been hard to write?

> It should have been broad daylight, but it was night. Black night. As black and as bloody and as bad as getting hurt again and again could ever be.
> It just went on and on. It didn't quit.

3. Repeating sounds is called *alliteration*. "He was big, bad and bold," emphasizes the *b* sound. What sound is repeated in the passage in question 2? How does this alliteration add to the description?

Discussing the Story

4. What is your opinion of the boy, Robert Peck? What is your opinion of his father, Haven Peck?

5. Someone said of this book: "It is about a coming to manhood." What can you find in the chapters you have read to show that Robert is growing up?

6. There is a great deal in the description of Robert's adventure with Apron to make you wince, even cringe. But do you feel any of it is "dirty" or indecent? Give reasons for your opinion.

Discussing the Author's Work

7. Robert Newton Peck lived a good deal of the story he tells. Why do you suppose many authors choose to write about things they know well?

A Day No Pigs Would Die

8. When you tell stories about your family, you probably refer to "my father" and "my mother." The author has Robert say "Papa" and "Mama." Why do you suppose he does this?

9. The story is written from the point of view of a character in the story, the boy Robert. Robert is telling the story about himself. He says "I" and "my" as if he were talking directly to you. This is called a *first-person narrative*. It is told from a *first-person point of view*. How does this technique make a story seem more real?

Writing Exercise

Tell a story that describes an experience you have had. Tell it as if you were speaking to a friend. In telling the story, do these things:

1. Have other people in the story speak. Make them speak just as they sounded to you—that is, use their dialect, and your own. (See how author Robert Newton Peck does this in his story.)

2. Use at least one simile. (Look back at part 3 of the lesson.)

3. Use at least one overstatement or understatement. (Look back at part 4 of the lesson.)

4. If possible, use an ironic statement. (Look back at part 4 of the lesson.)

Unit 4 Tone and Mood

To Kill a Mockingbird
BY HARPER LEE

About the Illustration

How would you describe what is happening in this scene? Point out some details in the drawing to support your response.

Here are some questions to help you think:

- ☐ What do you think this boy is feeling? What details make you think that?

- ☐ What effect does the background have on you? How would this scene be different if it took place on a sunny day?

Unit 4

Introduction	What the Novel Is About/What the Lesson Is About
Selection	**To Kill a Mockingbird**
Lesson	**Tone and Mood**
Activities	Comprehension Questions/Discussion Guides/Writing Exercise

Introduction

What the Novel Is About

To Kill a Mockingbird is about eight-year-old Jean Louise (Scout) Finch, her twelve-year-old brother, Jem, their father, Atticus Finch, and the people of Maycomb County, Alabama. There is no mother in the Finch family. She died when the children were small. In her place there are two women: Calpurnia, who is cook and nurse to the children; and Atticus's sister, Aunt Alexandra. The story takes place between 1933 and 1935.

Two parts of the story come together in the chapter you will read. One part involves Arthur (Boo) Radley, a next-door neighbor who is never seen. When he was a teen-ager, Boo got into some small trouble with the law. To keep him from the disgrace of jail, his father shut him up in the house. As far as anyone knows, he has not been out again in twenty-five years.

The children believe Boo is some sort of monster. Stories told about him say that he goes out at night peeking in windows and killing animals to eat raw. The Radley house, then, is something that children and many adults fear.

One summer, Scout, Jem and a friend named Dill decide they are going to be daring enough to get a look at Boo Radley. Making swift raids up to the Radley house becomes a game with them. Once they are even bold enough to try to peek through a window. They never do get to see Boo, but Boo Radley is watching them.

The other part of the story deals with Tom Robinson, a black man who has been wrongly accused of raping and beating a white girl, Mayella Ewell. Atticus Finch, who is a lawyer, is given the job of defending Tom. In court, Atticus proves that the girl was not raped, and that it was the girl's father, Bob Ewell—and not Tom—who beat her.

Bob Ewell, a mean and treacherous man, swears he will get Atticus Finch for shaming him in public. But Ewell is a coward. In a drunken rage he goes instead after Atticus's children, Scout and Jem.

Chapter 28 begins with Jem and Scout walking to a Halloween pageant being held in the school auditorium. The school is just around the corner from their house (past the Radley house) and across the schoolyard. Scout is going to be in the pageant dressed as a smoked ham, one of the products of Maycomb County. Her costume is made from chicken wire. The wire is bent in the shape of a ham, wide and round at the bottom and narrow at the top where the bone, or hock, is. The whole thing is covered with brown cloth.

What happens before, during and after the pageant is the subject of this chapter. You will meet Mrs. Merriweather, a town busybody who is in charge of the pageant. Atticus Finch appears in the last part of the chapter, and in the last few pages you will meet Dr. Reynolds and Sheriff Heck Tate.

One other character appears. He is described only as a "countryman" whom Scout has never seen before. He is the one who saves the children's lives when they are attacked. It will be up to you to figure out who he could be.

You will notice a reference to a mockingbird (a "mocker") early in the chapter. A mockingbird is a plain gray and white songbird that imitates the songs of other birds. It is one of the most delightful birds to listen to as it goes through its repetoire, or list, of songs it has learned from other birds.

The point is made in the novel that people sometimes kill these lovely songbirds for no better reason than that they are small, weak and defenseless. This mean streak in people is beyond explaining or understanding. The author uses this point to show how people sometimes kill other people in much the same way. Just as they might kill a mockingbird, the strong people in society will mistreat, even kill, other people for no better reason than that they are weak and defenseless.

To Kill a Mockingbird first appeared in 1960 and has been a best seller ever since. It was written by Harper Lee, who grew up in Monroeville, Alabama, during the Depression years in which the story is set. The town, in fact, is the Maycomb of the story. Her father was a lawyer there, and he served as a model for Atticus Finch. *To Kill a Mockingbird* won a Pulitzer Prize in 1961. It was made into a movie starring Gregory Peck as Atticus and often replays on television.

What the Lesson Is About

This lesson is about tone and mood. When you think of tone you probably think of a sound. A bell has a certain tone. Your voice has a tone when you speak or sing. You can change the tone of your voice to match your feelings. You shout when you are angry. You speak softly in a romantic mood.

Writing has tone as well, even if there is no sound. It shows up as a feeling. It can be said that a piece of writing has a sad tone, an angry tone, a sarcastic tone, a happy tone, and so on.

Mood is a feeling, too. Moods carry the same names as tone: happiness, sorrow, despair, excitement, boredom. You know what moods are because you have experienced them all yourself.

Tone and mood go together like a chicken and an egg. But like the chicken and the egg, it's hard to tell which comes first. Tones create moods, and moods create tones. As a writer writes, he or she is in a certain mood. The author has certain feelings and attitudes about the subject matter and the characters. This mood is reflected in the writing as tone. You can also detect the moods of the characters. And as a reader you notice the tone and adopt a mood to match it.

The questions below will help you to focus on tone and mood in the chapter from *To Kill a Mockingbird*. Read the chapter carefully and try to answer these questions as you go along:

1 Tone and mood constantly change in a story. Where are there changes of tone and mood in the chapter? Mark them as you find them. Try to label them as funny, tense, exciting, calm, frightening, or whatever you think they are.

2 How does the setting in the dark schoolyard affect the tone of the story, the mood of the characters, and your mood as a reader?

3 Special tones and moods may be associated with people you know. Tones and moods also go with characters in a novel. What tone and what mood do you sense when you read about Mrs. Merriweather? What tones are connected with other characters?

4 Authors create tone and mood with words and with the way they put words together. What words or expressions can you find in the story that seem to create a special tone or mood? Mark them as you find them.

To Kill a Mockingbird

Harper Lee

28.

The weather was unusually warm for the last day of October. We didn't even need jackets. The wind was growing stronger, and Jem said it might be raining before we got home. There was no moon.

The street light on the corner cast sharp shadows on the Radley house. I heard Jem laugh softly. "Bet nobody bothers them tonight," he said. Jem was carrying my ham costume, rather awkwardly, as it was hard to hold. I thought it gallant of him to do so.

"It is a scary place though, ain't it?" I said. "Boo doesn't mean anybody any harm, but I'm right glad you're along."

"You know Atticus wouldn't let you go to the schoolhouse by yourself," Jem said.

"Don't see why, it's just around the corner and across the yard."

"That yard's a mighty long place for little girls to cross at night," Jem teased. "Ain't you scared of haints?"

We laughed. Haints, Hot Steams, incantations, secret signs, had vanished with our years as mist with sunrise. "What was that old thing," Jem said, "Angel bright, life-in-death; get off the road, don't suck my breath."

"Cut it out, now," I said. We were in front of the Radley Place.

Jem said, "Boo must not be at home. Listen."

High above us in the darkness a solitary mocker poured out his repertoire in blissful unawareness of whose tree he sat in, plunging from the shrill kee, kee of the sunflower bird to the irascible qua-ack of a bluejay, to the sad lament of Poor Will, Poor Will, Poor Will.

We turned the corner and I tripped on a root growing in the road. Jem tried to help me, but all he did was drop my costume in the dust. I didn't fall, though, and soon we were on our way again.

We turned off the road and entered the schoolyard. It was pitch black.

"How do you know where we're at, Jem?" I asked, when we had gone a few steps.

"I can tell we're under the big oak because we're passin' through a cool spot. Careful now, and don't fall again."

We had slowed to a cautious gait, and were feeling our way forward so as not to bump into the tree. The tree was a single and ancient oak; two children could not reach around its trunk and touch hands. It was far away from teachers, their spies, and curious neighbors: it was near the Radley lot, but the Radleys were not curious. A small patch of earth beneath its branches was packed hard from many fights and furtive crap games.

The lights in the high school auditorium were blazing in the distance, but they blinded us, if anything. "Don't look ahead, Scout," Jem said. "Look at the ground and you won't fall."

"You should have brought the flashlight, Jem."

"Didn't know it was this dark. Didn't look like it'd be this dark earlier in the evening. So cloudy, that's why. It'll hold off a while, though."

Someone leaped at us.

"God amighty!" Jem yelled.

A circle of light burst in our faces, and Cecil Jacobs jumped in glee behind it. "Ha-a-a, gotcha!" he shrieked. "Thought you'd be comin' along this way!"

"What are you doin' way out here by yourself, boy? Ain't you scared of Boo Radley?"

Cecil had ridden safely to the auditorium with his parents, hadn't seen us, then had ventured down this far because he knew good and well we'd be coming along. He thought Mr. Finch'd be with us, though.

"Shucks, ain't much but around the corner," said Jem. "Who's scared to go around the corner?" We had to admit that Cecil was pretty good, though. He *had* given us a fright, and he could tell it all over the schoolhouse, that was his privilege.

"Say," I said, "ain't you a cow tonight? Where's your costume?"

"It's up behind the stage," he said. "Mrs. Merriweather says the pageant ain't comin' on for a while. You can put yours back of the stage by mine, Scout, and we can go with the rest of 'em."

This was an excellent idea, Jem thought. He also thought it a good thing that Cecil and I would be together. This way, Jem would be left to go with people his own age.

When we reached the auditorium, the whole town was there except Atticus and the ladies worn out from decorating, and the usual outcasts and shut-ins. Most of the county, it seemed, was there: the hall was teeming with slicked-up country people. The high school building had a wide downstairs hallway; people milled around booths that had been installed along each side.

"Oh Jem, I forgot my money," I sighed, when I saw them.

"Atticus didn't," Jem said. "Here's thirty cents, you can do six things. See you later on."

"Okay," I said, quite content with thirty cents and Cecil. I went with Cecil down to the front of the auditorium, through a door on one side, and backstage. I got rid of my ham costume and departed in a hurry, for Mrs. Merriweather was standing at a lectern in front of the first row of seats making last-minute, frenzied changes in the script.

"How much money you got?" I asked Cecil. Cecil had thirty cents, too, which made us even. We squandered our first nickels on the House of Horrors, which scared us not at all; we entered the black seventh-grade room and were led around by the temporary ghoul in residence and were made to touch several objects alleged to be component parts of a human being. "Here's his eyes," we were told when we touched two peeled grapes on a saucer. "Here's his heart," which felt like raw liver. "These are his innards," and our hands were thrust into a plate of cold spaghetti.

Cecil and I visited several booths. We each bought a sack of Mrs. Judge Taylor's homemade divinity. I wanted to bob for apples, but Cecil said it wasn't sanitary. His mother said he might catch something from everybody's heads having been in the same tub. "Ain't anything around town now to catch," I protested. But Cecil said his mother said it was unsanitary to eat after folks. I later asked Aunt Alexandra about this, and she said people who held such views were usually climbers.

We were about to purchase a blob of taffy when Mrs. Merriweather's runners appeared and told us to go backstage, it was time to get ready. The auditorium was filling with people; the Maycomb County High School band had assembled in front below the stage; the stage footlights were on and the red velvet curtain rippled and billowed from the scurrying going on behind it.

Backstage, Cecil and I found the narrow hallway teeming with people: adults in homemade three-corner hats, Confederate caps, Spanish-American War hats, and World War helmets. Children dressed as various agricultural enterprises crowded around the one small window.

"Somebody's mashed my costume," I wailed in dismay. Mrs. Merriweather galloped to me, reshaped the chicken wire, and thrust me inside.

To Kill a Mockingbird

"You all right in there, Scout?" asked Cecil. "You sound so far off, like you was on the other side of a hill."

"You don't sound any nearer," I said.

The band played the national anthem, and we heard the audience rise. Then the bass drum sounded. Mrs. Merriweather, stationed behind her lectern beside the band, said: "Maycomb County: Ad Astra Per Aspera." The bass drum boomed again. "That means," said Mrs. Merriweather, translating for the rustic elements, "from the mud to the stars." She added, unnecessarily, it seemed to me, "A pageant."

"Reckon they wouldn't know what it was if she didn't tell 'em," whispered Cecil, who was immediately shushed.

"The whole town knows it," I breathed.

"But the country folks've come in," Cecil said.

"Be quiet back there," a man's voice ordered, and we were silent.

The bass drum went boom with every sentence Mrs. Merriweather uttered. She chanted mournfully about Maycomb County being older than the state, that it was a part of the Mississippi and Alabama Territories, that the first white man to set foot in the virgin forests was the Probate Judge's great-grandfather five times removed, who was never heard of again. Then came the fearless Colonel Maycomb, for whom the county was named.

Andrew Jackson appointed him to a position of authority, and Colonel Maycomb's misplaced self-confidence and slender sense of direction brought disaster to all who rode with him in the Creek Indian Wars. Colonel Maycomb persevered in his efforts to make the region safe for democracy, but his first campaign was his last. His orders, relayed to him by a friendly Indian runner, were to move south. After consulting a tree to ascertain from its lichen which way was south, and taking no lip from the subordinates who ventured to correct him, Colonel Maycomb set out on a purposeful journey to rout the enemy and entangled his troops so far northwest in the forest primeval that they were eventually rescued by settlers moving inland.

Mrs. Merriweather gave a thirty-minute description of Colonel Maycomb's exploits. I discovered that if I bent my knees I could tuck them under my costume and more or less sit. I sat down, listened to Mrs. Merriweather's drone and the bass drum's boom and was soon fast asleep.

They said later that Mrs. Merriweather was putting her all into the grand finale, that she had crooned, "Po-ork," with a confidence born of pine trees and butterbeans entering on cue. She waited a few seconds, then called, "Po-ork?" When nothing materialized, she yelled, "Pork!"

I must have heard her in my sleep, or the band playing *Dixie* woke me, but it was when Mrs. Merriweather triumphantly mounted the stage with the state flag that I chose to make my entrance. Chose is incorrect: I thought I'd better catch up with the rest of them.

They told me later that Judge Taylor went out behind the auditorium and stood there slapping his knees so hard Mrs. Taylor brought him a glass of water and one of his pills.

Mrs. Merriweather seemed to have a hit, everybody was cheering so, but she caught me backstage and told me I had ruined her pageant. She made me feel awful, but when Jem came to fetch me he was sympathetic. He said he couldn't see my costume much from where he was sitting. How he could tell I was feeling bad under my costume I don't know, but he said I did all right, I just came in a little late, that was all. Jem was becoming almost as good as Atticus at making you feel right when things went wrong. Almost—not even Jem could make me go through that crowd, and he consented to wait backstage with me until the audience left.

"You wanta take it off, Scout?" he asked.

"Naw, I'll just keep it on," I said. I could hide my mortification under it.

To Kill a Mockingbird

"You all want a ride home?" someone asked.

"No sir, thank you," I heard Jem say. "It's just a little walk."

"Be careful of haints," the voice said. "Better still, tell the haints to be careful of Scout."

"There aren't many folks left now," Jem told me. "Let's go."

We went through the auditorium to the hallway, then down the steps. It was still black dark. The remaining cars were parked on the other side of the building, and their headlights were little help. "If some of 'em were goin' in our direction we could see better," said Jem. "Here Scout, let me hold onto your—hock. You might lose your balance."

"I can see all right."

"Yeah, but you might lose your balance." I felt a slight pressure on my head, and assumed that Jem had grabbed that end of the ham. "You got me?"

"Uh huh."

We began crossing the black schoolyard straining to see our feet. "Jem," I said, "I forgot my shoes, they're back behind the stage."

"Well let's go get 'em." But as we turned around the auditorium lights went off. "You can get 'em tomorrow," he said.

"But tomorrow's Sunday," I protested as Jem turned me homeward.

"You can get the Janitor to let you in . . . Scout?"

"Hm?"

"Nothing."

Jem hadn't started that in a long time. I wondered what he was thinking. He'd tell me when he wanted to, probably when we got home. I felt his fingers press the top of my costume, too hard, it seemed. I shook my head. "Jem, you don't hafta—"

"Hush a minute, Scout," he said, pinching me.

We walked along silently. "Minute's up," I said. "What-cha thinkin' about?" I turned to look at him, but his outline was barely visible.

"Thought I heard something," he said. "Stop a minute."

We stopped.

"Hear anything?" he asked.

"No."

We had not gone five paces before he made me stop again.

"Jem, are you tryin' to scare me? You know I'm too old—"

"Be quiet," he said, and I knew he was not joking.

The night was still. I could hear his breath coming easily beside me. Occasionally there was a sudden breeze that hit my bare legs, but it was all that remained of a promised windy night. This was the stillness before a thunderstorm. We listened.

"Heard an old dog just then," I said.

"It's not that," Jem answered. "I hear it when we're walkin' along, but when we stop I don't hear it."

"You hear my costume rustlin'. Aw, it's just Halloween got you. . . ."

I said it more to convince myself than Jem, for sure enough, as we began walking, I heard what he was talking about. It was not my costume.

"It's just old Cecil," said Jem presently. "He won't get us again. Let's don't let him think we're hurrying."

We slowed to a crawl. I asked Jem how Cecil could follow us in this dark, looked to me like he'd bump into us from behind.

"I can see you, Scout," Jem said.

"How? I can't see you."

"Your fat streaks are showin'. Mrs. Crenshaw painted 'em with some of that shiny stuff so they'd show up under the footlights. I can see you pretty well, an' I expect Cecil can see you well enough to keep his distance."

I would show Cecil that we knew he was behind us and we were ready for him. "Cecil Jacobs is a big wet he-en!" I yelled suddenly, turning around.

We stopped. There was no acknowledgement save he-en bouncing off the distant schoolhouse wall.

"I'll get him," said Jem. *"He-y!"*

Hay-e-hay-e-hay-ey, answered the schoolhouse wall.

It was unlike Cecil to hold out for so long; once he pulled a joke he'd repeat it time and again. We should have been leapt at already. Jem signaled for me to stop again.

He said softly, "Scout, can you take that thing off?"

"I think so, but I ain't got anything on under it much."

"I've got your dress here."

"I can't get it on in the dark."

"Okay," he said, "never mind."

"Jem, are you afraid?"

"No. Think we're almost to the tree now. Few yards from that, an' we'll be to the road. We can see the street light then." Jem was talking in an unhurried, flat toneless voice. I wondered how long he would try to keep the Cecil myth going.

"You reckon we oughta sing, Jem?"

"No. Be real quiet again, Scout."

We had not increased our pace. Jem knew as well as I that it was difficult to walk fast without stumping a toe, tripping on stones, and other inconveniences, and I was barefooted. Maybe it was the wind rustling the trees. But there wasn't any wind and there weren't any trees except the big oak.

Our company shuffled and dragged his feet, as if wearing heavy shoes. Whoever it was wore thick cotton pants; what I thought were trees rustling was the soft swish of cotton on cotton, wheek, wheek, with every step.

I felt the sand go cold under my feet and I knew we were near the big oak. Jem pressed my head. We stopped and listened.

Shuffle-foot had not stopped with us this time. His trousers swished softly and steadily. Then they stopped. He was running, running toward us with no child's steps.

"Run, Scout! Run! Run!" Jem screamed.

I took one giant step and found myself reeling: my arms useless, in the dark, I could not keep my balance.

"Jem, Jem, help me, Jem!"

Something crushed the chicken wire around me. Metal ripped on metal and I fell to the ground and rolled as far as I could, floundering to escape my wire prison. From somewhere near by came scuffling, kicking sounds, sounds of shoes and flesh scraping dirt and roots. Someone rolled against me and I felt Jem. He was up like lightning and pulling me with him but, though my head and shoulders were free, I was so entangled we didn't get very far.

We were nearly to the road when I felt Jem's hand leave me, felt him jerk backwards to the ground. More scuffling, and then came a dull crunching sound and Jem screamed.

I ran in the direction of Jem's scream and sank into a flabby male stomach. Its owner said, "Uff!" and tried to catch my arms, but they were tightly pinioned. His stomach was soft but his arms were like steel. He slowly squeezed the breath out of me. I could not move. Suddenly he was jerked backwards and flung on the ground, almost carrying me with him. I thought, Jem's up.

One's mind works very slowly at times. Stunned, I stood there dumbly. The scuffling noises were dying; someone wheezed and the night was still again.

Still but for a man breathing heavily, breathing heavily and staggering. I thought he went to the tree and leaned against it. He coughed violently, a sobbing, bone-shaking cough.

To Kill a Mockingbird

"Jem?"

There was no answer but the man's heavy breathing.

"Jem?"

Jem didn't answer.

The man began moving around, as if searching for something. I heard him groan and pull something heavy along the ground. It was slowly coming to me that there were now four people under the tree.

"Atticus . . . ?"

The man was walking heavily and unsteadily toward the road.

I went to where I thought he had been and felt frantically along the ground, reaching out with my toes. Presently I touched someone.

"Jem?"

My toes touched trousers, a belt buckle, buttons, something I could not identify, a collar, and a face. A prickly stubble on the face told me it was not Jem's. I smelled stale whiskey.

I made my way along in what I thought was the direction of the road. I was not sure, because I had been turned around so many times. But I found it and looked down to the street light. A man was passing under it. The man was walking with the staccato steps of someone carrying a load too heavy for him. He was going around the corner. He was carrying Jem. Jem's arm was dangling crazily in front of him.

By the time I reached the corner the man was crossing our front yard. Light from our front door framed Atticus for an instant; he ran down the steps, and together, he and the man took Jem inside.

I was at the front door when they were going down the hall. Aunt Alexandra was running to meet me. "Call Dr. Reynolds!" Atticus's voice came sharply from Jem's room. "Where's Scout?"

"Here she is," Aunt Alexandra called, pulling me along with her to the telephone. She tugged at me anxiously. "I'm all right, Aunty," I said, "you better call."

She pulled the receiver from the hook and said, "Eula May, get Dr. Reynolds, quick!"

"Agnes, is your father home? Oh God, where is he? Please tell him to come over here as soon as he comes in. Please, it's urgent!"

There was no need for Aunt Alexandra to identify herself; people in Maycomb knew each other's voices.

Atticus came out of Jem's room. The moment Aunt Alexandra broke the connection, Atticus took the receiver from her. He rattled the hook, then said, "Eula May, get me the sheriff, please."

"Heck? Atticus Finch. Someone's been after my children. Jem's hurt. Between here and the schoolhouse. I can't leave my boy. Run out there for me, please, and see if he's still around. Doubt if you'll find him now, but I'd like to see him if you do. Got to go now. Thanks, Heck."

"Atticus, is Jem dead?"

"No, Scout. Look after her, sister," he called, as he went down the hall.

Aunt Alexandra's fingers trembled as she unwound the crushed fabric and wire from around me. "Are you all right, darling?" she asked over and over as she worked me free.

It was a relief to be out. My arms were beginning to tingle, and they were red with small hexagonal marks. I rubbed them, and they felt better.

"Aunty, is Jem dead?"

"No—no, darling, he's unconscious. We won't know how badly he's hurt until Dr. Reynolds gets here. Jean Louise, what happened?"

"I don't know."

She left it at that. She brought me something to put on,

146   To Kill a Mockingbird

and had I thought about it then, I would have never let her forget it: in her distraction, Aunty brought me my overalls. "Put these on, darling," she said, handing me the garments she most despised.

She rushed back to Jem's room, then came to me in the hall. She patted me vaguely, and went back to Jem's room.

A car stopped in front of the house. I knew Dr. Reynolds's step almost as well as my father's. He had brought Jem and me into the world, had led us through every childhood disease known to man including the time Jem fell out of the treehouse, and he had never lost our friendship. Dr. Reynolds said if we had been boil-prone things would have been different, but we doubted it.

He came in the door and said, "Good Lord." He walked toward me, said, "You're still standing," and changed his course. He knew every room in the house. He also knew that if I was in bad shape, so was Jem.

After ten forevers Dr. Reynolds returned. "Is Jem dead?" I asked.

"Far from it," he said, squatting down to me. "He's got a bump on the head just like yours, and a broken arm. Scout, look that way—no, don't turn your head, roll your eyes. Now look over yonder. He's got a bad break, so far as I can tell now it's in the elbow. Like somebody tried to wring his arm off . . . now look at me."

"Then he's not dead?"

"No-o!" Dr. Reynolds got to his feet. "We can't do much tonight," he said, "except try to make him as comfortable as we can. We'll have to X-ray his arm—looks like he'll be wearing his arm 'way out by his side for a while. Don't worry, though, he'll be as good as new. Boys his age bounce."

While he was talking, Dr. Reynolds had been looking keenly at me, lightly fingering the bump that was coming on my forehead. "You don't feel broke anywhere, do you?"

Dr. Reynolds's small joke made me smile. "Then you don't think he's dead, then?"

He put on his hat. "Now I may be wrong, of course, but I think he's very alive. Shows all the symptoms of it. Go have a look at him, and when I come back we'll get together and decide."

Dr. Reynolds's step was young and brisk. Mr. Heck Tate's was not. His heavy boots punished the porch and he opened the door awkwardly, but he said the same thing Dr. Reynolds said when he came in. "You all right, Scout?" he added.

"Yes sir, I'm goin' in to see Jem. Atticus'n'them's in there."

"I'll go with you," said Mr. Tate.

Aunt Alexandra had shaded Jem's reading light with a towel, and his room was dim. Jem was lying on his back. There was an ugly mark along one side of his face. His left arm lay out from his body; his elbow was bent slightly, but in the wrong direction. Jem was frowning.

"Jem . . . ?"

Atticus spoke. "He can't hear you, Scout, he's out like a light. He was coming around, but Dr. Reynolds put him out again."

"Yes sir." I retreated. Jem's room was large and square. Aunt Alexandra was sitting in a rocking-chair by the fireplace. The man who brought Jem in was standing in a corner, leaning against the wall. He was some countryman I did not know. He had probably been at the pageant, and was in the vicinity when it happened. He must have heard our screams and come running.

Atticus was standing by Jem's bed.

Mr. Heck Tate stood in the doorway. His hat was in his hand, and a flashlight bulged from his pants pocket. He was in his working clothes.

"Come in, Heck," said Atticus. "Did you find anything? I can't conceive of anyone low-down enough to do a thing like this, but I hope you found him."

Mr. Tate sniffed. He glanced sharply at the man in the corner, nodded to him, then looked around the room—at Jem, at Aunt Alexandra, then at Atticus.

"Sit down, Mr. Finch," he said pleasantly.

Atticus said, "Let's all sit down. Have that chair, Heck. I'll get another one from the livingroom."

Mr. Tate sat in Jem's desk chair. He waited until Atticus returned and settled himself. I wondered why Atticus had not brought a chair for the man in the corner, but Atticus knew the ways of country people far better than I. Some of his rural clients would park their long-eared steeds under the chinaberry trees in the back yard, and Atticus would often keep appointments on the back steps. This one was probably more comfortable where he was.

"Mr. Finch," said Mr. Tate, "tell you what I found. I found a little girl's dress—it's out there in my car. That your dress, Scout?"

"Yes sir, if it's a pink one with smockin'," I said. Mr. Tate was behaving as if he were on the witness stand. He liked to tell things his own way, untrammeled by state or defense, and sometimes it took him a while.

"I found some funny-looking pieces of muddy-colored cloth—"

"That's m'costume, Mr. Tate."

Mr. Tate ran his hands down his thighs. He rubbed his left arm and investigated Jem's mantelpiece, then he seemed to be interested in the fireplace. His fingers sought his long nose.

"What is it, Heck?" said Atticus.

Mr. Tate found his neck and rubbed it. "Bob Ewell's lyin' on the ground under that tree down yonder with a kitchen knife stuck up under his ribs. He's dead, Mr. Finch."

Tone and Mood

People turn to entertainment mostly to change their moods. Say you feel bored. That is your mood of the moment. Seeking a change of mood, you decide to read or watch television. Now you are faced with a choice. "What am I in the mood for?" you ask yourself.

What you really mean is, "What mood would I like to be in?" If you want to be put in a lighthearted mood, you choose something funny, a comedy or a humorous book. There's soap opera or romance or tragic drama if you want a good cry. There's sports or adventure if you want to be lifted out of your seat.

A mood is the way you feel. The moods of a book are the way the characters feel and the way they make you feel in turn as a reader. Joy, anger, sorrow, fear, excitement—all of these and more are moods. What is tone? Tone is what carries the mood to you. A comedy is funny because it has a comic tone. A drama may be sad because it has a tragic tone. In a mystery, the tone is mysterious or ghostly or suspenseful. You respond, or the characters in the story respond, with a mood that is fearful or expectant.

Tone and mood work very closely together. The tone of a church is awe-inspiring. That tone may put you in a thoughtful or prayerful mood. The tone at a ball game is exciting. It puts you in a happy or eager mood. The tone at a funeral is quiet and mournful. You mood is sad accordingly.

But mood can create tone, too. In a classroom, an angry teacher can create a tone that is tense. One person's sour mood at a party can set a tone that is strained and unhappy for everyone.

In any case, the difference between tone and mood is this: tone is a manner or an attitude that carries—or *conveys*—a feeling. Mood, on the other hand, is the feeling itself. Or sometimes it is a state of mind.

Tone and mood work together in novels as they do everywhere else. The author is always in control of what is going on. It is the author who creates the tone and tells you about the moods of the characters. This is always done deliberately for a number of purposes.

First, the author wants to show the characters in all the different moods we expect from people in real life. So you may expect that moods will change. Second, the author usually has a feeling or attitude toward the characters in the novel and toward the subject matter of the story. By using tone carefully, a good author can communicate that attitude to readers, and even make them feel the same way. Thus, you always know when to cheer the hero and hiss at the villain. You can usually tell from the tone how the author feels in any passage. If there is a revolution, for example, you can tell at once from the tone which side the author is on.

Finally, the author wants you to be entertained. To be sure that you are, the author has to see to it that you are responding properly to the events of the story. Your mood can be controlled most easily, then, by the author's use of exactly the right tone.

We will look at four ways in which the author, Harper Lee, handles tone and mood:

1 Tone and mood are changed to make the story more entertaining and life-like.

2 Setting is used to convey tone and mood.

3 Tone and mood are used to let us know what we should feel about a certain character.

4 Tone and mood are created by carefully choosing different kinds of language.

No one is happy all the time. On any given day everyone has bad moments and good moments. You may be laughing one minute and ready to cry the next. Some part of your day will be exciting. The rest may be boring or just so-so. Moods change.

Tone and Mood

1 Changing Tones and Moods

Tones change, too. Think of a beautiful forest, for example. By day it might seem peaceful and put you in the mood for a quiet rest beside a stream. But at night, in the dark, branches seem to reach out like claws, and every sound sends a shiver down your spine. It's the same place, but a changed tone puts you into an entirely different mood.

Changes in tone and mood occur all the time in a novel. Such changes make the book more true to life. They also provide variety in your reading. Often, then, an author will use one kind of tone to emphasize its opposite. A serious event will seem more serious to you if something funny has happened just before it.

To Kill a Mockingbird treats some very serious ideas, like hate and prejudice. But Harper Lee has Scout tell the story as an eight-year-old girl would. Events in the story, then, can seem more amusing than they would if they were told by an older person. The tone of the story, as a result, often seems "cute" to us in the same way that small children often seem cute.

But events in the book often get deadly serious. And at these places, the tone become serious, frightening, or even sickening. The author has very clear feelings about what goes on in the story. She lets you know exactly how she feels through changes in tone.

Notice how tone and mood change from funny to quiet to something more serious in these passages. In the first example, Scout makes her appearance onstage in her ham costume and ruins Mrs. Merriweather's pageant.

> I must have heard her in my sleep, or the band playing *Dixie* woke me, but it was when Mrs. Merriweather triumphantly mounted the stage with the state flag that I choose to make my entrance. . . .
> They told me later that Judge Taylor went out behind the auditorium and stood there slapping his knees so hard Mrs. Taylor brought him a glass of water and one of his pills.

Scout has fallen asleep and missed her cue. The "ham" appears late, just when the program is most dramatic. The audience collapses in laughter and for a moment Scout thinks she is the hit of the evening—which in one way she is. The author has created a light, humorous tone for this scene. The audience is having a good time and readers are provided with a good chuckle. Everyone is in a good mood at this point. But the tone changes as Jem and Scout start home across the dark schoolyard.

> It was still black dark. The remaining cars were parked on the other side of the building, and their headlights were little help. . . . "Here Scout, let me hold onto your—hock. You might lose your balance."
> "I can see all right."
> . . . I felt a slight pressure on my head, and assumed that Jem had grabbed that end of the ham. "You got me?"
> "Uh huh."

This is a quieter tone. There is still a hint of the humor of the previous scene: Jem has to grab Scout's "hock." But it's dark now. And there is always a more somber tone in darkness. Then the tone changes once more.

> I felt his fingers press the top of my costume, too hard, it seemed. I shook my head. "Jem, you don't hafta—"
> "Hush a minute, Scout," he said, pinching me. . . .
> "Thought I heard something," he said. "Stop a minute."
> We stopped.
> "Hear anything?" he asked.
> "No."
> We had not gone five paces before he made me stop again.
> "Jem, are you tryin' to scare me? You know I'm too old—"
> "Be quiet," he said, and I knew he was not joking.

The tone is now tense and threatening. The mood of the children? Plainly they are frightened. Readers become tense and expectant. Perhaps this is another one of Cecil Jacobs's Halloween pranks. But somehow, from the tone of things, you get the feeling that this time it's something more serious. In the space of a little more than a page, the

To Kill A Mockingbird

author has changed the tone three times. The moods of characters and readers change, too.

Exercise A

The passage below is from the selection you have read. Answer the questions about this passage using what you have learned in this part of the lesson. Choose the best answer for each question. Put an *x* in the correct box or fill in the appropriate words.

"Sit down, Mr. Finch," he [Sheriff Tate] said pleasantly.

Atticus said, "Let's all sit down. Have that chair, Heck. I'll get another one from the livingroom." . . .

"Mr. Finch," said Mr. Tate, "tell you what I found. I found a little girl's dress—it's out there in my car. That your dress, Scout?"

"Yes sir, if it's a pink one with smockin'," I said. Mr. Tate was behaving as if he were on the witness stand. He liked to tell things his own way . . . and sometimes it took him a while. . . .

Mr. Tate ran his hands down his thighs. He rubbed his left arm and investigated Jem's mantelpiece. . . . His fingers sought his long nose.

"What is it, Heck?" said Atticus.

Mr. Tate found his neck and rubbed it. "Bob Ewell's lyin' on the ground under that tree down yonder with a kitchen knife stuck up under his ribs. He's dead, Mr. Finch."

1. Sheriff Tate begins speaking pleasantly. Atticus is pleasant and friendly. It seems like a friendly visit. How does the tone change as the passage goes along?

   ☐ a. From pleasant to businesslike to nervous

   ☐ b. From pleasant to angry to frightening

   ☐ c. From pleasant to humorous to calm

   ☐ d. From pleasant to threatening to humorous

2. A short sentence tells that Atticus's mood has changed. He has caught the mood of Sheriff Tate from his tone. Write the short sentence that shows Atticus has changed.

_____

_____

_____

Now check your answers using the Answer Key on page 436. Correct any wrong answer and review this part of the lesson if you don't understand why your answer was wrong.

Early in the lesson it was pointed out that places, by their very natures, have a certain tone about them. A church, a ball park, a funeral home—each has its own tone and creates its own mood in people. In describing a setting, authors try to do more than

just tell you what the place looks like. They try to give you a sense of the tone of the place. Once you have caught the tone, you know how the author feels, and how the characters must feel, how you as reader are supposed to feel. The mood is established, in other words.

If setting a scene were just a matter of describing the time and place, Harper Lee could have done something like this:

Time: October.

Place: The schoolyard in back of the Radley house.
You can see a single street light.

Characters: Enter Jem and Scout.

But the author does much more than this. In beginning the chapter she establishes a tone. From the tone, you catch the mood of the characters. And you, as a reader, are ready for what happens as the story goes along.

The weather was unusually warm for the last day of October. We didn't even need jackets. The wind was growing stronger, and Jem said it might be raining before we got home. There was no moon.

The street light on the corner cast sharp shadows on the Radley house. I heard Jem laugh softly. "Bet nobody bothers them tonight," he said. . . .

"It is a scary place though, ain't it?" I said. "Boo doesn't mean anybody any harm, but I'm right glad you're along."

"You know Atticus wouldn't let you go to the schoolhouse by yourself," Jem said.

"Don't see why, it's just around the corner and across the yard."

"That yard's a mighty long place for little girls to cross at night," Jem teased. "Ain't you scared of haints?"

We laughed. Haints, Hot Steams, incantations, secret signs, had vanished with our years as mist with sunrise.

It is the last day of October—Halloween. Though it is still warm in Alabama, it is windy this night. Windy nights are always a bit scary. There is no moon. It is dark and rain is threatening. The single street light is making sharp shadows on the Radley house. This place is frightening for children even in daytime. But the children are too old to believe in ghosts ("haints"). Jem is joking and teasing.

The whole passage gives off an uneasy feeling. There is nothing frightening—yet. But you can't help feeling that maybe something *might* happen. And of course the author has set things up just this way to prepare for the way the chapter works out in the end. She will return to this tone later and develop it into something terrifying.

But before that happens, there are several other scenes, each with its own tone and mood. Look at the one in Exercise B. This happens just before the pageant begins.

Exercise B

The passage below is from the selection you have read. Answer the questions about this passage using what you have learned in this part of the lesson. Choose the best answer for each question. Put an *x* in the correct box or fill in the appropriate words.

The auditorium was filling with people; the Maycomb County High School band had assembled in front below the stage; the stage footlights were on and the red velvet curtain rippled and billowed from the scurrying going on behind it.

Backstage, Cecil and I found the narrow hallway teeming with people. . . . Children dressed as various agricultural enterprises crowded around the one small window.

"Somebody's mashed my costume," I wailed in dismay. Mrs. Merriweather galloped to me, reshaped the chicken wire, and thrust me inside.

1. How would you describe the tone of this setting?

   ☐ a. Tense and angry

   ☐ b. Excited and confused

   ☐ c. Carefree and happy

   ☐ d. Orderly and serious

2. You get a sense that many people are rushing about in this scene. Copy down at least two expressions that give this feeling.

_____

_____

_____

Now check your answers using the Answer Key on page 436. Correct any wrong answer and review this part of the lesson if you don't understand why your answer was wrong.

Tone and Mood

3 Tone, Mood and Character

People often bring a certain tone to a place with just their presence. In *A Day No Pigs Would Die* (Unit 3), Robert, a twelve-year-old boy, says of his mother, "I could smell her goodness." As so many mothers do for their children, this mother carried her "goodness" with her into Robert's life. This was the tone she brought to the story. You can sense Robert's mood even though it is not spelled out by the author. He feels safe and secure in his mother's presence.

You can usually tell what an author thinks of a character by the tone that is used whenever that character appears. The author likes Scout. You can be sure something funny or endearing is going to happen when she's around. You like Scout because the author likes Scout. When Atticus is around, the tone is comfortable and secure. It is much like the tone provided by the mother and father in *A Day No Pigs Would Die*.

How does the author feel, and how do you feel, about Mrs. Merriweather in these passages?

> The bass drum went boom with every sentence Mrs. Merriweather uttered. She chanted mournfully about Maycomb County being older than the state, that it was a part of Mississippi and Alabama Territories, that the first white man to set foot in the virgin forests was the Probate Judge's great-grandfather five times removed, who was never heard of again. Then came the fearless Colonel Maycomb, for whom the county was named. . . .
>
> Mrs. Merriweather gave a thirty-minute description of Colonel Maycomb's exploits. . . . I sat down, listened to Mrs. Merriweather's drone and the bass drum's boom and was soon fast asleep.

Who wouldn't fall asleep! Mrs. Merriweather is an old bore. She is long-winded. She is full of her own cleverness and importance. But she is neither clever nor very important. This is the way the author feels about her. The reader knows this because of the tone the author uses whenever this character appears.

What mood does Mrs. Merriweather inspire in readers and other

To Kill A Mockingbird

characters in the story? We snicker at her. We can't wait for an excuse to laugh out loud at her. And this is exactly what Judge Taylor does when Scout marches onstage at the wrong time and breaks up Mrs. Merriweather's boring performance.

Exercise C

The passages below are from the selection you have read. Answer the questions about these passages using what you have learned in this part of the lesson. Choose the best answer for each question. Put an *x* in the correct box or fill in the appropriate words.

Dr. Reynolds's step was young and brisk. Mr. Heck Tate's was not. His heavy boots punished the porch and he opened the door awkwardly, but he said the same thing Dr. Reynolds had said when he came in. "You all right, Scout?" he added.

"Yes sir, I'm goin' in to see Jem. Atticus'n'them's in there."

"I'll go with you," said Mr. Tate.

1. How are you made to feel about Sheriff Tate from the tone of this short passage?

☐ a. He is probably a cruel and uncaring police officer.

☐ b. He is an awkward and comical dunce.

☐ c. He makes you feel nervous and afraid when he appears.

☐ d. He is tired from the responsibility of his job, but he is a concerned officer.

I knew Dr. Reynolds's step almost as well as my father's. He had brought Jem and me into the world, had led us through every childhood disease known to man including the time Jem fell out of the treehouse, and he had never lost our friendship.

2. By her tone, the author tells us that Dr. Reynolds is a man to be trusted. In the space provided, write the expression that best conveys this feeling.

_____

_____

_____

Now check your answers using the Answer Key on page 436. Correct any wrong answer and review this part of the lesson if you don't understand why your answer was wrong.

To Kill A Mockingbird

In a conversation you can tell the attitude, or tone, of the speakers from several things. You listen to the words used. Are they harsh or friendly? You watch facial expressions, listen to how the words are spoken, catch body movements and hand gestures. All of these things tell you how people feel.

4 Tone, Mood and Language

But in a book there are only words. Readers have to imagine the rest. Providing just the right tone through words is one of the arts of expert writing. What the author has to do is select just the right words and put them together in just the right way to achieve a desired effect. Let's look at some examples.

In the last section of the lesson you saw how Mrs. Merriweather was presented as a tiresome bore. The author didn't say, "She spoke sadly." The words chosen were, "She chanted mournfully." From this you can well imagine what it was like listening to this lady. The speech had the tone of a funeral. Even the sentences describing her are long and tiresome—just like the lady herself. By contrast, people weren't just moving around backstage. They were "scurrying." This one word makes you feel the hustle and bustle and confusion.

Words are chosen for their sound and their shade of meaning. "He *raced*" sounds faster than "he *ran*." "The bells *tinkled merrily*" puts you in a different mood from "the bells *rang*." "I heard *the sweet song* of the birds" has a different tone from "the birds *sang*."

It makes a difference, too, if sentences are long or short, straightforward or roundabout. It is much funnier to hear in a long sentence that Judge Taylor slapped his knees and had to take a pill, than to be told simply that he laughed heartily. Short sentences are frequently used in action scenes to build suspense and excitement. Long sentences are often used in describing calm, peaceful scenes. Try to see how some of these choices about language are used in the passage in Exercise D.

The passage below is from the selection you have read. Answer the questions about this passage using what you have learned in this part of the lesson. Choose the best answer for each question. Put an x in the correct box or fill in the appropriate words.

Maybe it was the wind rustling the trees. But there wasn't any wind and there weren't any trees except the big oak.

Our company shuffled and dragged his feet, as if wearing heavy shoes. Whoever it was wore thick cotton pants; what I thought were trees rustling was the soft swish of cotton on cotton, wheek, wheek, with every step.

I felt the sand go cold under my feet and I knew we were near the big oak. Jem pressed my head. We stopped and listened.

Shuffle-foot had not stopped with us this time. His trousers swished softly and steadily. Then they stopped. He was running, running toward us with no child's steps.

"Run, Scout! Run! Run!" Jem screamed.

1. There are many sounds described in this scene. What kind of tone does the author use when she describes the sounds?

   ☐ a. Hushed and threatening

   ☐ b. Loud and exciting

   ☐ c. Quiet and peaceful

   ☐ d. Harsh and annoying

2. There are at least six expressions in the passage that provide tone by describing sounds with words. Write

down at least three of these expressions. (Example: wind rustling the trees)

_____

_____

_____

Use the Answer Key on page 436 to check your answers. Correct any wrong answer and review this part of the lesson if you don't understand why your answer was wrong. Now go on to do the Comprehension Questions.

Comprehension Questions

Answer these questions without looking back at the selection. Choose the best answer to each question and put an *x* in the box beside it.

Recalling
Facts

1. It was October. The weather was

  ☐ a. warm, with rain threatening.

  ☐ b. chilly and damp.

  ☐ c. wet, cold and windy.

  ☐ d. warm and damp like summer.

Keeping
Events in
Order

2. When did Cecil Jacobs frighten Jem and Scout?

  ☐ a. When they were crossing the schoolyard after the pageant

  ☐ b. While everyone was waiting for the pageant to begin

  ☐ c. When they were crossing the schoolyard before the pageant

  ☐ d. Just before the children were attacked

Recognizing
Words in
Context

3. What is a *pageant*?

  ☐ a. A musical comedy

  ☐ b. A costume show dealing with historical events

  ☐ c. A play, usually a tragedy

  ☐ d. A festival with games and other booths

4. What was it that Scout and Cecil Jacobs did while waiting for the pageant?

☐ a. They waited behind the stage.

☐ b. They fussed with Mrs. Merriweather.

☐ c. They tried the games and shows.

☐ d. They played in the schoolyard.

5. "After consulting a tree to *ascertain* . . . which way was south . . . Colonel Maycomb set out." The word *ascertain* means

☐ a. find out.

☐ b. make ready.

☐ c. cover up.

☐ d. pretend.

6. After Scout's appearance the pageant seemed to be a hit. Everyone cheered. But Mrs. Merriweather told Scout she had ruined the pageant. Why?

☐ a. Nothing had gone right all night.

☐ b. People were laughing at the most serious moment.

☐ c. Scout had ruined things on purpose.

☐ d. Mrs. Merriweather just didn't understand her success.

7. When Jem and Scout were attacked, they were

☐ a. near the auditorium.

☐ b. near the oak tree.

☐ c. under the street light.

☐ d. in front of the Radley house.

8. Two people saved Scout from harm. Who were they?

☐ a. Jem and the man who carried Jem

☐ b. Atticus and Heck Tate

☐ c. Jem and Aunt Alexandra

☐ d. Jem and Sheriff Tate

9. After the fight, Scout felt about with her toes. She "touched trousers, a belt buckle, buttons, *something I could not identify,* a collar, and a face." A clue at the end of the story lets us know that the "something" she could not identify was

☐ a. a whiskey bottle.

☐ b. a knife.

☐ c. a whip.

☐ d. a club.

10. Jem's conduct during this chapter was

☐ a. childish and panicky.

☐ b. foolish and risky.

☐ c. frightened but controlled.

☐ d. cocky and assured.

11. When did Scout arrive at the house after the attack?

☐ a. Before anyone else did

☐ b. After Jem and the man carrying him

☐ c. At the same time as Dr. Reynolds

☐ d. Before Dr. Reynolds but after Heck Tate

12. Atticus was a lawyer. "Some of his rural clients would park their long-eared steeds in the back yard." In other words,

☐ a. the sheriffs and deputies parked their cars in the yard.

☐ b. the yard was reserved parking for other lawyers and their horses.

☐ c. delivery wagons from nearby farms used the back door.

☐ d. some of his country customers parked their mules in the yard.

13. Bob Ewell was killed

☐ a. while chasing the children.

☐ b. after the children were safely home.

☐ c. when Sheriff Tate caught him.

☐ d. during the scuffle with the children.

14. How did Sheriff Tate seem to feel about finding Bob Ewell's body?

☐ a. He felt nothing.

☐ b. He was proud of himself.

☐ c. He seemed upset.

☐ d. He seemed calm and relieved.

15. How did Jem feel toward Scout?

☐ a. Protective

☐ b. Annoyed

☐ c. Bossy

☐ d. Uncaring

Tone and Mood

Now check your answers using the Answer Key on page 436. Correct any wrong answers you have by putting a check (✓) in the box next to the right answer. Count the number of questions you answered correctly and plot the total on the Comprehension Scores graph on page 444.

Next, look at the questions you answered incorrectly. What types of questions were they? Count the number of each type and enter the numbers in the spaces below:

Recognizing Words in Context   _____

Recalling Facts   _____

Keeping Events in Order   _____

Making Inferences   _____

Understanding Main Ideas   _____

Now use these numbers to fill in the Comprehension Skills Profile on page 445.

Discussion Guides

The questions below will help you to think about the selection and the lesson you have just read. If you don't discuss these questions in class, try to think about them or discuss them with your classmates.

Discussing Tone and Mood

1. Sometimes it's hard to tell which comes first—tone or mood. Think of yourself as a writer. What would you be most concerned with: your own feelings, the plot, the characters, or the reader?

2. Tone reflects the author's attitude. Judging from the tone, how do you think Harper Lee feels about Jem?

3. When the sheriff appears, this is all you are told about him directly: "Mr. Heck Tate stood in the doorway. His hat was in his hand, and a flashlight bulged from his pants pocket. He was in his working clothes." This sets a serious tone for the sheriff's visit. It puts you in a mood to expect trouble. How does it do this?

Discussing the Story

4. Describe a time when you were in a play or a pageant. How was it like the pageant that Scout was in?

5. Jem, Scout and other people were nervous about the Radley house. Most people know a place that makes them nervous. Tell about a place that seems scary or unnerving to you.

6. Bob Ewell was an evil man. He attacked the children in darkness and someone killed him. It was not legal to kill Bob Ewell. Was it right or wrong? Can there be a difference between an action's being legal and being right? Explain you opinions.

Discussing the Author's Work

7. The author tells the story thinking back to the time when she was eight. Find passages that sound like an eight-year-old. Find other passages that sound like an adult. What is it that makes one passage sound childish, the other adult?

8. The story is written using the pronoun *I* frequently. It is written as if Scout were telling the story—Scout, now grown up. This is called a first-person point of view. Several of the stories in this text are written this way. *A Day No Pigs Would Die* (Unit 3) is one of them. How are the two stories different in the way they sound?

9. Harper Lee makes fun of the "glorious" history of Maycomb County. Find a place where she does this. Explain how she makes fun while appearing to be serious.

Writing Exercise

Here is a group of sentences. A number of words and expressions follow each sentence. Rewrite each sentence at least two ways using the words and expressions you are given. Change the tone of the sentence each time you rewrite it. Use your own words if you prefer.

Example: The bird sat in the tree and sang.

(pesky; songster; squawked; sweet; perched; green leaves; hidden; warbled; tune)

The pesky bird perched in the tree and squawked.
The sweet songster hidden among the leaves warbled a tune.

1. Freda said, "Is that the way you treat a lady?"

   (scowled; screamed; raised her eyebrows; swallowed hard; stuttered; for shame; smiled; dear friend; laughed; lovely)

   _____

   _____

   _____

   _____

2. There was an explosion.

(broke the stillness; like thunder; like a cork popping; rumbled in the distance; burst; just as I turned; I waited patiently; shook my soul; curled my toes)

_____

_____

_____

_____

3. Pete Mosler stepped up to the plate, swung, and missed the ball.

(staggered; fanned; didn't come near; swaggered; struck a mighty blow; gave it all he had; sneaky; captain)

_____

_____

_____

_____

4. The speech was about the founding fathers of Maycomb County.

(dragged on for hours; dramatic history; stirring; cast a spell; fun-filled; senseless; merry men; fiddle-faddle; strength; heartening)

_____

_____

_____

_____

Unit 5   Conflict

Of Mice and Men
BY JOHN STEINBECK

About the Illustration

How would you describe the relationship between these two men? Point out some details in the drawing to support your response.

Here are some questions to help you think:

☐ How do you know that the man on the right is angry?

☐ What do you think the man on the left is doing? What are his feelings? How do you know?

☐ How well do these two men know each other? What makes you think so?

Unit 5

Introduction	**What the Novel Is About/What the Lesson Is About**
Selection	**Of Mice and Men**
Lesson	**Conflict**
Activities	Comprehension Questions/Discussion Guides/Writing Exercise

Introduction

What the Novel Is About

Of Mice and Men is about George Milton and Lennie Small, two very different men who travel and work together. They are migrant farm workers and drifters who move from ranch to ranch in the Salinas Valley country of California.

The time is the mid-1930s. These were Depression years when one-third of the workers in the United States were jobless. Many thousands of these people came to California in search of work harvesting the fruits and vegetables that grew in abundance there. They traveled the highways and rode railroad boxcars from one place to another, going wherever work might be.

It was a lonely life. At night they might "jungle up," which meant camping with other travelers for protection and company. Often they were looked upon as common tramps, hoboes, or "bindle-bums" as some called them then.

Most of these people dreamed that someday there would be something better for them. Though others thought of them as bums, they did not think of themselves that way. They planned somehow to save enough from their pitiful wages to buy little places of their own. "A little place and a couple of acres" is the way George puts it in the story. Unfortunately, it seldom happened that they could ever get that far ahead. They were doomed to spend their lives in endless poverty and loneliness.

George is pretty good at finding work for himself and Lennie. But their lives are complicated by the fact that Lennie is mentally retarded. The two men are exact opposites. George is small, quick and shrewd. Lennie is huge, powerful and slow. But Lennie is also childlike and so timid he wouldn't hurt a fly. Even a hint of violence terrifies him. Since he has no memory, he forgets things and never learns from his mistakes. This forgetfulness and his love of petting soft things get him in trouble constantly. And it is George who has to keep getting Lennie out of trouble. When the chapter you will read opens, George and Lennie have just been forced to leave a town called Weed because of some trouble Lennie got into there. George has to take care of Lennie and keep them both in work.

Why, then, does George stay with Lennie? As you read the chapter, this is the most important question to think about.

The author, John Steinbeck, may already be familiar to you. He was born and raised in the Salinas Valley of California and many of his best stories are set there. His California stories and novels include *The Grapes of Wrath, Tortilla Flat, The Pearl, The Leader of the People,* and *Cannery Row.* Steinbeck was awarded the Nobel Prize for Literature in 1962.

What the Lesson Is About

The lesson which follows the reading selection is about conflict.

When you hear the word *conflict,* you probably think of a fight or battle of some sort. This is exactly what conflict is. Only most of the time the worst conflicts are not waged with fists or guns. Many of life's conflicts involve a struggle to get along with other people. For example, there are conflicts with people at school and on the job. These conflicts are rarely violent, but you are still in a fight to get along and get ahead. And there are also the constant struggles you wage to get along with yourself. Sometimes when you try to make decisions, you can feel a conflict in yourself. Should you choose one thing or another? Should you act one way or another? And how do you feel after you have made your choice? Feeling self-doubt or guilt is also a kind of conflict in yourself.

Because of all these conflicts, there is a story that can be told about anyone's life. What makes these stories interesting is seeing how each person acts when facing up to conflicts. In this lesson you will see how conflict is used in fiction to create a story and move it along.

The questions below will help you to focus on conflict in the chapter from *Of Mice and Men*. Read the chapter carefully and try to answer these questions as you go along:

1   There are different kinds of conflict. Sometimes people fight with other people. Sometimes the struggle is within a person. Can you find examples of both kinds of conflict in the chapter?

2   Facing up to a conflict usually means doing something about it. You are moved to action by the conflict. How do George's conflicts make him act?

3   How a person handles conflict tells you a great deal about that person's character. What do you learn about Lennie and George from the way they handle their conflicts?

4   Conflict makes the plot or storyline of a novel move along so that a story is told. Conflict also ties all the different actions of a story together. How do Lennie's problems (conflicts) make things happen in the story, and how do they move the story along?

Of Mice and Men

John Steinbeck

A few miles south of Soledad, the Salinas River drops in close to the hillside bank and runs deep and green. The water is warm too, for it has slipped twinkling over the yellow sands in the sunlight before reaching the narrow pool. On one side of the river the golden foothill slopes curve up to the strong and rocky Gabilan mountains, but on the valley side the water is lined with trees—willows fresh and green with every spring, carrying in their lower leaf junctures the debris of the winter's flooding; and sycamores with mottled, white, recumbent limbs and branches that arch over the pool. On the sandy bank under the trees the leaves lie deep and so crisp that a lizard makes a great skittering if he runs among them. Rabbits come out of the brush to sit on the sand in the evening, and the damp flats are covered with the night tracks of 'coons, and with the spread pads of dogs from the ranches, and with the split-wedge tracks of deer that come to drink in the dark.

There is a path through the willows and among the sycamores, a path beaten hard by boys coming down from the ranches to swim in the deep pool, and beaten hard by tramps who come wearily down from the highway in the evening to jungle-up near water. In front of the low horizontal limb of a giant sycamore there is an ash pile made by many fires; the limb is worn smooth by men who have sat on it.

Evening of a hot day started the little wind to moving among the leaves. The shade climbed up the hills toward the top. On the sand banks the rabbits sat as quietly as little gray, sculptured stones. And then from the direction of the state highway came the sound of footsteps on crisp sycamore leaves. The rabbits hurried noiselessly for cover. A stilted heron labored up into the air and pounded down river. For a moment the place was lifeless, and then two men emerged from the path and came into the opening by the green pool.

They had walked in single file down the path, and even in the open one stayed behind the other. Both were dressed in denim trousers and in denim coats with brass buttons. Both wore black, shapeless hats and both carried tight blanket rolls slung over their shoulders. The first man was small and quick, dark of face, with restless eyes and sharp, strong features. Every part of him was defined: small, strong hands, slender arms, a thin and bony nose. Behind him walked his opposite, a huge man, shapeless of face, with large, pale eyes, with wide, sloping shoulders; and he walked heavily, dragging his feet a little, the way a bear drags his paws. His arms did not swing at his sides, but hung loosely.

The first man stopped short in the clearing, and the follower nearly ran over him. He took off his hat and wiped the sweat-band with his forefinger and snapped the moisture off. His huge companion dropped his blankets and flung himself down and drank from the surface of the green pool; drank with long gulps, snorting into the water like a horse. The small man stepped nervously beside him.

"Lennie!" he said sharply. "Lennie, for God' sakes don't drink so much." Lennie continued to snort into the pool. The small man leaned over and shook him by the shoulder. "Lennie. You gonna be sick like you was last night."

Lennie dipped his whole head under, hat and all, and then he sat up on the bank and his hat dripped down on his blue coat and ran down his back. "Tha's good," he said. "You drink some, George. You take a good big drink." He

Of Mice and Men

smiled happily.

George unslung his bindle and dropped it gently on the bank. "I ain't sure it's good water," he said. "Looks kinda scummy."

Lennie dabbled his big paw in the water and wiggled his fingers so the water arose in little splashes; rings widened across the pool to the other side and came back again. Lennie watched them go. "Look, George. Look what I done."

George knelt beside the pool and drank from his hand with quick scoops. "Tastes all right," he admitted. "Don't really seem to be running, though. You never oughta drink water when it ain't running, Lennie," he said hopelessly. "You'd drink out of a gutter if you was thirsty." He threw a scoop of water into his face and rubbed it about with his hand, under his chin and around the back of his neck. Then he replaced his hat, pushed himself back from the river, drew up his knees and embraced them. Lennie, who had been watching, imitated George exactly. He pushed himself back, drew up his knees, embraced them, looked over to George to see whether he had it just right. He pulled his hat down a little more over his eyes, the way George's hat was.

George stared morosely at the water. The rims of his eyes were red with sun glare. He said angrily, "We could just as well of rode clear to the ranch if that bastard bus driver knew what he was talkin' about. 'Jes' a little stretch down the highway,' he says. 'Jes' a little stretch.' God damn near four miles, that's what it was! Didn't wanta stop at the ranch gate, that's what. Too God damn lazy to pull up. Wonder he isn't too damn good to stop in Soledad at all. Kicks us out and says, 'Jes' a little stretch down the road.' I bet it was *more* than four miles. Damn hot day."

Lennie looked timidly over to him. "George?"

"Yeah, what ya want?"

"Where we goin', George?"

The little man jerked down the brim of his hat and scowled over at Lennie. "So you forgot that awready, did you? I gotta tell you again, do I? Jesus Christ, you're a crazy bastard!"

"I forgot," Lennie said softly. "I tried not to forget. Honest to God I did, George."

"O.K.—O.K. I'll tell ya again. I ain't got nothing to do. Might jus' as well spen' all my time tellin' you things and then you forget 'em, and I tell you again."

"Tried and tried," said Lennie, "but it didn't do no good. I remember about the rabbits, George."

"The hell with the rabbits. That's all you ever can remember is them rabbits. O.K.! Now you listen and this time you got to remember so we don't get in no trouble. You remember settin' in that gutter on Howard Street and watchin' that blackboard?"

Lennie's face broke into a delighted smile. "Why sure, George. I remember that . . . . but . . . . what'd we do then? I remember some girls come by and you says . . . . you say . . . ."

"The hell with what I says. You remember about us goin' into Murray and Ready's, and they give us work cards and bus tickets?"

"Oh, sure, George. I remember that now." His hands went quickly into his side coat pockets. He said gently, "George . . . . I ain't got mine. I musta lost it." He looked down at the ground in despair.

"You never had none, you crazy bastard. I got both of 'em here. Think I'd let you carry your own work card?"

Lennie grinned with relief. "I . . . . I thought I put it in my side pocket." His hand went into the pocket again.

George looked sharply at him. "What'd you take outa that pocket?"

"Ain't a thing in my pocket," Lennie said cleverly.

"I know there ain't. You got it in your hand. What you got

in your hand—hidin' it?"

"I ain't got nothin', George. Honest."

"Come on, give it here."

Lennie held his closed hand away from George's direction. "It's on'y a mouse, George."

"A mouse? A live mouse?"

"Uh-uh. Jus' a dead mouse, George. I didn' kill it. Honest! I found it. I found it dead."

"Give it here!" said George.

"Aw, leave me have it, George."

"Give it here!"

Lennie's closed hand slowly obeyed. George took the mouse and threw it across the pool to the other side, among the brush. "What you want of a dead mouse, anyways?"

"I could pet it with my thumb while we walked along," said Lennie.

"Well, you ain't petting no mice while you walk with me. You remember where we're goin' now?"

Lennie looked startled and then in embarrassment hid his face against his knees. "I forgot again."

"Jesus Christ," George said resignedly, "Well—look, we're gonna work on a ranch like the one we come from up north."

"Up north?"

"In Weed."

"Oh, sure. I remember. In Weed."

"That ranch we're goin' to is right down there about a quarter mile. We're gonna go in an' see the boss. Now, look —I'll give him the work tickets, but you ain't gonna say a word. You jus' stand there and don't say nothing. If he finds out what a crazy bastard you are, we won't get no job, but if he sees ya work before he hears ya talk, we're set. Ya got that?"

"Sure, George. Sure I got it."

"O.K. Now when we go in to see the boss, what you gonna do?"

"I . . . . I," Lennie thought. His face grew tight with thought. "I . . . . ain't gonna say nothin'. Jus' gonna stan' there."

"Good boy. That's swell. You say that over two, three times so you sure won't forget it."

Lennie droned to himself softly, "I ain't gonna say nothin' . . . . I ain't gonna say nothin' . . . . I ain't gonna say nothin'."

"O.K.," said George. "An' you ain't gonna do no bad things like you done in Weed, neither."

Lennie looked puzzled. "Like I done in Weed?"

"Oh, so ya forgot that too, did ya? Well, I ain't gonna remind ya, fear ya do it again."

A light of understanding broke on Lennie's face. "They run us outa Weed," he exploded triumphantly.

"Run us out, hell," said George disgustedly. "We run. They was lookin' for us, but they didn't catch us."

Lennie giggled happily. "I didn't forget that, you bet."

George lay back on the sand and crossed his hands under his head, and Lennie imitated him, raising his head to see whether he were doing it right. "God, you're a lot of trouble," said George. "I could get along so easy and so nice if I didn't have you on my tail. I could live so easy and maybe have a girl."

For a moment Lennie lay quiet, and then he said hopefully, "We gonna work on a ranch, George."

"Awright. You got that. But we're gonna sleep here because I got a reason."

The day was going fast now. Only the tops of the Gabilan mountains flamed with the light of the sun that had gone from the valley. A water snake slipped along on the pool, its head held up like a little periscope. The reeds jerked slightly in the current. Far off toward the highway a man shouted something, and another man shouted back. The sycamore limbs rustled under a little wind that died immediately.

"George—why ain't we goin' on to the ranch and get some supper? They got supper at the ranch."

George rolled on his side. "No reason at all for you. I like it here. Tomorra we're gonna go to work. I seen thrashin' machines on the way down. That means we'll be bucking grain bags, bustin' a gut. Tonight I'm gonna lay right here and look up. I like it."

Lennie got up on his knees and looked down at George. "Ain't we gonna have no supper?"

"Sure we are, if you gather up some dead willow sticks. I got three cans of beans in my bindle. You get a fire ready. I'll give you a match when you get the sticks together. Then we'll heat the beans and have supper."

Lennie said, "I like beans with ketchup."

"Well, we ain't got no ketchup. You go get wood. An' don't you fool around. It'll be dark before long."

Lennie lumbered to his feet and disappeared in the brush. George lay where he was and whistled softly to himself. There were sounds of splashings down the river in the direction Lennie had taken. George stopped whistling and listened. "Poor bastard," he said softly, and then went on whistling again.

In a moment Lennie came crashing back through the brush. He carried one small willow stick in his hand. George sat up. "Awright," he said brusquely. "Gi'me that mouse!"

But Lennie made an elaborate pantomime of innocence. "What mouse, George? I ain't got no mouse."

George held out his hand. "Come on. Give it to me. You ain't puttin' nothing over."

Lennie hesitated, backed away, looked wildly at the

brush line as though he contemplated running for his freedom. George said coldly, "You gonna give me that mouse or do I have to sock you?"

"Give you what, George?"

"You know God damn well what. I want that mouse."

Lennie reluctantly reached into his pocket. His voice broke a little. "I don't know why I can't keep it. It ain't nobody's mouse. I didn't steal it. I found it lyin' right beside the road."

George's hand remained outstretched imperiously. Slowly, like a terrier who doesn't want to bring a ball to its master, Lennie approached, drew back, approached again. George snapped his fingers sharply, and at the sound Lennie laid the mouse in his hand.

"I wasn't doin' nothing bad with it, George. Jus' strokin' it."

George stood up and threw the mouse as far as he could into the darkening brush, and then he stepped to the pool and washed his hands. "You crazy fool. Don't you think I could see your feet was wet where you went acrost the river to get it?" He heard Lennie's whimpering cry and wheeled about. "Blubberin' like a baby! Jesus Christ! A big guy like you." Lennie's lip quivered and tears started in his eyes. "Aw, Lennie!" George put his hand on Lennie's shoulder. "I ain't takin' it away jus' for meanness. That mouse ain't fresh, Lennie; and besides, you've broke it pettin' it. You get another mouse that's fresh and I'll let you keep it a little while."

Lennie sat down on the ground and hung his head dejectedly. "I don't know where there is no other mouse. I remember a lady used to give 'em to me—ever' one she got. But that lady ain't here."

George scoffed. "Lady, huh? Don't even remember who that lady was. That was your own Aunt Clara. An' she stopped givin' 'em to ya. You always killed 'em."

Lennie looked sadly up at him. "They was so little," he said, apologetically. "I'd pet 'em, and pretty soon they bit my fingers and I pinched their heads a little and then they was dead—because they was so little.

"I wish't we'd get the rabbits pretty soon, George. They ain't so little."

"The hell with the rabbits. An' you ain't to be trusted with no live mice. Your Aunt Clara give you a rubber mouse and you wouldn't have nothing to do with it."

"It wasn't no good to pet," said Lennie.

The flame of the sunset lifted from the mountaintops and dusk came into the valley, and a half darkness came in among the willows and the sycamores. A big carp rose to the surface of the pool, gulped air and then sank mysteriously into the dark water again, leaving widening rings on the water. Overhead the leaves whisked again and little puffs of willow cotton blew down and landed on the pool's surface.

"You gonna get that wood?" George demanded. "There's plenty right up against the back of that sycamore. Flood-water wood. Now you get it."

Lennie went behind the tree and brought out a litter of dried leaves and twigs. He threw them in a heap on the old ash pile and went back for more and more. It was almost night now. A dove's wings whistled over the water. George walked to the fire pile and lighted the dry leaves. The flame cracked up among the twigs and fell to work. George undid his bindle and brought out three cans of beans. He stood them about the fire, close in against the blaze, but not quite touching the flame.

"There's enough beans for four men," George said.

Lennie watched him from over the fire. He said patiently, "I like 'em with ketchup."

A / "Well, we ain't got any," George exploded. "Whatever we ain't got that's what you want. God a'mighty, if I was alone I could live so easy. I could go get a job an' work, an' no trouble. No mess at all, and when the end of the month come I could take my fifty bucks and go into town and get whatever I want. Why, I could stay in a cat house all night. I could eat any place I want, hotel or any place, and order any damn thing I could think of. An' I could do all that every damn month. Get a gallon of whisky, or set in a pool room and play cards or shoot pool." Lennie knelt and looked over the fire at the angry George. And Lennie's face was drawn with terror. "An' whatta I got," George went on furiously. "I got you! You can't keep a job and you lose me ever' job I get. Jus' keep me shovin' all over the country all the time. An' that ain't the worst. You get in trouble. You do bad things and I got to get you out." His voice rose nearly to a shout. "You crazy son-of-a-bitch. You keep me in hot water all the time." He took on the elaborate manner of little girls when they are mimicking one another. "Jus' wanted to feel that girl's dress—jus' wanted to pet it like it was a mouse—— Well, how the hell did she know you jus' wanted to feel her dress? She jerks back and you hold on like it was a mouse. She yells and we got to hide in a irrigation ditch all day with guys lookin' for us, and we got to sneak out in the dark and get outta the country. All the time somethin' like that—all the time. I wisht I could put you in a cage with about a million mice an' let you have fun." His anger left him suddenly. He looked across the fire at Lennie's anguished face, and then he looked ashamedly at the flames.

It was quite dark now, but the fire lighted the trunks of the trees and the curving branches overhead. Lennie crawled slowly and cautiously around the fire until he was close to George. He sat back on his heels. George turned the bean cans so that another side faced the fire. He pretended to be unaware of Lennie so close beside him.

"George," very softly. No answer. "George!"

"Whatta you want?"

"I was only foolin', George. I don't want no ketchup. I wouldn't eat no ketchup if it was right here beside me."

"If it was here, you could have some."

"But I wouldn't eat none, George. I'd leave it all for you. You could cover your beans with it and I wouldn't touch none of it."

George still stared morosely at the fire. "When I think of the swell time I could have without you, I go nuts. I never get no peace."

Lennie still knelt. He looked off into the darkness across the river. "George, you want I should go away and leave you alone?"

"Where the hell could you go?"

"Well, I could. I could go off in the hills there. Some place I'd find a cave."

"Yeah? How'd you eat. You ain't got sense enough to find nothing to eat."

"I'd find things, George. I don't need no nice food with ketchup. I'd lay out in the sun and nobody'd hurt me. An' if I foun' a mouse, I could keep it. Nobody'd take it away from me."

George looked quickly and searchingly at him. "I been mean, ain't I?"

"If you don' want me I can go off in the hills an' find a cave. I can go away any time."

"No—look! I was jus' foolin', Lennie. 'Cause I want you to stay with me. Trouble with mice is you always kill 'em." He paused. "Tell you what I'll do, Lennie. First chance I get I'll give you a pup. Maybe you wouldn't kill *it*. That'd be better than mice. And you could pet it harder."

Lennie avoided the bait. He had sensed his advantage. "If you don't want me, you only jus' got to say so, and I'll go off in those hills right there—right up in those hills and live by myself. An' I won't get no mice stole from me."

George said, "I want you to stay with me, Lennie. Jesus Christ, somebody'd shoot you for a coyote if you was by yourself. No, you stay with me. Your Aunt Clara wouldn't like you running off by yourself, even if she is dead."

Lennie spoke craftily, "Tell me—like you done before."

"Tell you what?"

"About the rabbits."

George snapped, "You ain't gonna put nothing over on me."

Lennie pleaded, "Come on, George. Tell me. Please, George. Like you done before."

"You get a kick outta that, don't you? Awright, I'll tell you, and then we'll eat our supper. . . ."

George's voice became deeper. He repeated his words rhythmically as though he had said them many times before. "Guys like us, that work on ranches, are the loneliest guys in the world. They got no family. They don't belong no place. They come to a ranch an' work up a stake and then they go inta town and blow their stake, and the first thing you know they're poundin' their tail on some other ranch. They ain't got nothing to look ahead to."

Lennie was delighted. "That's it—that's it. Now tell how it is with us."

George went on. "With us it ain't like that. We got a future. We got somebody to talk to that gives a damn about us. We don't have to sit in no bar room blowin' our jack jus' because we got no place else to go. If them other guys gets in jail they can rot for all anybody gives a damn. But not us."

Lennie broke in. *"But not us! An' why? Because . . . ."*

because I got you to look after me, and you got me to look after you, and that's why." He laughed delightedly. "Go on now, George!"

"You got it by heart. You can do it yourself."

"No, you. I forget some a' the things. Tell about how it's gonna be."

"O.K. Someday—we're gonna get the jack together and we're gonna have a little house and a couple of acres an' a cow and some pigs and——"

"An' live off the fatta the lan'," Lennie shouted. "An' have *rabbits.* Go on, George! Tell about what we're gonna have in the garden and about the rabbits in the cages and about the rain in the winter and the stove, and how thick the cream is on the milk like you can hardly cut it. Tell about that, George."

"Why'n't you do it yourself? You know all of it."

"No . . . . you tell it. It ain't the same if I tell it. Go on . . . . George. How I get to tend the rabbits."

"Well," said George, "we'll have a big vegetable patch and a rabbit hutch and chickens. And when it rains in the winter, we'll just say the hell with goin' to work, and we'll build up a fire in the stove and set around it an' listen to the rain comin' down on the roof—Nuts!" He took out his pocket knife. "I ain't got time for no more." He drove his knife through the top of one of the bean cans, sawed out the top and passed the can to Lennie. Then he opened a second can. From his side pocket he brought out two spoons and passed one of them to Lennie.

They sat by the fire and filled their mouths with beans and chewed mightily. A few beans slipped out of the side of Lennie's mouth. George gestured with his spoon. "What you gonna say tomorrow when the boss asks you questions?"

Lennie stopped chewing and swallowed. His face was

concentrated. "I . . . . I ain't gonna . . . . say a word."

"Good boy! That's fine, Lennie! Maybe you're gettin' better. When we get the coupla acres I can let you tend the rabbits all right. 'Specially if you remember as good as that."

Lennie choked with pride. "I can remember," he said.

George motioned with his spoon again. "Look, Lennie. I want you to look around here. You can remember this place, can't you? The ranch is about a quarter mile up that way. Just follow the river?"

"Sure," said Lennie. "I can remember this. Di'n't I remember about not gonna say a word?"

" 'Course you did. Well, look. Lennie—if you jus' happen to get in trouble like you always done before, I want you to come right here an' hide in the brush."

"Hide in the brush," said Lennie slowly.

"Hide in the brush till I come for you. Can you remember that?"

"Sure I can, George. Hide in the brush till you come."

"But you ain't gonna get in no trouble, because if you do, I won't let you tend the rabbits." He threw his empty bean can off into the brush.

"I won't get in no trouble, George. I ain't gonna say a word."

"O.K. Bring your bindle over here by the fire. It's gonna be nice sleepin' here. Lookin' up, and the leaves. Don't build up no more fire. We'll let her die down."

They made their beds on the sand, and as the blaze dropped from the fire the sphere of light grew smaller; the curling branches disappeared and only a faint glimmer showed where the tree trunks were. From the darkness Lennie called, "George—you asleep?"

"No. Whatta you want?"

"Let's have different color rabbits, George."

"Sure we will," George said sleepily. "Red and blue and green rabbits, Lennie. Millions of 'em."

"Furry ones, George, like I seen in the fair in Sacramento."

"Sure, furry ones."

" 'Cause I can jus' as well go away, George, an' live in a cave."

"You can jus' as well go to hell," said George. "Shut up now."

The red light dimmed on the coals. Up the hill from the river a coyote yammered, and a dog answered from the other side of the stream. The sycamore leaves whispered in a little night breeze.

Conflict

Author Katherine Porter once wrote a memorable story called "Rope." It is about a man and his wife who have just moved to the country. The man goes to town for groceries. He buys his groceries and comes home. In addition to the groceries, he gets a length of rope he might need "someday." And he forgets to get the coffee his wife wants.

That's no story, you might say. And of course you'd be right. These simple actions need something more to turn them into a story. They need something to capture your interest. In a successful story, that something is conflict. Conflict is a struggle between two or more people, forces, ideas or feelings. What makes "Rope" so unforgettable is not the action, but the conflict that arises between the man and his wife set off by the purchase of the rope.

Even if the action in a story is more exciting than a trip to buy groceries, it will not hold your interest for long if it does not involve conflict of some sort. Conflict changes a plain description of actions into a story that has meaning and emotional impact.

For example, James Dickey's novel, *Deliverance*, is about four men who take a canoe trip. During the trip one man is killed. The others, after severe hardships, return safely. You can see that there is a lot of action in the story, but it still doesn't seem very interesting. Yet *Deliverance* is one of the most exciting novels of recent years—so exciting it was made into a movie. It is the conflict in the story, not all the action, which makes it exciting. Once you are exposed to the conflict, you can't put the book down. The men are challenged by hardships in nature. They are attacked by other men and must fight back. These outer conflicts lead to inner ones: each man must search his soul because of what happens. Their old ways of living and thinking come into conflict with what they learn on the trip. They have hard choices to make. These are the conflicts that make the story.

This lesson is about conflict and how conflict works to make a story. We will consider four ways in which the author, John Steinbeck, uses conflict:

1 The author uses different kinds of conflict.

2 The author uses conflict as a moving, or motivating, force.

3 The author reveals characters through conflict.

4 The author uses conflict to produce the plot, or storyline, of the novel.

In general, there are four kinds of conflict: conflict between people, conflict with oneself, conflict with nature, and conflict with society. The most common conflict is between people. A fist fight, for example, is certainly conflict between two people. Competition

1 Kinds of Conflict

for the job of head cheerleader or class president is also conflict among people. But there are other kinds of conflict among people that are not quite so obvious. There are quiet conflicts between children and parents, and students and teachers. There are conflicts over jobs in business.

People also find conflict within themselves. A guilty conscience is a form of inner conflict. Struggling to decide what to do in a certain situation is also a personal conflict. Will you go to college or not? Will you follow someone else's advice or your own? Will you break off with a friend? All of these questions that require soul-searching and decision-making are personal or inner conflicts.

Conflicts with the forces of nature arise, too. A trapper lost in a blizzard is in conflict with nature. So is someone who is slogging through the jungle. And fighting a raging river on a raft is also conflict with nature.

Finally, a person may be in conflict with society. This would describe a criminal with a grudge against the world. Or a conflict with society might involve a homeowner whose house is in the way of a new highway. An animal character faced with the destruction of its forest home is also in conflict with society.

The most important conflicts in a story always involve the main characters, sometimes called the *protagonists*. George and Lennie are the protagonists in *Of Mice and Men*. What kinds of conflict involving George and Lennie do you see in the passage below? (There may be more than one kind of conflict in any situation.)

> . . . George exploded. "Whatever we ain't got, that's what you want. God a'mighty, if I was alone I could live so easy. I could go get a job an' work, an' no trouble." . . . . Lennie knelt and looked over the fire at the angry George. And Lennie's face was drawn with terror. "An' whatta I got,"

George went on furiously. "I got you! You can't keep a job and you lose me ever' job I get. . . . An' that ain't the worst. You get in trouble. You do bad things and I got to get you out." His voice rose nearly to a shout. . . . "Jus' wanted to feel that girl's dress—jus' wanted to pet it like it was a mouse——Well, how the hell did she know you jus' wanted to feel her dress?. . . . She yells and we got to hide in a irrigation ditch all day with guys lookin' for us. . . . I wisht I could put you in a cage with about a million mice an' let you have fun." His anger left him suddenly. He looked across the fire at Lennie's anguished face, and then he looked ashamedly at the flames.

George is fiercely angry. His anger seems directed at Lennie. Lennie is terrified of George's anger. Clearly there is a conflict between two people.

But there is another kind of conflict here. George is doing a good bit of soul-searching. He is really asking himself why he stays with Lennie and takes care of him. Then George is suddenly ashamed of his anger. He is ashamed of what he is doing to Lennie. This causes a personal or inner conflict for George that is important throughout the novel.

And there is one other kind of conflict in the story. It seems that Lennie, in a very innocent way, patted a girl's dress. The girl screamed, not understanding that Lennie was simple and harmless. This brought the whole town down on both Lennie and George, and they had to flee for their lives. Society then, as now, was a long way from understanding the mentally retarded. Because of this, Lennie and George are in direct conflict with society.

Exercise A

The following passage is from the selection you have read. Answer the questions about this passage using what you have learned in this part of the lesson. Choose the best answer for each question. Put an x in the correct box or fill in the appropriate words.

George lay back on the sand and crossed his hands under his head, and Lennie imitated him, raising his head to see whether he were doing it right. "God, you're a lot of trouble," said George. "I could get along so easy and so nice if I didn't have you on my tail."

1. What kind of conflict can you see here?

    ☐ a. Conflict between people: George is making Lennie angry.

    ☐ b. Conflict with nature: George and Lennie hate sleeping outdoors.

    ☐ c. Inner conflict: George is thinking out loud about his problems.

    ☐ d. Conflict with society: George thinks Lennie will get him into trouble.

2. There must be two opposing forces or ideas in order for there to be conflict. One idea that George has here is that Lennie is "a lot of trouble." What is the opposing idea that George has about what he'd like his life to be like? Copy George's words that express that idea.

_____

_____

_____

Now check your answers using the Answer Key on page 437. Correct any wrong answer and review this part of the lesson if you don't understand why your answer was wrong.

Conflict
2 **Conflict as Motivation**

Conflict always involves a struggle of some sort, either with forces outside you or tensions inside you. That's why conflicts are usually disturbing or upsetting. Most people don't enjoy being in an argument or a fight, nor do they enjoy worrying about a decision or coping with fears. Conflict, then, often becomes a *motive* for action. If you are in conflict, you do something in order to end the conflict. To put it another way, conflict often gives you the *motivation* to settle the problem. It leads you to action or a decision.

On a very simple level, think of a pesky fly buzzing about. You are in conflict with this fly: it wants to stay, you want it to go. This conflict will motivate you to take some action to get rid of the fly. In a sense, a story is unfolding, a life-and-death battle between you and the fly which you might title "The SWAT Team."

This relation between conflict and motivation happens in stories just as it does in life. Often, conflicts arise when you, or a character in a story, are pursuing a goal. The goal may be small (catching a fly) or big (graduating from school). As you move toward your goal, new conflicts will arise. These new conflicts motivate you to new action, and that's how a story develops. We will see more about this in the section on conflict and plot.

In *Of Mice and Men*, there are motivating forces at work that keep George and Lennie together. These forces are the result of certain inner conflicts. The conflicts motivate Lennie and George to act the way they do. What they do creates new conflicts, and so the story goes.

The passage below shows the inner conflict that motivates George and Lennie to stick together.

> "Guys like us, that work on ranches, are the loneliest guys in the world. They got no family. They don't belong no place. They come to a ranch an' work up a stake and then they go inta town and blow their stake, and the first thing you know they're poundin' their tail on some other ranch. They ain't got nothing to look ahead to."
> Lennie was delighted. "That's it—that's it. Now tell how it is with us."

Of Mice and Men

George went on. "With us it ain't like that. We got a future. We got somebody to talk to that gives a damn about us. We don't have to sit in no bar room blowin' our jack jus' because we got no place else to go. If them other guys gets in jail they can rot for all anybody gives a damn. But not us."

Lennie broke in. *"But not us! An' why? Because. . . . because I got you to look after me, and you got me to look after you, and that's why."* He laughed delightedly.

It is easy to see why Lennie needs George. Lennie is like a small child who needs a parent to look after him. But what motivates George to stay with Lennie?

George doesn't want to be a lonely drifter like other ranch workers he sees. "We got a future," he says. This is like saying, "We have a goal. We have a purpose in life, which is each other."

Keeping this relationship is George's goal. The motivation to work for this goal has come from an inner conflict—George's dread of a lonely and purposeless life is stronger than his anger at all the trouble that Lennie gets them into. As we have seen, this motivation has led to conflicts in the past. It will create new conflicts as the story unfolds.

Exercise B

The passage below is from the selection you have read. Answer the questions about this passage using what you have learned in this part of the lesson. Choose the best answer for each question. Put an *x* in the correct box or fill in the appropriate words.

[George is answering Lennie's plea to "Tell about how it's gonna be."]

"O.K. Someday—we're gonna get the jack together and we're gonna have a little house and a couple of acres an' a cow and some pigs and——"

"An' live off the fatta the lan'," Lennie shouted.

"An' have *rabbits*. Go on George! Tell about what we're gonna have in the garden and about the rabbits in the cages. . . ."

"Well," said George, "we'll have a big vegetable patch and a rabbit hutch and chickens. And when it rains in the winter, we'll just say the hell with goin' to work, and we'll build up a fire in the stove and set around it an' listen to the rain comin' down on the roof—Nuts!" He took out his pocket knife. "I ain't got time for no more."

1. What goal is suggested here that will probably motivate future conflict and action in the story?

   ☐ a. A dream of owning a large ranch

   ☐ b. A wish for security and independence

   ☐ c. A vision of life without work

   ☐ d. A desire to escape from life

2. Because of something George says, we can feel that the distant goal is in conflict with what is real at the moment. The conflict raises a doubt that they can reach their goal. Write down the expression that shows George has serious doubts.

   _____

   _____

   _____

Now check your answers using the Answer Key on page 437. Correct any wrong answer and review this part of the lesson if you don't understand why your answer was wrong.

Of Mice and Men

People act differently under pressure from the way they act at other times. A very calm, friendly person may become a monster if given trouble on a job. Other people are unflappable. No matter how difficult a situation, they come through like the Rock of Gibraltar. Take a person, apply pressure, and you will soon see what kind of a character you are dealing with.

3 Conflict and Character

Life is filled with conflicts. How a person reacts to conflict is one very good measure of that person's character. This is also true in fiction. In a novel, as in real life, you can learn a lot about a character when you see how the character reacts to the conflicts that arise in the story. What is more, you can see how the character's life is being affected by these conflicts and how the course of the story changes as a result. Conflict, character and story march along together through a book, you might say.

The conflict in the passage below is a small one. It is an argument over a dead mouse. But this small conflict tells us a great deal about George and Lennie and their relationship. It also tells us something about Lennie that will be very important later in the novel.

> George sat up. "Awright," he said brusquely. "Gi'me that mouse!"
>
> But Lennie made an elaborate pantomime of innocence. "What mouse, George? I ain't got no mouse."
>
> George held out his hand. "Come on. Give it to me. You ain't puttin' nothing over."
>
> Lennie hesitated, backed away, looked wildly at the brush line as though he contemplated running for his freedom. George said coldly, "You gonna give me that mouse or do I have to sock you?". . . .
>
> Lennie reluctantly reached into his pocket. His voice broke a little. "I don't know why I can't keep it. It ain't nobody's mouse. I didn't steal it. I found it lyin' right beside the road."

George's hand remained outstretched imperiously. Slowly, like a terrier who doesn't want to bring a ball to its master, Lennie approached, drew back, approached again. George snapped his fingers sharply, and at the sound Lennie laid the mouse in his hand.

This is not what you would call an earth-shaking conflict. It's more like a conflict between a devoted dog and its master. And that's one important thing we learn about George and Lennie. George is the master and Lennie is the obedient pet. Lennie, as big as he is, is frightened of George, or at least in awe of him. This gives us a clue that, though Lennie is a giant, he is quite harmless. He's timid, in fact. He is easily upset by even a hint of violence. This character trait will become extremely important later in the novel.

George seems cold and ill-tempered here. But take a look at how different he seems in the passage in Exercise C.

Exercise C

The passage below is from the selection you have read. Answer the questions about this passage using what you have learned in this part of the lesson. Choose the best answer for each question. Put an *x* in the correct box or fill in the appropriate words.

"I wasn't doin' nothing bad with it, George. Jus' strokin' it."

George stood up and threw the mouse as far as he could into the darkening brush. . . . "You crazy fool. Don't you think I could see your feet was wet where you went acrost the river to get it?" He heard Lennie's whimpering cry and wheeled about. "Blubberin' like a baby! Jesus Christ! A big guy like you." Lennie's lip quivered and tears started in his eyes. "Aw Lennie!" George put his hand on Lennie's shoulder. "I ain't takin' it away jus' for meanness. That mouse ain't fresh, Lennie; and besides, you've broke it pettin' it. You get another mouse that's fresh and I'll let you keep it a little while."

1. This conflict shows some important points about Lennie's character. We can see that he

   □ a. is bad by nature and won't admit it.

   □ b. has a mean streak in him like George.

   □ c. is not as fearful as George might think.

   □ d. doesn't realize how strong he is.

2. There is a short expression that shows George's mood has suddenly changed. A soft side of his character is coming out. What is the short expression that begins the change? Write it in the space provided.

   _____

   _____

Now check your answers using the Answer Key on page 437. Correct any wrong answer and review this part of the lesson if you don't understand why your answer was wrong.

Conflict	
4	**Conflict and Plot**

The plot of a novel is made up of all the actions that occur in the story. But an author can't just throw a bunch of actions together helter-skelter and expect them to come out as something you would want to read. All that results from writing down one action after another is a list of events, not a story. To hold your interest, these actions must be arranged according to some order or plan.

For this reason, in many stories actions arise from conflicts that have already been carefully described. Because we understand the conflict, we see the reason for the actions that result. If we know that there is a certain conflict in a character, we'll be interested in seeing the action taken to end that conflict. And these actions may lead to new conflicts with other characters, with society, or with nature. These new conflicts can result in still more action. In this way, conflict and action build on each other to make the story. There is progress in the plot.

Notice how much we can tell about the plot of John Steinbeck's novel from looking at the conflict in the first chapter. Lennie has gotten into trouble in Weed (conflict with society). This explains why he and George have come to look for work on the ranch (action). Because they have had to run away, there are arguments about the way Lennie acts (conflict between people). This conflict leads George to make plans for how to get work when they get to the ranch (action).

We suspect that this cycle of conflict and action will continue when they get to the ranch. And this is indeed the case. Conflict and action will continue to build on one another until they reach a high point of suspense and excitement. This high point is called the *climax* of the plot. The action that solves the final conflict and brings the story to a close is called the *resolution*.

Below is an early episode in the chapter. It tells of two problems (conflicts) and hints at action that may occur later in the novel as a result of these conflicts. George is speaking:

> "That ranch we're goin' to is right down there about a quarter mile. We're gonna go in an' see the boss. Now, look—I'll give him the work tickets, but you ain't gonna

Of Mice and Men

say a word. You jus' stand there and don't say nothing. . . . if he sees ya work before he hears ya talk, we're set. Ya got that?"

"Sure, George. Sure I got it."

"O.K. Now when we go in to see the boss, what you gonna do?"

"I . . . . I," Lennie thought. His face grew tight with thought. "I . . . . ain't gonna say nothin'. Jus' gonna stan' there."

"Good boy. That's swell. You say that over two, three times so you sure won't forget it. . . . An' you ain't gonna do no bad things like you done in Weed, neither."

The two problems we are told about are that Lennie forgets and that he does "bad things." The trouble in George's life comes from trying to manage Lennie and the problems he creates. There are hints of conflict to come at the ranch. Getting Lennie a job is always a tricky business. George is coaching Lennie to avoid the two things that cause the worst trouble. "Don't say nothing" and "you ain't gonna do no bad things," he tells Lennie.

We suspect that, as usual, Lennie will forget. There will surely be conflict arising from Lennie's doing something bad. These conflicts will, in fact, be exactly what lead the plot to its climax.

Exercise D

The passage below is from the selection you have read. Answer the questions about this passage using what you have learned in this part of the lesson. Choose the best answer for each question. Put an x in the correct box or fill in the appropriate words.

Lennie . . . looked off into the darkness across the river. "George, you want I should go away and leave you alone?"

"Where the hell could you go?"

"Well, I could. I could go off in the hills there. Some place I'd find a cave." . . . .

George looked quickly and searchingly at him. "I been mean,

ain't I?. . . . No—look! I was jus' foolin', Lennie. 'Cause I want you to stay with me. Trouble with mice is you always kill 'em." He paused. "Tell you what I'll do, Lennie. First chance I get I'll give you a pup. Maybe you wouldn't kill *it*. That'd be better than mice. And you could pet it harder."

1. You have now seen several conflicts between George and Lennie in the chapter. What happens in the plot as a result of these conflicts?

   ☐ a. George and Lennie dislike each other more and more.

   ☐ b. Lennie and George seem to come closer together.

   ☐ c. Lennie seems to be improving and will soon be normal.

   ☐ d. George is coming to the end of his patience.

2. To resolve their conflict, George hints at a future action that may affect the plot. Write down the sentence that suggests the future action.

   _____

   _____

   _____

Use the Answer Key on page 437 to check your answers. Correct any wrong answer and review this part of the lesson if you don't understand why your answer was wrong. Now go on to do the Comprehension Questions.

Comprehension Questions

Answer these questions without looking back at the selection. Choose the best answer to each question and put an *x* in the box beside it.

Recalling
Facts

1. Where are George and Lennie during this chapter?

   ☐ a. On a ranch

   ☐ b. Camped beside a river

   ☐ c. Somewhere in the desert

   ☐ d. In a dense forest

Understanding
Main Ideas

2. Which of these sayings might help explain an important idea in the story?

   ☐ a. Having somebody is better than having nobody at all.

   ☐ b. My right hand doesn't know what my left is doing.

   ☐ c. It ain't a fit night for man or beast.

   ☐ d. Every penny saved is a penny earned.

Recalling
Facts

3. How would you describe George?

   ☐ a. Big and powerful

   ☐ b. Heavy and humorous

   ☐ c. Small and quick

   ☐ d. Skinny and dull

4. Why would Lennie imitate anything George did?

☐ a. Lennie was making fun of George.

☐ b. Lennie admired George.

☐ c. Lennie couldn't do anything else.

☐ d. Lennie was smarter than he seemed.

5. Which of these statements is correct?

☐ a. Lennie and George got off the bus and decided to go to the ranch the next day.

☐ b. Lennie and George went to the ranch, didn't like it, and went to the river.

☐ c. Lennie and George camped out on their way to Weed.

☐ d. Having lost their jobs, Lennie and George were on their way to get new job tickets.

6. What does George think of Lennie as a ranch worker?

☐ a. George thinks Lennie can't remember how to work.

☐ b. George lets Lennie try, but he doesn't expect much.

☐ c. George knows Lennie is an excellent worker.

☐ d. George is sure Lennie will be fired when the boss sees him work.

Of Mice and Men

7. "Lennie . . . looked wildly at the brush line as though he *contemplated* running for his freedom." "He *contemplated*" probably means that he

☐ a. was afraid to do it.

☐ b. didn't like it.

☐ c. forgot about it.

☐ d. thought about it.

8. What was Lennie fond of doing?

☐ a. He was fond of swimming.

☐ b. He enjoyed the trees and soft breeze.

☐ c. He liked to pet soft things.

☐ d. He liked to torture animals.

9. "George undid his *bindle* and brought out three cans of beans." A *bindle* is probably

☐ a. a bundle of possessions.

☐ b. a garment like an overcoat.

☐ c. a box of groceries.

☐ d. a camping outfit.

10. Why does George explode when Lennie asks for ketchup?

☐ a. George doesn't like ketchup.

☐ b. George is probably worried because they don't have much of anything.

☐ c. George is sick of the way that Lennie always wastes ketchup.

☐ d. Lennie would break the bottle as he does everything else.

11. Lennie threatens to leave

☐ a. after George complains about his behavior.

☐ b. before he and George camp near the river.

☐ c. during the long bus ride.

☐ d. before he and George leave Weed.

12. The story is concerned mostly with showing us about

☐ a. racial prejudice in small-town America.

☐ b. methods of surviving outdoors.

☐ c. labor unions among migrant workers.

☐ d. strains and bonds in a relationship.

13. "George *gestured* with his spoon." This means he probably

☐ a. banged it on the bean can.

☐ b. made a motion with it.

☐ c. threw the spoon away.

☐ d. dipped it in the water.

14. Lennie and George hid from the townspeople of Weed

☐ a. after getting angry at the bus driver.

☐ b. while they were hunting for rabbits.

☐ c. after Lennie held onto a girl's dress.

☐ d. before they left Aunt Clara's place.

15. The title of the story, *Of Mice and Men,* is from a poem. Which of these quotations would also make a good title?

☐ a. "I have a dream . . . ."

☐ b. "This little pig . . . ."

☐ c. "Wagon soldier's shout . . . ."

☐ d. "The highwayman came riding . . . ."

Now check your answers using the Answer Key on page 437. Correct any wrong answers you have by putting a check (✓) in the box next to the right answer. Count the number of questions you answered correctly and plot the total on the Comprehension Scores graph on page 444.

Next, look at the questions you answered incorrectly. What types of questions were they? Count the number of each type and enter the numbers in the spaces below:

Recognizing Words in Context	_____
Recalling Facts	_____
Keeping Events in Order	_____
Making Inferences	_____
Understanding Main Ideas	_____

Now use these numbers to fill in the Comprehension Skills Profile on page 445.

Discussion Guides

The questions below will help you to think about the selection and the lesson you have just read. If you don't discuss these questions in class, try to think about them or discuss them with your classmates.

Discussing Conflict

1. How would you explain George's inner conflict about staying with Lennie?

2. Lennie is not very bright, but he has inner conflicts, too. What are they? How do they affect the story?

3. Try to predict what conflicts with society George and Lennie may have at the ranch.

Discussing the Story

4. The title of the novel comes from these lines in a poem by Robert Burns:

   > The best laid schemes of mice and men
   > *Gang aft agley.*

   Gang aft agley means "go often wrong." Judging from what you have read, how do you think these lines fit the story?

5. What can you find that is lovable or endearing about Lennie?

6. *Of Mice and Men* is often described as a story that touches your heart in some way. How does it do this?

Discussing the Author's Work

7. John Steinbeck was awarded a Nobel Prize for his work. He writes in very plain and simple language about working people, and usually poor people. Why do you think he received such a high award for this?

8. In his later years Steinbeck made his home in New York City. He liked New York, he said, because it is "the world, with every vice and blemish and beauty." Can this same description be given of the world of Lennie and George which Steinbeck created?

9. When he wrote *Of Mice and Men,* John Steinbeck wanted to see how much he could make a novel sound like a play (or movie). Read a page of conversation from the chapter with someone else. One person should take the part of Lennie, the other should be George. Is it like a play? In what ways?

Writing Exercise

Below you will find a list of actions in the order in which they happened. Write a paragraph or two that describes how an author might turn these events into a story by adding conflict. Be sure to tell about some of the conflicts that could occur in this situation.

The Actions:

1. A man comes home from work.

2. His wife comes home from work an hour later.

3. The man leaves shortly after his wife arrives.

4. He returns two hours later and they sit down to a late supper.

Unit 6　Theme

Mom, the Wolf Man and Me
BY NORMA KLEIN

About the Illustration

How would you describe the
way that this girl feels?
Point out some details in
the drawing to support your
answer.

Here are some questions to
help you think:

☐ How would you describe
the expression on the
girl's face? Why do you
think she is looking at
the boy rather than at
the woman at the table?

☐ What expression would
you expect to see on the
boy's face if he turned
around?

☐ How do you know that
both the boy and the girl
find something about
this woman unusual?

Unit 6

Introduction	**What the Novel Is About/What the Lesson Is About**
Selection	**Mom, the Wolf Man and Me**
Lesson	**Theme**
Activities	**Comprehension Questions/Discussion Guides/Writing Exercise**

Introduction

What the Novel Is About

Brett is eleven. She lives with her mother in a New York City apartment house, and she is much like any other girl her age. Her life at home is pleasant, and she gets along well with her mother.

There is only one problem. Her mother has never been married and Brett does not know her father. As a result, Brett has become very conscious of the households of her friends. There's Evelyn, whose mother is divorced and looking for another husband. There's Andrew, who has a "regular" family—mother and father at home—though neither parent is very nice.

"The only part that I really mind about Mom not being married," Brett says, "is when people ask questions." People are nosey. They always look for something "different" about others to ask and talk about. So even though Brett is completely happy and comfortable with her mother, fathers are much on her mind.

What if her mother were to marry? What if the new father were like Andrew's father? Even if she liked her mother's choice, it wouldn't be the same. Brett couldn't be as close to her mother if her mother were to marry. Certainly their life together would change.

All things considered, Brett seems to prefer things to go on as they are. But living involves change. And the Wolf Man comes into their lives.

Who the Wolf Man is and what he means to Brett and her mother is what the rest of the book is about. To find out who he is and how things work out for Brett, you'll have to read the rest of the novel.

What the Lesson Is About

This lesson is about themes in literature. In music, a theme is a tune or refrain. Usually it is something that is repeated or emphasized in some way. In literature, a theme is an idea that is repeated or emphasized. It is part of the message an author offers to readers along with the story.

Several ideas are offered to readers as themes in *Mom, the Wolf Man and Me*. One theme explores the relationships between parents and their children. Another theme deals with the idea of change. As you will see, Brett is uncomfortable with changes in her life.

The questions below will help you to focus on themes in the chapter from *Mom, the Wolf Man and Me*. Read the chapter carefully and try to answer these questions as you go along:

1 How do the actions of Mary Jane Wakowski and the doorman at Brett's new home point to a theme in the story?

2 How is Brett's mother different from Evelyn's mother? How do these two characters add to the "parent" theme in the story?

3 Which conversations show that Brett isn't entirely comfortable about not having a father?

4 Who else besides Brett do you sympathize with in this story?

Mom, the Wolf Man and Me

Norma Klein

Chapter 1
Father's Day

"Where's your father? Did he have to go to work or something?"

It was Father's Day at school and Mary Jane Wakowski was eyeing me with this funny expression. Her father, a sort of fat man with glasses, was off in the corner talking to Mrs. Darling. I gave her a kind of steady, blank look and just said, "No."

"So, where is he?"

"I don't have a father." You've got to say this just the right way and, in fact, I was out of practice, because for years I'd always gone to the same school and everybody knew and didn't ask. I don't really mind if they do, but if they haven't for a long time, you tend not to think of good, quick answers. Evelyn, this girl who lives in my building, says it's the same with her birthmark. She has a birthmark on her leg, a brown spot, and she says there are months and months when practically everyone she meets says, "What's that *thing* on your leg?" or "Did you fall and hit yourself?" (Once she said some little boy asked, "Did a dog go against your leg?") So she has to think of something to say that will sort of put the person in his place or make him feel a little dumb for asking. But then, she says, there are months when nobody asks about it and she forgets it's there. Then, when somebody mentions it again, she's forgotten all her good remarks. That's the way it is with me.

Mary Jane's got a wise expression. She thinks she's very smart because her father, who's a teacher, is always teaching her things at home like algebra so she knows them before anyone at school. "Oh, your parents are divorced, I guess," she said.

"Nope," I said.

Her eyes got bigger. "What do you mean? What are they, then?"

"They aren't divorced," I said. "They were never married."

Some days I kind of like going through this routine, even though it might be easier to say "They're divorced," since it wouldn't really matter. But I like seeing that expression on people's faces—*sometimes* I like it.

"They have to have been married," she said, almost mad. "You couldn't have been born otherwise."

I smiled.

"Everybody has a mother and a father," she went on. "That's how people get born."

"Is it?" I said.

"A mommy can't do it all by herself," Mary Jane said. "She can't sit on an egg or something."

"Gee, can't she?" I said, looking as bland as vanilla pudding, I hoped.

"You *know* she can't," said Mary Jane, ruffled.

"All I said was, they didn't get married," I said. "I didn't say she sat on an *egg*."

Maybe the light was beginning to dawn in Mary Jane's head, but she still kept looking at me in this funny, puzzled way. Finally, she said, "I never heard of anything like *that*."

Mary Jane is the type who if she never heard of it, thinks it should never have happened. "Live and learn," I said and walked over to the corner to play.

That's the trouble with starting in a new school. The reason I did was that we moved to a different part of New York, and we were in a different district. I was sorry we moved anyway. We used to live in the Village on this little street with trees, where it was quiet most of the time. But Mom said they were going to raise our rent, and she heard of an apartment in a new building uptown right near "a very good school." I guess the school is good, but I don't like the apartment building. It's *too* new. The doorman asks everyone who comes up who they are and that makes a lot of people nervous. He even asks people who've been there before. Mom doesn't like that either. She's always telling him just to let people up if they want to visit us, but he always says, "That's my job, Mrs. Levin."

Mom doesn't mind being called Mrs. Levin, even if she's not married. She says it's a convenience. I guess she doesn't like explaining all the time either. But the people at work call her Miss Levin. When they call up, they ask for her by that name or sometimes just by her first name, Deborah. She's a photographer for a magazine. She takes pictures, mostly of actors and actresses, sometimes of criminals and people along the street and things like that. When I was a baby, and even now, she took hundreds of pictures of me. If I'm just sitting there reading, I'll look up and there's Mom, sneaking up on me with her camera. Sometimes she lets me look through it, and she said that for my next birthday, when I'm twelve, she'll let me have my own camera. Then she says we can go to Africa together and take pictures of wild animals. That's something Mom has always wanted to do and I'd like to do it, too, since I love animals.

The only part that I really mind about Mom not being married is when people ask questions. Otherwise we have a good time, better in some ways than lots of my friends who have mothers *and* fathers. Like, when I visit Andrew, who was my best friend from my old school, everything has to be done at just a certain time. First we have to do our homework, then we can play, and at just a certain time, we have to have dinner. "Don't you see what time it is?" Andrew's mother keeps saying. In our house we hardly even have clocks. Mom never cares what time it is or when we eat. She says I have to go to bed more or less on time but if I don't, she doesn't really care. Maybe it's because her schedule is so odd. She works at night lots of times, developing pictures in our little back room. Sometimes she works all night and then just leaves me breakfast. I eat it by myself and go off to school by myself, too. Sometimes—which seems funny to some people—she's just getting up when I come home from school. Once she was just having breakfast when Andrew and I came in. "How come your mother is in her pajamas?" he said. "Is she sick?"

I felt funny then. I guess I wanted her to be like Andrew's mother, who is always dressed up and greets us at the door with sandwiches or cookies. So I said she was sick and when Andrew went home, I told Mom she shouldn't just be in pajamas at three in the afternoon. The good thing about Mom is that you can tell her these things. She never gets mad, but she doesn't always do them either. But after that, she tried sleeping in her blue jeans and shirt so that, even if she was just getting up, my friends wouldn't know. I thought that was okay, even though not that many mothers wear blue jeans either. But Mom is just sort of like that. She wears her hair in a pony tail, too, and she never gets dressed up like Evelyn's mother and never puts on makeup. Evelyn and I sometimes watch her mother get dressed up for dates and it takes her hours. She sits in front of this big mirror, that makes her face look gigantic, like a pumpkin. Then she puts on all sorts of stuff and lets us try some too—moon drops and blushers and eye makeup and perfume. Mom never uses that stuff. If she goes out, she just washes her hair and maybe puts on something different, but not that different from what she was wearing already. She's just that way. Even Andrew says mothers are just a certain way, whatever that way is, and it's silly to think they will ever change. But on the whole, I like Mom the way she is and don't especially mind not having a father.

Andrew's father, for instance, isn't nice at all. He never wants to play with him and he's always telling Andrew he isn't good at things. So mainly he makes Andrew feel worse than he would if he never had a father. There are lots of fathers like that, so I'd rather have none than one of those. Of course, it would be nice to have a great one. Sometimes I pretend Wally, this man that Mom works with, is my real father. (I know he isn't, because Mom said my real father lives in some other city and doesn't even know he's my real father, or that I was even born.) Wally has a wife, actually, but he doesn't like her. Mom says she doesn't like her either. But even though I like Wally, I don't know if I'd want him for a father all the time. He has a funny face, which is one thing I like—it's very round, like a moon, with a long dark moustache that he always pulls on when he's thinking. He always says to me, "Hi, kid. What's new?" He never calls me by my real name, Brett. What I like best is that sometimes, as a special treat, he brings over his movie projector and on Sunday nights, which is the time he has his children visit him, (he has Nicky who is two years younger than me and Marshall who's just three) he shows us all movies and we have pizza sent up and it's a lot of fun. If he lived with us, though, we'd do that every week, and it might not be so much fun. Also, I couldn't do as many things with Mom the way I do now. Most mothers and fathers go off together and leave their children with a babysitter, but Mom lets me come along if I want. If I had a father, maybe she wouldn't.

It's funny. Evelyn, whose parents are divorced, really wants a father. Her mother spends practically all her time going out on dates. Once Evelyn said to me, "That's her work."

"Going out on dates isn't work," I said.

"It *is*," said Evelyn. "She does it to find a father. She

doesn't even like it, but she knows she has to."

"Why does she have to?" I said. "Mine doesn't."

"She has to. She goes to look them all over. If she finds a good one, she'll pick him."

There must be a lot of bad ones, because Evelyn's mother has been going on dates for years. Whenever Evelyn and I play, she usually thinks of some game about fathers. Or she'll say, "Wouldn't it be great to have Pat as a father?"

Pat is one of the doormen in our building and he's always joking and telling Evelyn that her uncle's dog, Miffy, this poodle, is in a wooden box that is in the lobby. "I've got him in there. Should I let him out?" He always says that and I don't think it's so funny anymore, but Evelyn really likes him. He always gives Miffy a biscuit, but he makes her dance around on her hind legs, even though she's quite old. Evelyn says Miffy likes that, but I think it's cruel.

"What would be so good about having a father who was a doorman?" I'd say.

"Oh, you'd see him all the time," Evelyn said. "If you came home from school, he'd be right there. And you could play in the lobby if you wanted."

"I guess so."

Personally I can think of things I'd rather do than play in the lobby of our building all afternoon, but Evelyn is like that. She'd give almost anything to have a father. Whenever we go places where you can make a wish, you know she's always wishing about that. Once I even used my wish to wish it for her, but later, when it didn't happen, I was sorry that I threw the wish away. I don't think it ever works if you use your wish up on someone else.

The day they had Father's Day at school, not all of the fathers came. Melinda's mother is divorced and so is Kenneth's, and some of the fathers work, so I didn't feel funny about it. I just don't feel funny about being the only one not to do things. I guess it's my personality. People like my teacher at my old school think I'm pretending about that. I can tell that sometimes they feel sorry for me and they even say I'm being "brave," even if the thing has nothing to do with being brave. It's funny. But, even if all the fathers had come on Father's Day, I wouldn't have minded so much. It's just that they all didn't. But when I came home from school and was having a snack with Mom, I could see she was worried about it.

"Oh, there weren't so many fathers," I said. I even made it seem like there were hardly any so she wouldn't worry about it.

"I could've had Wally come," she said. "He had today off."

"Mom, it didn't matter," I said. "Anyway, Wally's not my father and so it's silly to make things up."

Mom sort of sighed and cut another brownie. "I just hate these rituals!" she said. "All these holidays!"

"I don't," I said. "Some of them are nice."

"It's such a waste of time," she said.

"It's funny," I said. "They don't have a *Mother's* Day at school."

Mom frowned. "Ya, Scratcher, that is funny. Why don't they? . . . I guess it's because some mothers are at the school all the time. They have nothing better to do."

"I guess that's it," I said. I wish Mom wouldn't worry so much about this stuff, but she's that way. Unlike me, she really cares if she's the only one doing something a certain way. And the trouble is, usually she *is* the only one. That's the funny part.

Theme

Authors express their ideas in books. Both novels and books of nonfiction set forth the ideas their authors want to get across to readers. In nonfiction—a history text let's say—it's rather easy to spot these ideas. The author spells them out for you in "topic sentences." Such statements as, "These are the causes of the Civil War. . . ," tell you at once what ideas will be discussed.

In a novel, though, ideas are not stated directly. Instead they emerge as part of the story. Ideas that are repeated or emphasized are called themes of the story. When you are asked what a story is about, you can answer in two ways. One way is to recite the action of the story: "Tex Jones came to town and was hired by Lily Goodthing. A gang of outlaws was trying to take Lily's ranch away from her." You would go on to tell about the gun battles and the romance and so on.

But a better way to tell what the story is about is to describe its themes: "The story is about the rights of settlers. Tex and Lily fight the forces of evil in the Old West." These are the ideas or themes of the story.

There are minor and major themes. A major theme is an idea the author returns to time and again. It becomes one of the most important things that the story is about. Minor themes are ideas that may appear from time to time. In our story about Tex and Lily, the battle between good and evil will probably appear often. Thus, you would call it a major theme. Along the way there may be lessons about the value of friendships. There may be ideas about how to get along with animals. Since these are not of key importance in the story, they would be minor themes.

In *Mom, the Wolf Man and Me*, readers are asked to think about problems faced by the daughter of a single parent. Brett Levin's problems with being different are the kind that most people have at one time or another. They are well worth thinking about, and they are presented as major themes of the novel. Along the way, the author, Norma Klein, talks about people who are vain and those who are not. She talks about how people react to the curiosity of others. These are minor themes in the story.

Themes in novels are expressed in several ways. In this lesson, we'll look at four ways that author Norma Klein expresses themes:

1 Actions, the events in the story, are used to suggest themes.

2 Themes are pointed at through the use of characters.

3 Themes and ideas are presented in thoughts and conversations.

4 Themes are emphasized by the way the author makes us feel.

It isn't at all unusual for people to express their ideas and feelings through their actions. Holding hands or kissing clearly expresses love. If, after a visit to the doctor, a person gives up smoking, he or she has made a very plain statement. This action says, "I am afraid smoking is injuring my health."

<table>
<tr><td></td><td>Theme</td></tr>
<tr><td>1</td><td>Theme and Action</td></tr>
</table>

Authors carefully pick and choose to find the actions they wish to include in their stories. One way of choosing is to ask what an action will "say" in the story. In other words, how will the action express an idea or theme? What does author Norma Klein seem to be getting at in the passage below? What ideas emerge from the way Brett Levin and Mary Jane are acting?

> "Where's your father? Did he have to go to work or something?"
>
> It was Father's Day at school and Mary Jane Wakowski was eyeing me with this funny expression. Her father, a sort of fat man with glasses, was off in the corner talking to Mrs. Darling. I gave her a kind of steady, blank look and just said, "No."
>
> "So, where is he?"
>
> "I don't have a father." You've got to say this just the right way and, in fact, I was out of practice, because for years I'd always gone to the same school and everybody knew and didn't ask. I don't really mind if they do, but if they haven't for a long time, you tend not to think of good, quick answers.

One point is made by the way Mary Jane is acting. The author is showing that people can be nosey. Mary Jane is asking for information that is none of her business. The way that Brett acts in response makes another point. She is clearly uncomfortable at being asked such questions. She tries to stop Mary Jane by staring at her and giving a short answer rather than a detailed explanation. She finally says, "I don't have a father," to confuse Mary Jane. Everyone has a father, of course. Brett's just doesn't happen to be married to her mother.

So what you see here is a small fencing match with words between the two girls. Mary Jane is trying to satisfy her curiosity. And Brett is annoyed. As Brett says a little further on, "The only part I really mind about Mom not being married is when people ask questions." Through the girls' actions here, the author is telling us to pay attention to two points. One point is that people may be a little uncomfortable or self-conscious about the way that their lives are different from other people's. This will prove to be a major theme in the story. The second point is that people can be nosey, and this will be a minor theme in the story.

Exercise A

The passage below is from the selection you have read. Answer the questions about this passage using what you have learned in this part of the lesson. Choose the best answer for each question. Put an x in the correct box or fill in the appropriate words.

That's the trouble with starting in a new school. The reason I did was that we moved to a different part of New York, and we were in a different district. I was sorry we moved anyway. We used to live in the Village on this little street with trees, where it was quiet most of the time. But Mom said they were going to raise our rent, and she heard of an apartment in a new building uptown right near "a very good school." I guess the school is good, but I don't like the apartment building. It's *too* new. The doorman asks everyone who comes up who they are and that makes a lot of people nervous. He even asks people who've been there before.

1. This passage talks about what it's like to move to a new home. Which of the following themes can be related to the action of moving?

   ☐ a. Talking with doormen

   ☐ b. Dealing with change

   ☐ c. Living in the Village

   ☐ d. Living in peace and quiet

2. You saw that Mary Jane Wakowski was nosey about Brett's family life. Another example of this theme appears here. Write down at least one sentence from the passage that points to unnecessary prying.

_____

_____

_____

Now check your answers using the Answer Key on page 438. Correct any wrong answer and review this part of the lesson if you don't understand why your answer was wrong.

2 Theme and Character

You may know someone who is mean and stingy. Perhaps that person is so stingy that whenever you think of stinginess, you think of that person. In Charles Dickens's story "A Christmas Carol," there is a character like this named Scrooge. Dickens uses Scrooge in the story to present the theme of meanness and miserliness in the world. In fact, Dickens makes old Scrooge so mean and stingy that, for readers of the story and even for those who have only heard of it, Scrooge has come to stand for stinginess in the world.

You can probably think of a story where a character is linked with good, or with evil. In another story, an animal character may have been linked with faithfulness. The authors probably used these characters to discuss themes. Perhaps the theme of one story was that goodness is often opposed by evil. Perhaps the theme of another story pointed out the value of loyalty in the world.

Two themes, one major and one minor, are expressed through the characters of the mothers in this next passage.

> But Mom is just sort of like that. She wears her hair in a pony tail, too, and she never gets dressed up like Evelyn's mother and never puts on makeup. Evelyn and I sometimes watch her mother get dressed up for dates and it takes her hours. She sits in front of this big mirror, that makes her face look gigantic, like a pumpkin. Then she puts on all sorts of stuff and lets us try some, too—moon drops and blushers and eye makeup and perfume. Mom never uses that stuff. If she goes out, she just washes her hair and maybe puts on something different, but not that different from what she was wearing already. She's just that way. Even Andrew says mothers are just a certain way, whatever that way is, and it's silly to think they will ever change.

The two mothers are very different. Evelyn's mother is very concerned about her appearance. Perhaps she is very vain. Or maybe she worries about what people will think of her. Brett's mother seems more relaxed about her appearance.

Mom, the Wolf Man and Me

The easy-going nature of Brett's mother is a minor theme in the story. The fact that there are differences among people is a major theme. As Brett remembers her friend saying, "Mothers are just a certain way . . . and it's silly to think they will ever change." Further along in the novel, readers meet many people—and not just mothers—who don't seem likely to change. Brett must learn to accept the differences among people. And other people must accept the differences in Brett.

Exercise B

The passage below is from the selection you have read. Answer the questions about this passage using what you have learned in this part of the lesson. Choose the best answer for each question. Put an *x* in the correct box or fill in the appropriate words.

Sometimes—which seems funny to some people—she's [Brett's mother] just getting up when I come home from school. Once she was just having breakfast when Andrew and I came in. "How come your mother is in her pajamas?" he said. "Is she sick?"

I felt funny then. I guess I wanted her to be like Andrew's mother, who is always dressed up and greets us at the door with sandwiches or cookies. So I said she was sick and when Andrew went home, I told Mom she shouldn't just be in pajamas at three in the afternoon. The good thing about Mom is that you can tell her these things. She never gets mad, but she doesn't always do them either. But after that, she tried sleeping in her blue jeans and shirt so that, even if she was just getting up, my friends wouldn't know.

1. Reread the last three sentences carefully. An important theme is emphasized through this description of character. Which sentence below best states the theme?

   ☐ a. Brett and her mother can talk to one another and come to agreements.

   ☐ b. Brett is spoiled and her mother is trying to unspoil her.

   ☐ c. Brett's mother is a selfish person even though she seems to be easy-going.

   ☐ d. Brett's mother never gets angry, which means no one should ever get angry.

2. You can often spot a theme when an idea is repeated in a story. Here Brett again expresses the idea that she is self-conscious about her home life. Write down the short sentence and half of a longer one that points to this theme.

_____

_____

_____

Now check your answers using the Answer Key on page 438. Correct any wrong answer and review this part of the lesson if you don't understand why your answer was wrong.

Mom, the Wolf Man and Me

A careful writer puts nothing in a novel without a good reason for doing so. Thus, only actions and events that will move the story along, explain a character or develop a theme are used. Thoughts and conversations of characters are used for the same reasons.

Brett's conversation with Mary Jane at the start of the novel does several things. It gets the story rolling. It introduces Brett and tells about her family life. It also gives you an idea of how Brett feels about her life and about some of her friends. And, as you have seen in part one, it introduces two themes.

The author has set up the story so that it is told by Brett. When Brett is not talking to another character, you could say she is talking directly to the readers. Or, you might say she is thinking, or explaining her thoughts to herself. This method of telling a story is called a *first-person narrative.*

In other novels, the conversation—dialogue—appears as it does here. But the author drops in from time to time to tell you what characters are thinking. This is called a *third-person narrative.*

However the thinking and talking are done in a story, they are used to advance the plot, reveal a character or develop a theme. The following passage is a combination of thought and conversation. Notice how it brings out a theme about fathers. As you have noticed, fathers are much on Brett's mind.

Most mothers and fathers go off together and leave their children with a babysitter, but Mom lets me come along if I want. If I had a father, maybe she wouldn't.

It's funny. Evelyn, whose parents are divorced, really wants a father. Her mother spends practically all her time going out on dates. Once Evelyn said to me, "That's her work."

"Going out on dates isn't work," I said.

"It *is*,"said Evelyn. "She does it to find a father. She doesn't even like it, but she knows she has to."

"Why does she have to?" I said. "Mine doesn't."

"She has to. She goes to look them all over. If she finds a good one, she'll pick him."

There must be a lot of bad ones, because Evelyn's mother
has been going on dates for years.

It seems that Evelyn's mother is searching for a father for her daughter. The search may be for herself as well. She wants the companionship of a husband. Searching has become a kind of "work" for her. And
you can't help but feel sympathy for her difficulties and disappoint-
ments.

Brett says that her mother doesn't search for a father. But Brett is
certainly aware of fathers throughout the novel. The story begins with
Father's Day at school. In other passages Brett thinks about Andrew's
father. Sometimes she thinks about what it might be like to have Wally
as a father. She figures, and rightly so, that if she had a father, her life
would be quite different.

Through Brett's thoughts and conversations, the author asks readers
to consider several questions. How important is it to have a father in
the home? How important is it for the child? How important is it for the
mother? How would having a new father change the relationship between mother and daughter? These questions arise again and again in
the thoughts and conversations of the novel. This is one way the author
calls your attention to an important theme.

Exercise C

The passage below is from the selection you have read. Answer
the questions about this passage using what you have learned in
this part of the lesson. Choose the best answer for each question.
Put an x in the correct box or fill in the appropriate words.

[Brett is speaking with her mother about Father's Day at school.]

"Oh, there weren't so many fathers," I said. I even made it seem
like there were hardly any so she wouldn't worry about it.
"I could've had Wally come," she said. "He had today off."
"Mom, it didn't matter," I said. "Anyway, Wally's not my father
and so it's silly to make things up."

Mom sort of sighed and cut another brownie. "I just hate these rituals!" she said. "All these holidays!"

"I don't," I said. "Some of them are nice."

"It's such a waste of time," she said. . . .

I wish Mom wouldn't worry so much about this stuff, but she's that way. Unlike me, she really cares if she's the only one doing something a certain way. And the trouble is, usually she *is* the only one. That's the funny part.

1. One of the themes of the story deals with the relationship between Brett and her mother. What does this conversation tell you about that?

   ☐ a. They don't think much about one another.

   ☐ b. They just don't understand one another.

   ☐ c. They seem to worry about one another.

   ☐ d. They wish there were no fathers.

2. You have seen that Brett is a bit troubled by having a home life that is different from other children's. This is an important theme in the novel. But in a sentence near the end of this passage she says the opposite. She says it's not her but her mother who worries about being different. Copy this sentence in the space provided.

   _____

   _____

   _____

Now check your answers using the Answer Key on page 438. Correct any wrong answer and review this part of the lesson if you don't understand why your answer was wrong.

4 Theme

Themes and Feelings

Themes are important in a book because they teach us something. In *Mom, the Wolf Man and Me*, author Norma Klein wants to do more than just tell the story of one person, Brett Levin, who has an unusual family life. She wants readers to feel what it is like to be in some way different from most people. She also wants us to think about how we treat people who are different from us. In other words, she wants us to learn something about our own lives from the theme in *Mom, the Wolf Man and Me.*

One way that authors make sure that we learn something from themes is by guiding our feelings about what happens in a book. You've seen, for example, how we sympathize with Brett when she has to face Mary Jane's questions about her father. Because we share Brett's feelings in that scene, we learn how hard it is to be different even though we may not have had that experience in our own lives. Norma Klein makes us share Brett's feelings—makes us feel them with Brett—by letting us see how awkward Brett feels in this situation. By doing that, she makes us understand an important theme about how hard it is to be different.

But the author also guides our feelings to show us how easy it is to be critical of differences in other people if we're not careful. See whose feelings you share in the passage below.

> Evelyn and I sometimes watch her mother get dressed up for dates and it takes her hours. She sits in front of this big mirror that makes her face look gigantic, like a pumpkin. . . . Her mother spends practically all her time going out on dates. Once Evelyn said to me, "That's her work. . . . She does it to find a father. She doesn't even like it, but she knows she has to. . . . If she finds a good one, she'll pick him."

The author wants us to feel a little sorry for Evelyn's mother. She shows us how hard Evelyn's mother is working at something that is supposed to be fun. We can see that Evelyn's mother is probably not very happy, and we sympathize with her. By contrast, Brett seems to think that Evelyn's mother is a little funny. She points out that her face looks "like a pumpkin." She also makes a joke about how much time Evelyn's mother spends going out on dates.

Because we sympathize with Evelyn's mother, we can see that Brett is being a little unfair. She is critical of the ways that Evelyn's mother is different from her own mother. Her mother doesn't get dressed up or put on make-up to go out on dates. She doesn't "work" at getting a father for Brett. Brett doesn't realize that she is being unfair, but we do because of the way we feel about Evelyn's mother in this description. We learn something about how easy it is to be critical of those who are different from us if we're not careful. Norma Klein emphasizes her theme about differences by guiding the way we feel about what happens in this scene.

How are your feelings being guided to reveal a theme in the passage in Exercise D?

Exercise D

The passage below is from the selection you have read. Answer the questions about this passage using what you have learned in this part of the lesson. Choose the best answer for each question. Put an *x* in the correct box or fill in the appropriate words.

[Brett is talking to Evelyn.]

"What would be so good about having a father who is a doorman?" I'd say.

"Oh, you'd get to see him all the time," Evelyn said. If you came home from school, he'd be right there. And you could play in the lobby if you wanted."

"I guess so."

Personally I can think of things I'd rather do than play in the lobby of our building all the time, but Evelyn is like that. She'd give anything to have a father.

1. What does Brett think about Evelyn in this scene?

   ☐ a. She thinks Evelyn is a little silly.

   ☐ b. She agrees with Evelyn about the doorman.

   ☐ c. She thinks Evelyn is smart.

   ☐ d. She likes the way Evelyn imagines new situations.

2. Write the sentence that tells us that we should feel some sympathy for Evelyn.

   _____

   _____

   _____

Use the Answer Key on page 438 to check your answers. Correct any wrong answer and review this part of the lesson if you don't understand why your answer was wrong. Now go on to do the Comprehension Questions.

Comprehension Questions

Answer these questions without looking back at the selection. Choose the best answer to each question and put an *x* in the box beside it.

Recalling
Facts

1. On a visiting day at school, Mary Jane Wakowski was puzzled because Brett

   ☐ a. came from a different neighborhood.

   ☐ b. was lying to her.

   ☐ c. said she had no father.

   ☐ d. didn't tell her mother about the event.

Keeping
Events in
Order

2. When did Brett and her mother move into their new neighborhood?

   ☐ a. After Brett met Mary Jane Wakowski

   ☐ b. When Brett's mother became a photographer

   ☐ c. Before Brett and Andrew became friends

   ☐ d. Just before the Father's Day party at school

Understanding
Main Ideas

3. What did the doorman and Mary Jane Wakowski have in common that Brett didn't like?

   ☐ a. Asking questions

   ☐ b. Arguing

   ☐ c. Making jokes

   ☐ d. Disliking Brett

4. Mary Jane Wakowski became *ruffled* during her conversation with Brett. In other words, she

☐ a. shouted loudly.

☐ b. became very quiet.

☐ c. was amused.

☐ d. was upset.

5. Brett's mother

☐ a. was divorced.

☐ b. had never married.

☐ c. was a widow.

☐ d. had a husband who deserted her.

6. The story is about a young girl whose home life is

☐ a. always upset and in turmoil.

☐ b. somewhat different from her friends'.

☐ c. like that of any other family.

☐ d. in need of something to make it better.

7. Brett's mother was a(n)

☐ a. photographer.

☐ b. teacher.

☐ c. fashion model.

☐ d. actress.

8. Sometimes Brett's mother stayed up late *developing* pictures. She was

☐ a. coloring them.

☐ b. thinking about them.

☐ c. treating film with chemicals.

☐ d. sketching them.

9. Brett's mother complained about rituals

☐ a. whenever the doorman announced a visitor.

☐ b. after Brett told her about the Father's Day at school.

☐ c. after she learned of Andrew's daily schedule.

☐ d. before she became friends with Wally.

10. You could probably say that the life Brett and her mother lead is

☐ a. governed by a strict schedule.

☐ b. troublesome and annoying.

☐ c. rather relaxed and informal.

☐ d. unconcerned with important things.

11. The author uses Evelyn's mother to show that some single parents

☐ a. do not treat their children kindly.

☐ b. would do anything to stay single.

☐ c. try very hard to get married.

☐ d. don't care one way or another about marriage.

12. How would you describe the feeling between Brett and her mother?

☐ a. Strained and uncomfortable

☐ b. Very wishy-washy

☐ c. Rather like strangers

☐ d. Very close

13. When did Brett have a chat with her mother about Father's Day at school?

☐ a. Several days later

☐ b. Right after school that day

☐ c. Before Brett left for school

☐ d. A couple of days before the event

14. Brett's mother said she hated *rituals*. In other words, she disliked

☐ a. formal ways of doing things.

☐ b. wealthy people.

☐ c. pictures and decorations.

☐ d. fancy ways of dressing.

15. How does Brett feel about the thought of having a father?

☐ a. She is not sure if she would want a father or not.

☐ b. She is certain she would rather not have a father.

☐ c. She wants a father very badly.

☐ d. She will leave home if her mother marries.

Now check your answers using the Answer Key on page 438. Correct any wrong answers you have by putting a check (✓) in the box next to the right answer. Count the number of questions you answered correctly and plot the total on the Comprehension Scores graph on page 444.

Next, look at the questions you answered incorrectly. What types of questions were they? Count the number of each type and enter the numbers in the spaces below:

Recognizing Words in Context   _____

Recalling Facts   _____

Keeping Events in Order   _____

Making Inferences   _____

Understanding Main Ideas   _____

Now use these numbers to fill in the Comprehension Skills Profile on page 445.

Discussion Guides

The questions below will help you to think about the selection and the lesson you have just read. If you don't discuss these questions in class, try to think about them or discuss them with your classmates.

Discussing Theme

1. A major theme in the story deals with changes in life and how people face these changes. How would you feel if there were important changes in your life? As examples of change, think about moving to a new city, changing schools or having someone come to live with you.

2. Brett mentions in the chapter that her mother wears blue jeans. She mentions it in other chapters, too. What does this detail tell us about Brett's mother? How might this detail point to a theme in the story? How might blue jeans represent a theme in your own life?

3. Find and listen to a record of *Peter and the Wolf* by the composer Prokofiev. See if you can pick out musical themes or repeated refrains. There are themes for Peter, for the Wolf and for various other characters.

Discussing the Story

4. Why is changing schools and apartments a problem for Brett? What kinds of changes would occur if she suddenly acquired a father?

5. Some people might say that the relationship between Brett and her mother was *too* informal. Was it? How should parents and children behave toward one another?

6. Brett says it bothers her when people ask questions about her Mom not being married. At the end of the chapter she says she doesn't care if she is different. Judging from what you have read, do you think Brett does or doesn't care about the differences? Give reasons for your opinion.

Discussing the Author's Work

7. Several of the chapters used in this text are written in the first person. This is where a character in the story tells the story and uses the pronoun "I" in telling it [*A Day No Pigs Would Die* (Unit 3), *To Kill a Mockingbird* (Unit 4), *Summer of My German Soldier* (Unit 2)]. Do you like books written this way? Explain your opinion.

8. *Mom, the Wolf Man and Me* is a first-person narrative. It gives you Brett's idea of her life in her own words, the words an eleven-year-old girl would use. How would the story change if it were a third-person narrative? For example, think about how the description of Wally's family life might change.

9. Mary Jane Wakowski isn't a bad person, but she is curious, as many people are. Still, after reading about her, you probably don't like her. That's the author's doing. How does the author manage to control your feelings about this character?

Writing Exercise

Try one of these writing tasks.

1. Create a conversation between two people that deals with one of the themes in the list below.

2. Tell of an event or action that is based on one of the themes in the list below.

3. Describe a character who brings out one of the themes on the list below.

List of Themes

Selfishness	Love	Growing Up
Change	Kindness	The Power of Money
Bravery	Evil	Cruelty
Fear	Goodness	Old Age

Unit 7   Symbolism

A Separate Peace

BY JOHN KNOWLES

About the Illustration

How do you know that this tree has a special importance to this man? Point out some details in the drawing to support your answer.

Here are some questions to help you think:

☐ How would you describe this tree? What effect does the way it looks have on you?

☐ What makes this tree stand out from the rest of the scene?

☐ What kind of feeling do you think the man has about this tree?

Unit 7

Introduction What the Novel Is About/What the Lesson Is About

Selection **A Separate Peace**

Lesson **Symbolism**

Activities Comprehension Questions/Discussion Guides/Writing Exercise

Introduction

What the Novel Is About

During World War II Gene Forrester was a student at the Devon School. Fifteen years later Gene returns to the school and seeks out two places that have special meaning for him. One place is a marble staircase. The other place is a tree by the river. A bit of innocent horseplay among boys at the tree had begun a chain of events that had led to tragedy. The tragedy had come to its climax at the marble staircase.

After briefly presenting Gene Forrester as a man, *A Separate Peace* flashes back to when he was a boy in school. The time is summer, 1942. World War II hovers in the background. The boys in school who are sixteen and seventeen will soon be draft age. Many of the teachers have already gone into military service or other war work.

Gene's close friend at school is Phineas, known as Finny. Finny is a very unusual fellow. He is the school's best athlete and he enjoys meeting challenges head-on. His joy is in accomplishing something difficult or dangerous just for the sake of doing it. He is not a braggart or a wise guy. In fact, he would like his friend Gene to have some of his own self-confidence. He has a reputation for being fearless, though some think him foolhardy in the chances he takes. Still, he is the envy and wonder of students and masters alike.

Gene, on the other hand, is more like most of the rest of us. He has many fears. Challenges upset him. He would rather bow to authority than defy it. Finny, his opposite, is always at Gene's side urging him to behave with more self-confidence. At one point in the story it becomes evident that Finny loves Gene like a brother. Gene feels the same way about Finny, but he hasn't the courage to confess even this.

Readers call this a story of betrayal. In a terrible, unexplained moment Gene jostles his friend from a tree limb. Finny falls, shattering his leg. This leads to an even more tragic series of events, and that is what the book is about.

John Knowles, like Gene Forrester, was educated at one of New England's best preparatory schools, and later at Yale University. *A Separate Peace* is his first novel, appearing in 1960. It won several awards as a novel for adults, but it was quickly adopted by high-school students who made it their own. It is now called a perpetual best seller in schools, along with *The Catcher in the Rye* and *Lord of the Flies*. If you enjoy reading *A Separate Peace,* you may wish to try another of John Knowles's books with a similar theme: *The Paragon*. This novel is set at Yale in 1953.

What the Lesson Is About

The lesson that follows the reading selection is about symbolism.

The novel is about two boys at school and the tragic consequences of an accident that happens to them there. But on another level, the story is about fear and overcoming fear.

Fear is one of our most powerful and most puzzling emotions. It can make people hate, it can paralyze us, it can make us physically and mentally ill. When dealing with a subject as difficult as this, authors often use symbols to help explain complex ideas and feelings. They use a common object to stand for something that can't be seen or grasped so easily.

When one thing stands for another, it is called a symbol. A flag is a symbol that represents a country. A dollar bill is a symbol of value in goods and services. An anchor may symbolize hope, while a cross, a star or a crescent moon may symbolize faith.

In *A Separate Peace,* John Knowles uses the setting, the actions and the characters as symbols. Together they help us feel how puzzling and powerful an emotion fear really is.

A Separate Peace

The questions below will help you to focus on symbolism in the chapter from *A Separate Peace*. Read the chapter carefully and try to answer these questions as you go along:

1 Gene Forrester returns to Devon School and finds it seems to have been "preserved." What does he mean by this? What is the school a symbol of?

2 What does Finny mean to Gene?

3 What different ways of looking at life are shown by the behavior of the boys at the river?

4 What theme is introduced by Gene's description of the tree near the river?

A Separate Peace

John Knowles

ONE

I went back to the Devon School not long ago, and found it looking oddly newer than when I was a student there fifteen years before. It seemed more sedate than I remembered it, more perpendicular and strait-laced, with narrower windows and shinier woodwork, as though a coat of varnish had been put over everything for better preservation. But, of course, fifteen years before there had been a war going on. Perhaps the school wasn't as well kept up in those days; perhaps varnish, along with everything else, had gone to war.

I didn't entirely like this glossy new surface, because it made the school look like a museum, and that's exactly what it was to me, and what I did not want it to be. In the deep, tacit way in which feeling becomes stronger than thought, I had always felt that the Devon School came into existence the day I entered it, was vibrantly real while I was a student there, and then blinked out like a candle the day I left.

Now here it was after all, preserved by some considerate hand with varnish and wax. Preserved along with it, like stale air in an unopened room, was the well known fear which had surrounded and filled those days, so much of it that I hadn't even known it was there. Because, unfamiliar with the absence of fear and what that was like, I had not been able to identify its presence.

Looking back now across fifteen years, I could see with great clarity the fear I had lived in, which must mean that in the interval I had succeeded in a very important undertaking; I must have made my escape from it.

I felt fear's echo, and along with that I felt the unhinged, uncontrollable joy which had been its accompaniment and opposite face, joy which had broken out sometimes in those days like Northern Lights across black sky.

There were a couple of places now which I wanted to see. Both were fearful sites, and that was why I wanted to see them. So after lunch at the Devon Inn I walked back toward the school. It was a raw, nondescript time of year, toward the end of November, the kind of wet, self-pitying November day when every speck of dirt stands out clearly. Devon luckily had very little of such weather—the icy clamp of winter, or the radiant New Hampshire summers, were more characteristic of it—but this day it blew wet, moody gusts all around me.

I walked along Gilman Street, the best street in town. The houses were as handsome and as unusual as I remembered. Clever modernizations of old Colonial manses, extensions in Victorian wood, capacious Greek Revival temples lined the street, as impressive and just as forbidding as ever. I had rarely seen anyone go into one of them, or anyone playing on a lawn, or even an open window. Today with their failing ivy and stripped, moaning trees the houses looked both more elegant and more lifeless than ever.

Like all old, good schools, Devon did not stand isolated behind walls and gates but emerged naturally from the town which had produced it. So there was no sudden moment of encounter as I approached; the houses along Gilman Street began to look more defensive, which meant that I was near the school, and then more exhausted, which meant that I was in it.

It was early afternoon and the grounds and buildings were deserted, since everyone was at sports. There was

A Separate Peace

nothing to distract me as I made my way across a wide yard, called the Far Common, and up to a building as red brick and balanced as the other major buildings, but with a large cupola and a bell and a clock and Latin over the doorway — the First Academy Building.

In through swinging doors I reached a marble foyer, and stopped at the foot of a long white marble flight of stairs. Although they were old stairs, the worn moons in the middle of each step were not very deep. The marble must be unusually hard. That seemed very likely, only too likely, although with all my thought about these stairs this exceptional hardness had not occurred to me. It was surprising that I had overlooked that, that crucial fact.

There was nothing else to notice; they of course were the same stairs I had walked up and down at least once every day of my Devon life. They were the same as ever. And I? Well, I naturally felt older—I began at that point the emotional examination to note how far my convalescence had gone—I was taller, bigger generally in relation to these stairs. I had more money and success and "security" than in the days when specters seemed to go up and down them with me.

I turned away and went back outside. The Far Common was still empty, and I walked alone down the wide gravel paths among those most Republican, bankerish of trees, New England elms, toward the far side of the school.

Devon is sometimes considered the most beautiful school in New England, and even on this dismal afternoon its power was asserted. It is the beauty of small areas of order —a large yard, a group of trees, three similar dormitories, a circle of old houses—living together in contentious harmony. You felt that an argument might begin again any time; in fact it had: out of the Dean's Residence, a pure and authentic Colonial house, there now sprouted an ell with a big bare picture window. Some day the Dean would probably live entirely encased in a house of glass and be happy as a sandpiper. Everything at Devon slowly changed and slowly harmonized with what had gone before. So it was logical to hope that since the buildings and the Deans and the curriculum could achieve this, I could achieve, perhaps unknowingly already had achieved, this growth and harmony myself.

I would know more about that when I had seen the second place I had come to see. So I roamed on past the balanced red brick dormitories with webs of leafless ivy clinging to them, through a ramshackle salient of the town which invaded the school for a hundred yards, past the solid gymnasium, full of students at this hour but silent as a monument on the outside, past the Field House, called The Cage—I remembered now what a mystery references to "The Cage" had been during my first weeks at Devon, I had thought it must be a place of severe punishment—and I reached the huge open sweep of ground known as the Playing Fields.

Devon was both scholarly and very athletic, so the playing fields were vast and, except at such a time of year, constantly in use. Now they reached soggily and emptily away from me, forlorn tennis courts on the left, enormous football and soccer and lacrosse fields in the center, woods on the right, and at the far end a small river detectable from this distance by the few bare trees along its banks. It was such a gray and misty day that I could not see the other side of the river, where there was a small stadium.

I started the long trudge across the fields and had gone some distance before I paid any attention to the soft and muddy ground, which was dooming my city shoes. I didn't stop. Near the center of the fields there were thin lakes of muddy water which I had to make my way around, my

A Separate Peace

unrecognizable shoes making obscene noises as I lifted them out of the mire. With nothing to block it the wind flung wet gusts at me; at any other time I would have felt like a fool slogging through mud and rain, only to look at a tree.

A little fog hung over the river so that as I neared it I felt myself becoming isolated from everything except the river and the few trees beside it. The wind was blowing more steadily here, and I was beginning to feel cold. I never wore a hat, and had forgotten gloves. There were several trees bleakly reaching into the fog. Any one of them might have been the one I was looking for. Unbelievable that there were other trees which looked like it here. It had loomed in my memory as a huge lone spike dominating the riverbank, forbidding as an artillery piece, high as the beanstalk. Yet here was a scattered grove of trees, none of them of any particular grandeur.

Moving through the soaked, coarse grass I began to examine each one closely, and finally identified the tree I was looking for by means of certain small scars rising along its trunk, and by a limb extending over the river, and another thinner limb growing near it. This was the tree, and it seemed to me standing there to resemble those men, the giants of your childhood, whom you encounter years later and find that they are not merely smaller in relation to your growth, but that they are absolutely smaller, shrunken by age. In this double demotion the old giants have become pigmies while you were looking the other way.

The tree was not only stripped by the cold season, it seemed weary from age, enfeebled, dry. I was thankful, very thankful that I had seen it. So the more things remain the same, the more they change after all—*plus c'est la même chose, plus ça change.* Nothing endures, not a tree, not love, not even a death by violence.

Changed, I headed back through the mud. I was drenched; anybody could see it was time to come in out of the rain.

The tree was tremendous, an irate, steely black steeple beside the river. I was damned if I'd climb it. The hell with it. No one but Phineas could think up such a crazy idea.

He of course saw nothing the slightest bit intimidating about it. He wouldn't, or wouldn't admit it if he did. Not Phineas.

"What I like best about this tree," he said in that voice of his, the equivalent in sound of a hypnotist's eyes, "what I like is that it's such a cinch!" He opened his green eyes wider and gave us his maniac look, and only the smirk on his wide mouth with its droll, slightly protruding upper lip reassured us that he wasn't completely goofy.

"Is that what you like best?" I said sarcastically. I said a lot of things sarcastically that summer; that was my sarcastic summer, 1942.

"Aey-uh," he said. This weird New England affirmative —maybe it is spelled "aie-huh"—always made me laugh, as Finny knew, so I had to laugh, which made me feel less sarcastic and less scared.

There were three others with us—Phineas in those days almost always moved in groups the size of a hockey team —and they stood with me looking with masked apprehension from him to the tree. Its soaring black trunk was set with rough wooden pegs leading up to a substantial limb which extended farther toward the water. Standing on this limb, you could by a prodigious effort jump far enough out into the river for safety. So we had heard. At least the seventeen-year-old bunch could do it; but they had a crucial year's advantage over us. No Upper Middler, which was the name for our class in the Devon School, had ever tried.

A Separate Peace

Naturally Finny was going to be the first to try, and just as naturally he was going to inveigle others, us, into trying it with him.

We were not even Upper Middler exactly. For this was the Summer Session, just established to keep up with the pace of the war. We were in shaky transit that summer from the groveling status of Lower Middlers to the near-respectability of Upper Middlers. The class above, seniors, draft-bait, practically soldiers, rushed ahead of us toward the war. They were caught up in accelerated courses and first-aid programs and a physical hardening regimen, which included jumping from this tree. We were still calmly, numbly reading Virgil and playing tag in the river farther downstream. Until Finny thought of the tree.

We stood looking up at it, four looks of consternation, one of excitement. "Do you want to go first?" Finny asked us, rhetorically. We just looked quietly back at him, and so he began taking off his clothes, stripping down to his underpants. For such an extraordinary athlete—even as a Lower Middler Phineas had been the best athlete in the school—he was not spectacularly built. He was my height—five feet eight and a half inches (I had been claiming five feet nine inches before he became my roommate, but he had said in public with that simple, shocking self-acceptance of his, "No, you're the same height I am, five-eight and a half. We're on the short side"). He weighed a hundred and fifty pounds, a galling ten pounds more than I did, which flowed from his legs to torso around shoulders to arms and full strong neck in an uninterrupted, unemphatic unity of strength.

He began scrambling up the wooden pegs nailed to the side of the tree, his back muscles working like a panther's. The pegs didn't seem strong enough to hold his weight. At last he stepped onto the branch which reached a little farther toward the water. "Is this the one they jump from?" None of us knew. "If I do it, you're all going to do it, aren't you?" We didn't say anything very clearly. "Well," he cried out, "here's my contribution to the war effort!" and he sprang out, fell through the tips of some lower branches, and smashed into the water.

"Great!" he cried, bobbing instantly to the surface again, his wet hair plastered in droll bangs on his forehead. "That's the most fun I've had this week. Who's next?"

I was. This tree flooded me with a sensation of alarm all the way to my tingling fingers. My head began to feel unnaturally light, and the vague rustling sounds from the nearby woods came to me as though muffled and filtered. I must have been entering a mild state of shock. Insulated by this, I took off my clothes and started to climb the pegs. I don't remember saying anything. The branch he had jumped from was slenderer than it looked from the ground and much higher. It was impossible to walk out on it far enough to be well over the river. I would have to spring far out or risk falling into the shallow water next to the bank. "Come on," drawled Finny from below, "stop standing there showing off." I recognized with automatic tenseness that the view was very impressive from here. "When they torpedo the troop-ship," he shouted, "you can't stand around admiring the view. Jump!"

What was I doing up here anyway? Why did I let Finny talk me into stupid things like this? Was he getting some kind of hold over me?

"Jump!"

With the sensation that I was throwing my life away, I jumped into space. Some tips of branches snapped past me and then I crashed into the water. My legs hit the soft mud of the bottom, and immediately I was on the surface being congratulated. I felt fine.

"I think that was better than Finny's," said Elwin—better known as Leper—Lepellier, who was bidding for an ally in the dispute he foresaw.

"All right, pal," Finny spoke in his cordial, penetrating voice, that reverberant instrument in his chest, "don't start awarding prizes until you've passed the course. The tree is waiting."

Leper closed his mouth as though forever. He didn't argue or refuse. He didn't back away. He became inanimate. But the other two, Chet Douglass and Bobby Zane, were vocal enough, complaining shrilly about school regulations, the danger of stomach cramps, physical disabilities they had never mentioned before.

"It's you, pal," Finny said to me at last, "just you and me." He and I started back across the fields, preceding the others like two seigneurs.

We were the best of friends at that moment.

"You were very good," said Finny good-humoredly, "once I shamed you into it."

"You didn't shame anybody into anything."

"Oh, yes I did. I'm good for you that way. You have a tendency to back away from things otherwise."

"I never backed away from anything in my life!" I cried, my indignation at this charge naturally stronger because it was so true. "You're goofy!"

Phineas just walked serenely on, or rather flowed on, rolling forward in his white sneakers with such unthinking unity of movement that "walk" didn't describe it.

I went along beside him across the enormous playing fields toward the gym. Underfoot the healthy green turf was brushed with dew, and ahead of us we could see a faint green haze hanging above the grass, shot through with the twilight sun. Phineas stopped talking for once, so that now

I could hear cricket noises and bird cries of dusk, a gymnasium truck gunning along an empty athletic road a quarter of a mile away, a burst of faint, isolated laughter carried to us from the back door of the gym, and then over all, cool and matriarchal, the six o'clock bell from the Academy Building cupola, the calmest, most carrying bell toll in the world, civilized, calm, invincible, and final.

The toll sailed over the expansive tops of all the elms, the great slanting roofs and formidable chimneys of the dormitories, the narrow and brittle old housetops, across the open New Hampshire sky to us coming back from the river. "We'd better hurry or we'll be late for dinner," I said breaking into what Finny called my "West Point stride." Phineas didn't really dislike West Point in particular or authority in general, but just considered authority the necessary evil against which happiness was achieved by reaction, the backboard which returned all the insults he threw at it. My "West Point stride" was intolerable; his right foot flashed into the middle of my fast walk and I went pitching forward into the grass. "Get those hundred and fifty pounds off me!" I shouted, because he was sitting on my back. Finny got up, patted my head genially, and moved on across the field, not deigning to glance around for my counterattack, but relying on his extrasensory ears, his ability to feel in the air someone coming on him from behind. As I sprang at him he side-stepped easily, but I just managed to kick him as I shot past. He caught my leg and there was a brief wrestling match on the turf which he won. "Better hurry," he said, "or they'll put you in the guardhouse." We were walking again, faster; Bobby and Leper and Chet were urging us from ahead for God's sake to hurry up, and then Finny trapped me again in his strongest trap, that is, I suddenly became his collaborator. As we walked rapidly along I abruptly resented the bell and my West Point stride and hurrying and conforming. Finny was right. And there was only one way to show him this. I threw my hip against his, catching him by surprise, and he was instantly down, definitely pleased. This was why he liked me so much. When I jumped on top of him, my knees on his chest, he couldn't ask for anything better. We struggled in some equality for a while, and then when we were sure we were too late for dinner, we broke off.

He and I passed the gym and came on toward the first group of dormitories, which were dark and silent. There were only two hundred of us at Devon in the summer, not enough to fill most of the school. We passed the sprawling Headmaster's house—empty, he was doing something for the government in Washington; past the Chapel—empty again, used only for a short time in the mornings; past the First Academy Building, where there were some dim lights shining from a few of its many windows, Masters at work in their classrooms there; down a short slope into the broad and well clipped Common, on which light fell from the big surrounding Georgian buildings. A dozen boys were loafing there on the grass after dinner, and a kitchen rattle from the wing of one of the buildings accompanied their talk. The sky was darkening steadily, which brought up the lights in the dormitories and the old houses; a loud phonograph a long way off played *Don't Sit Under the Apple Tree,* rejected that and played *They're Either Too Young or Too Old,* grew more ambitious with *The Warsaw Concerto,* mellower with *The Nutcracker Suite,* and then stopped.

Finny and I went to our room. Under the yellow study lights we read our Hardy assignments; I was halfway through *Tess of the D'Urbervilles,* he carried on his baffled struggle with *Far from the Madding Crowd,* amused that there should be people named Gabriel Oak and Bathsheba Everdene. Our illegal radio, tuned too low to be intelligible, was broadcasting the news. Outside there was a rustling early summer movement of the wind; the seniors, allowed out later than we were, came fairly quietly back as the bell sounded ten stately times. Boys ambled past our door toward the bathroom, and there was a period of steadily pouring shower water. Then lights began to snap out all over the school. We undressed, and I put on some pajamas, but Phineas, who had heard they were unmilitary, didn't; there was the silence in which it was understood we were saying some prayers, and then that summer school day came to an end.

Symbolism

A well-known author once said, "We live in a world of symbols." To see that he was right, you have only to look at something as common as the dollar. From the front of a dollar, George Washington looks out at you. He is a symbol: the "father" of our country. To the right of Washington is the Treasury seal with its symbols, a scale and a key. On the reverse side is the Great Seal of the United States, an emblem made up of many symbols. The eagle symbolizes power and freedom. The arrows and olive branch it is clutching are symbols of war and peace. The thirteen stars stand for the first thirteen states.

We have symbols for our religions and symbols for our businesses. A group that forms a team always looks for a symbol to represent the team spirit. There are Lions and Bears and Hawks and Trojans and Vikings—all brave and fierce fighters.

People use symbols to express what is difficult to put into words—feelings and ideas. Thus, when you want to express respect for flag and country, you use an action that is a symbol. You place your hand over your heart. A symbol for education is often shown as a lamp that lights the darkness of ignorance.

You have probably noticed by now that symbols can take three forms. There are symbolic objects—flags, animals, a lamp, a tree. There are symbolic characters—Abe Lincoln, for example, is held up as a symbol of honesty. And there are symbolic actions—saluting, clapping, cheering or jeering.

As the Chinese proverb says, "One picture is worth more than ten thousand words." Authors, realizing that this is true, create as many pictures as they can with words to express feelings and ideas in their stories. There may be a forest that stands for fear and darkness. There may be a wizard who symbolizes evil or good. A fearless, persistent old person might symbolize enduring traditions.

You don't have to be aware of the symbolism in a story in order to enjoy the story. But you will find most stories pack more punch for you when you can see and appreciate the symbols an author holds out to you. It's not hard to spot symbolism once you realize it is always there. Simply think of a book as a "world of symbols," just like the world you live in.

In this lesson, we will look at four ways an author can develop symbols:

1 Objects may be used as symbols.

2 Characters may be used as symbols.

3 Actions may be symbolic.

4 Themes may be presented through symbols.

In literature, an author may seize upon almost anything and use it for a symbol. Poets especially like symbolic objects. Robert Frost used a fence that kept falling apart to symbolize a separation between neighbors. William Shakespeare used a bare tree limb

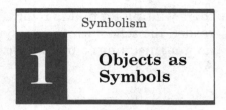

Symbolism

1 **Objects as Symbols**

in winter to symbolize his feelings about old age. This doesn't mean that a fence or a tree limb always has these meanings. You may think of something quite different when you see these objects. But a writer can make ordinary objects like fences and trees have larger symbolic meanings because of the way that he or she describes them.

John Knowles begins *A Separate Peace* using the Devon School as a symbol. Gene Forrester returns to this campus fifteen years after he finished school there. He describes it as he walks through. Notice how the author makes this description tell more than simply what the buildings look like. He makes the school take on symbolic meaning because of the language he describes it in.

> I went back to the Devon School not long ago, and found it looking oddly newer than when I was a student there fifteen years before. It seemed more sedate than I remembered it, more perpendicular and strait-laced, with narrower windows and shinier woodwork, as though a coat of varnish had been put over everything for better preservation. . . .
> I didn't entirely like this glossy new surface, because it made the school look like a museum, and that's exactly what it was to me, and what I did not want it to be.

Clearly this is no simple description of the way the Devon School looks. You couldn't draw a picture of the campus after reading this. Instead, you are given a sense of what the school means in Gene's mind. It is a symbol of everything that is stiff and proper and unchanging. The author creates this symbolic meaning by using words like "strait-laced" and "sedate" and "perpendicular" in his description.

But the school has another symbolic meaning for Gene. When he returns to Devon, he is struck by memories of his youth. He compares the school to a museum. It is as if all his memories are stored and displayed there waiting for him to return. In Gene's mind, and in the mind of the reader, the school becomes a symbol of Gene's past life. And there's yet another meaning connected with this symbol, as you will see in Exercise A.

Exercise A

The passage below is from the selection you have read. Answer the questions about this passage using what you have learned in this part of the lesson. Choose the best answer for each question. Put an *x* in the correct box or fill in the appropriate words.

Now here it was after all, preserved by some considerate hand with varnish and wax. Preserved along with it, like stale air in an unopened room, was the well known fear which had surrounded and filled those days, so much of it that I hadn't even known it was there. Because, unfamiliar with the absence of fear and what that was like, I had not been able to identify its presence.

Looking back now across fifteen years, I could see with great clarity the fear I had lived in, which must mean that in the interval I had succeeded in a very important undertaking: I must have made my escape from it.

1. Gene says that the school was "preserved by some considerate hand with varnish and wax." This is a symbolic way of speaking. Gene means that

  ☐ a. the groundskeeper does a good job.

  ☐ b. the school is much the way he remembers it.

  ☐ c. the students spend a lot of time cleaning.

  ☐ d. the school could use a new coat of paint.

2. What feeling has been "preserved" here along with the school? The word describing it appears three times in the passage. Write the word here.

_____

Now check your answers using the Answer Key on page 439. Correct any wrong answer and review this part of the lesson if you don't understand why your answer was wrong.

2 Characters as Symbols

Symbolic characters are everywhere, not just in books. There are probably people in your own life who have some symbolic meaning. For example, think of someone you admire. Doesn't that person symbolize success of some sort to you? When you think of ideas like courage or cowardice, don't people you know come to mind? To put it another way, you probably associate some of the people you know with larger ideas. As a result, they have a symbolic meaning for you.

A character in a book becomes symbolic in much the same way. An author will associate certain qualities with a character. Then that character comes to have a symbolic meaning in the story. Finny becomes a symbolic character in *A Separate Peace*. Notice how the qualities associated with Finny give him symbolic meaning to Gene and to the reader.

> The tree was tremendous, an irate, steely black steeple beside the river. I was damned if I'd climb it. The hell with it. No one but Phineas could think up such a crazy idea.
>
> He of course saw nothing the slightest bit intimidating about it. He wouldn't, or wouldn't admit it if he did. Not Phineas.
>
> "What I like best about this tree," he said in that voice of his, the equivalent in sound of a hypnotist's eyes, "what I like is that it's such a cinch!"
>
> . . . .
>
> . . . even as a Lower Middler Phineas had been the best athlete in the school. . . . He weighed a hundred and fifty pounds . . . which flowed from his legs to torso around shoulders to arms and full strong neck in an uninterrupted, unemphatic unity of strength.
>
> He began scrambling up the wooden pegs nailed to the side of the tree, his back muscles working like a panther's.

To Gene and to us, Finny is clearly a symbol of confidence, strength and courage. He dares to do anything, and he is good at everything he tries. He is well-liked and admired. He is, in short, everything Gene would like to be, but isn't.

Gene becomes symbolic as a contrast to Finny. Gene is associated with fear and with an effort to overcome fear. The author reminds us of these qualities in Gene as often as he reminds us of the opposite qualities in Finny. Notice the way Gene is presented in the passage below.

> This tree flooded me with a sensation of alarm all the way to my tingling fingers. My head began to feel unnaturally light, and the vague rustling sounds from the nearby woods came to me as though muffled and filtered. I must have been entering a mild state of shock. . . .
>
> What was I doing up here anyway? Why did I let Finny talk me into stupid things like this? Was he getting some kind of hold over me? . . .
>
> With the sensation that I was throwing my life away, I jumped into space. . . . My legs hit the soft mud of the bottom, and immediately I was on the surface being congratulated. I felt fine.

Gene is frightened at the thought of following Finny's jump from the tree. He thinks he entered "a mild state of shock." And yet, in this scene and others, Gene manages to overcome his fear and follow Finny's lead. Through the use of these repeated associations with larger ideas like fear and courage, the author makes characters symbolic.

Exercise B

The passage below is from the selection you have read. Answer the questions about this passage using what you have learned in this part of the lesson. Choose the best answer for each question. Put an *x* in the correct box or fill in the appropriate words.

> "I think that [Gene's jump] was better than Finny's," said Elwin —better known as Leper—Lepellier, who was bidding for an ally in the dispute he foresaw.

"All right, pal," Finny spoke in his cordial, penetrating voice . . . "don't start awarding prizes until you've passed the course. The tree is waiting."

Leper closed his mouth as though forever. He didn't argue or refuse. He didn't back away. He became inanimate. But the other two, Chet Douglas and Bobby Zane, were vocal enough, complaining shrilly about school regulations, the danger of stomach cramps, physical disabilities they had never mentioned before.

"It's you, pal," Finny said to me at last, "just you and me." He and I started back across the fields, preceding the others like two seigneurs.

1. Leper, Chet and Bobby represent two common ways that people react to fear. Which of the following are they?

   ☐ a. Good sense and patience

   ☐ b. Bravery and determination

   ☐ c. Panic and flight

   ☐ d. Excuses and paralysis

2. Find a sentence which suggests the two symbolic characters, Finny and Gene, are closely linked. Write the sentence here.

   _____

   _____

   _____

Now check your answers using the Answer Key on page 439. Correct any wrong answer and review this part of the lesson if you don't understand why your answer was wrong.

A Separate Peace

The only way you can know what people are like is by looking at the way they act. In the same way, you can only know what characters in a novel are like by looking at what they do and say. Authors choose the actions they include in a story very carefully.

The meaning an action has is one of the reasons for including it. In other words, an action can represent an idea. When it does, it is called a symbolic action.

Not all actions in a story are symbolic. An author may include an action just to move the story along or to provide a bit of humor. Actions become symbolic only when they are associated with some larger meaning or idea in the story. For example, the actions at the tree reveal something about courage, fear, and the effort to overcome fear. For this reason, these actions are symbolic ones. It is when actions are used to deal with ideas that they become symbols. Finny is fearless and jumps quickly and easily. Gene is fearful, but controls his fear and finally dares to jump. The other boys remain on the ground. Each way of acting symbolizes a way of looking at life.

The next passages are about actions that are also symbolic. This time, however, the larger idea the author is writing about is authority.

> "We'd better hurry or we'll be late for dinner," I said, breaking into what Finny called my "West Point stride." Phineas didn't really dislike West Point in particular or authority in general, but just considered authority the necessary evil against which happiness was achieved by reaction, the backboard which returned all the insults he threw at it. My "West Point stride" was intolerable; his right foot flashed into the middle of my fast walk and I went pitching forward into the grass.

Finny doesn't trip Gene because he wants to hurt him. He trips Gene because he wants to make a point. Finny's action has a symbolic meaning. But how do we know this? And how do we know exactly what the action symbolizes? We have to look closely at the way the author describes what happens.

A school rule says that the boys must go to dinner at a certain time. The dinner bell has rung and Gene starts to hurry. Gene is clearly worried about breaking the rule. The author emphasizes the way Gene is conforming to the rules by mentioning his "West Point stride." He is suggesting that Gene is following rules as if he were in the army.

Finny, by contrast, sees rules and authority as a "necessary evil." He feels he must rebel against them. When Finny trips Gene, his action becomes a symbol of that rebellion against authority. Finny will not hurry to be on time for dinner. Gene gets caught up in this mood, and his actions take on a different symbolic meaning in Exercise C.

Exercise C

The passage below is from the selection you have read. Answer the questions about this passage using what you have learned in this part of the lesson. Choose the best answer for each question. Put an *x* in the correct box or fill in the appropriate words.

"Better hurry," he [Finny] said, "or they'll put you in the guardhouse." We were walking again, faster; Bobby and Leper and Chet were urging us from ahead for God's sake to hurry up, and then Finny trapped me again in his strongest trap, that is, I suddenly became his collaborator. As we walked rapidly along I abruptly resented the bell and my West Point stride and hurrying and conforming. Finny was right. And there was only one way to show him this. I threw my hip against his, catching him by surprise, and he was instantly down, difinitely pleased. This was why he liked me so much. When I jumped on top of him, my knees on his chest, he couldn't ask for anything better. We struggled in some equality for a while, and then when we were sure we were too late for dinner, we broke off.

1. Which of the following phrases from the passage shows Gene acting the same way as he did in the tree episode—following Finny's lead?

   ☐ a. "I threw my hip against his. . . ."

   ☐ b. "We struggled in some equality. . . ."

   ☐ c. "I suddenly became his collaborator. . . ."

   ☐ d. "We were walking again, faster. . . ."

2. What pharse tells you that by taking this action and wrestling Finny to the ground, Gene momentarily becomes Finny's equal? Write it here.

   _____

   _____

   _____

Now check your answers using the Answer Key on page 439. Correct any wrong answer and review this part of the lesson if you don't understand why your answer was wrong.

4 Symbols and Themes

A theme is a larger idea that an author wants to explore or express in a book. On one level, *A Separate Peace* is a story about two boys at school. On a thematic level, it is about fear, and about how people handle that troubling emotion.

You've seen that symbols are connected with larger ideas, too. For example, you've seen how a character, Finny, can become a symbol of courage and confidence. It's not surprising, then, that authors often use symbols to help them develop their themes. Both symbols and themes are connected with the ideas that a book is expressing.

John Knowles introduces the theme of fear in *A Separate Peace* through the use of a symbolic object. The tree that Finny and Gene jump from as boys plays a major role in Chapter 1, which you have just read. The tree is a symbol of the fear that Gene experienced as a youth. In creating this symbol, John Knowles is announcing to us what his theme is.

> There were several trees bleakly reaching into the fog. Any one of them might have been the one I was looking for. Unbelievable that there were other trees which looked like it here. It had loomed in my memory as a huge lone spike dominating the riverbank, forbidding as an artillery piece, high as a beanstalk.

Once we see what this tree means, we understand more clearly what other scenes mean. By showing us how people respond to this symbolic tree, John Knowles is developing his theme about fear. Some people, like Finny, seem to welcome the challenge of it. Others, like Leper, Chet and Bobby, back away and make excuses. And people like Gene are almost overwhelmed by it, but learn to overcome their fear.

By showing how Gene's attitude towards this tree changes, John Knowles can tell us more of his idea about fear. When Gene returns to Devon as an adult, the tree seems different to him: "Yet here was a scattered grove of trees, none of them of any particular grandeur." The tree doesn't seem frightening to Gene any more. Knowles is developing his theme through this change in the symbolic object. Fear can be paralyzing, but it can also be overcome. We can grow out of it, as Gene has done. Notice how Gene responds to the tree in the passage in Exercise D. What is John Knowles telling us about his theme of fear?

Exercise D

The passage below is from the selection you have read. Answer the questions about this passage using what you have learned in this part of the lesson. Choose the best answer for each question. Put an *x* in the correct box or fill in the appropriate words.

This was the tree, and it seemed to me standing there to resemble those men, the giants of your childhood, whom you encounter years later and find that they are not merely smaller in relation to your growth, but that they are absolutely smaller, shrunken by age. . . .

The tree was not only stripped by the cold season, it seemed weary from age, enfeebled, dry. I was thankful, very thankful that I had seen it. . . . Nothing endures, not a tree, not love, not even a death by violence.

1. For Gene, the tree symbolizes the "giants of . . . childhood" who grow smaller as time passes. What giants does he mean?

  ☐ a. Authority figures—such as parents, teachers and other adults

  ☐ b. Storybook giants from fairy tales

  ☐ c. Giants that many children see in their dreams

  ☐ d. Trees that die or lose their leaves in winter

2. How does Gene feel when he finds that the tree no longer seems frightening to him? In the passage, one word that is repeated twice sums up Gene's feeling. Write it on the line provided.

_____

Use the Answer Key on page 439 to check your answers. Correct any wrong answer and review this part of the lesson if you don't understand why your answer was wrong. Now go on to do the Comprehension Questions.

A Separate Peace

Comprehension Questions

Answer these questions without looking back at the selection. Choose the best answer to each question and put an *x* in the box beside it.

Making
Inferences

1. When Gene Forrester came back to school, he wanted to see two "fearful" sites: a tree and a marble staircase. Why?

   ☐ a. They provided unforgettable thrills.

   ☐ b. He wondered if they would still seem fearful.

   ☐ c. He had a little extra time to kill.

   ☐ d. It was a school tradition.

Recalling
Facts

2. Where was the Devon School?

   ☐ a. South Carolina

   ☐ b. Maryland

   ☐ c. New Hampshire

   ☐ d. New York

Recognizing
Words in
Context

3. "In through swinging doors I reached a marble *foyer* . . ." A *foyer* is a(n)

   ☐ a. statue.

   ☐ b. fountain and pool.

   ☐ c. entrance hall.

   ☐ d. closet.

4. Two things were emphasized at Devon School. What were they?

☐ a. Military training and discipline

☐ b. Studies and athletics

☐ c. Architecture and history

☐ d. The buddy system and war games

5. One of the following expressions sums up an important idea mentioned several times in the chapter. Which one of the following is it?

☐ a. Things change.

☐ b. Once afraid always afraid.

☐ c. Now is the hour.

☐ d. Time is forever.

6. The tree *loomed* in Gene's memory "as a huge lone spike." When the tree *loomed,* it

☐ a. grew very large.

☐ b. faded away.

☐ c. shrank in size.

☐ d. vanished.

7. When did Gene return to look at the tree?

☐ a. Right after wrestling with Finny

☐ b. During World War II

☐ c. The day before he missed dinner

☐ d. Right after he came back to visit Devon

8. Finny said, "What I like best about this tree . . . is that it's such a cinch!" What did he really like about this tree?

☐ a. The view it permitted

☐ b. The memory it suggested

☐ c. The challenge it presented

☐ d. The privacy it gave

9. Why was it dangerous to jump out of the tree?

☐ a. The water was too deep.

☐ b. It was difficult to reach deep water.

☐ c. It was an extremely large tree.

☐ d. The wind was too strong.

10. Why were seniors at Devon School taking special courses?

☐ a. They were making up for failures.

☐ b. They were afraid not to try harder.

☐ c. Senior year is always a difficult one.

☐ d. They would soon be in military service.

11. When did Gene jump from the tree?

☐ a. Before Finny jumped

☐ b. Before summer session began

☐ c. After Leper jumped

☐ d. After Finny urged him to jump

12. Finny had a *"cordial, penetrating* voice." This means it was

☐ a. friendly and impressive.

☐ b. knotty and oily.

☐ c. rasping and harsh.

☐ d. fierce and commanding.

13. Gene had a fast way of walking. What did Finny call it?

☐ a. A jogging pace

☐ b. A West Point stride

☐ c. An army gallop

☐ d. A navy roll

14. Why did Gene tend to follow Finny's lead?

☐ a. He had no mind of his own.

☐ b. It was a fashionable thing to do.

☐ c. Finny had the best judgment of all the boys.

☐ d. Gene probably wanted to be more like Finny.

15. When did Gene and Finny miss dinner?

☐ a. After their wrestling and fooling around

☐ b. Before jumping from the tree

☐ c. After they rushed home to study

☐ d. While the other boys were delaying

Now check your answers using the Answer Key on page 439. Correct any wrong answers you have by putting a check (√) in the box next to the right answer. Count the number of questions you answered correctly and plot the total on the Comprehension Scores graph on page 444.

Next, look at the questions you answered incorrectly. What types of questions were they? Count the number of each type and enter the numbers in the spaces below:

Recognizing Words in Context   _____

Recalling Facts   _____

Keeping Events in Order   _____

Making Inferences   _____

Understanding Main Ideas   _____

Now use these numbers to fill in the Comprehension Skills Profile on page 445.

Discussion Guides

The questions below will help you to think about the selection and the lesson you have just read. If you don't discuss these questions in class, try to think about them or discuss them with your classmates.

Discussing Symbolism

1. At the end of the novel Gene says about World War II: "My war ended before I ever put on a uniform; I was on active duty all my time at school; I killed my enemy there." What do you suppose was Gene's "war" at school?

2. The Devon School represents everything in society that is prim, proper, well-organized and civilized. How does the author make this point?

3. World War II becomes an important symbol as the story goes along. How does it seem important in this chapter?

Discussing the Story

4. What is your opinion of Finny? And Gene?

5. When afraid, some people run away. Others fight or strike out at what they are afraid of. Leper did nothing. Why can this be the worst way to face fear?

6. What were you afraid of ten years ago that you are not afraid of now? Why did you change? Why did Gene change?

Discussing the Author's Work

7. The chapter starts with five pages of description, no conversation and very little action. Still, the author manages to hold your attention. How?

8. The tone and mood of the story change when the story changes from 1958 to 1942. How do they change and *why* do they change?

9. *A Separate Peace* has been called "a piercingly accurate recollection of life in a boy's preparatory school." In what ways do you find it "piercingly accurate"?

Writing Exercise

Write a short essay of about 100 words that describes a feeling you have had or an idea you feel strongly about. Use a symbol in the essay to represent your feeling or idea.

Begin by describing the symbol. Later in your essay, show how the symbol matches your idea or feeling.

You may choose one of the suggestions from the following list if you prefer.

Idea or Feeling	Symbol
Freedom	A hawk
Fear	A swamp
Something lasting	A mountain
Love	A rose
Welcome	The Statue of Liberty
A personal problem	A forest
Life	A road
Excitement	A powerful motor
Peace	A calm lake
War	A fire-breathing dragon

Unit 8 Autobiography and Biography

Anne Frank: The Diary of
a Young Girl BY ANNE FRANK

About the Illustration

How do you know that something frightening and sad is happening to these three people? Point out some details in the drawing to support your response.

Here are some questions to help you think:

☐ How would you describe the expressions on their faces?

☐ What is unusual about the way they look?

☐ How do they look different from the other two men in the drawing?

Unit 8

Introduction	What the Diary Is About/What the Lesson Is About
Selection	**Anne Frank: The Diary of a Young Girl**
Lesson	**Autobiography and Biography**
Activities	Comprehension Questions/Discussion Guides/Writing Exercise

Introduction

What the Diary Is About

During World War II, Nazi soldiers broke into an apartment in Amsterdam where two Jewish families were hiding. Their job was to remove all Jews from Holland. The Jews were to be sent to forced labor camps and gas chambers in Germany and Eastern Europe.

Part of the soldiers' job was to loot or destroy anything they found. They were to leave behind no record of their evil work for the rest of the world to see. During a search, one sergeant in charge found a briefcase. "Are there any jewels?" he asked. "No," said Otto Frank, now under arrest with his family and friends, "there are only papers."

The sergeant dumped the papers on the floor in disgust. He put some silverware and a candlestick in the briefcase and left with the prisoners.

With this act the sergeant had botched his job. Among the papers he had dumped on the floor was a document that would one day shout to the world about the Nazi horror. It was a diary written by a young Jewish girl, Anne Frank, during two years in hiding.

Anne Frank received her diary as a gift for her thirteenth birthday. A month later, she, her father, mother and older sister, Margot, were forced to go into hiding to avoid arrest by the Nazis. Another family, the Van Daans, went with them. This second family consisted of Mr. and Mrs. Van Daan and their son, Peter, two years older than Anne. A dentist, Mr. Dussel, joined them later.

So they were eight in all. Their hiding place was a large apartment behind the office building where Otto Frank had worked as a manager. Business friends who still worked there kept the secret. They also kept the fugitives supplied with food and other necessities.

The diary is not a record of horrors endured. It is a simple record of life lived in hiding. Anne tells of ordinary daily events and of news on the radio. She records her thoughts and feelings. It is this that makes her diary an autobiography, as you will see.

Anne's writing showed great promise. Had she lived, there is little doubt that she would have become a great writer. Instead, not yet sixteen, she died in the Belsen concentration camp in Germany, barely two months before the end of the war in Europe.

Of the eight who went into hiding, only Otto Frank survived. Mrs. Frank, Anne's mother, died mentally deranged from her experience at the Auschwitz camp. Mr. Frank watched Mr. Van Daan taken off to be gassed. Mr. Dussel died in another camp and Peter Van Daan was taken away, never to be heard from again. Mrs. Van Daan and Margot died at Belsen shortly before Anne.

When Otto Frank returned to Amsterdam after the War, the friends who had helped him in hiding gave him the papers they had found dumped on the floor. Among them was Anne's diary.

After some years the diary was published and Anne belonged to the world. Her diary has become one of the most widely read autobiographies of our time. It was made into a prize-winning play in 1956 and a movie in 1959. It was adapted for television in 1967 and is seen over and over again.

The house where Anne lived in hiding for two years is now kept as a memorial to her. There are other memorials to her in Germany, Israel, the United States and other countries around the world. But her diary is her greatest living memorial.

It is probably worthwhile to note that there are no memorials to Adolf Hitler, her great tormentor. While *Anne Frank: The Diary of a Young Girl* is very much alive, Hitler's autobiography, *Mein Kampf,* is a dusty curiosity of hate on library shelves.

What the Lesson Is About

The lesson that follows the reading selection is about biography and autobiography.

Biography is the story of a person's life. *Autobiography* is also such a story, but it's written by the person whose life is described.

Biography looks at a person against the background of his or her environment. It tries to give a feeling for the time and place the subject lives in. Biography also looks at the whole person. It is not the job of biography to praise or make a hero out of the subject. Good biography tells the bad with the good, the failures with the successes, the good judgments and the bad ones. And, above all, it tries to describe the innermost feelings of the subject.

A diary is not strictly an autobiography. Diaries are usually written as a day-to-day record of events and thoughts. They do not do the job of examining a person's entire life and times the way biography and autobiography do. They are generally written for the benefit of the diarist and no one else.

Anne Frank used a technique, however, that turned her diary into true autobiography. She addressed her writing to "Kitty," an imaginary friend, and thus gave herself an audience of one. As a result, she was not writing just for herself. For Kitty, she examined her own character and described those around her. She discussed the times and looked at her life in relation to those times. You will soon see that what she wrote is considerably more than a record of events.

The questions below will help you to focus on some characteristics of autobiography in *Anne Frank: The Diary of a Young Girl*. Read the selections carefully and try to answer these questions as you go along:

1 What effect do time and place have on Anne's life? What was it like to be Jewish in Holland in 1942?

2 We see Anne's character as she speaks of what she needs, wants, or longs for in life. What are some of her desires, and what do they show about her?

3 What do you learn about Anne and Peter from stories of their friendship?

4 What facts of history do you learn from your reading? How do historical events affect Anne?

Anne Frank: The Diary of a Young Girl

Anne Frank

Saturday, 20 June, 1942

I haven't written for a few days, because I wanted first of all to think about my diary. It's an odd idea for someone like me to keep a diary; not only because I have never done so before, but because it seems to me that neither I—nor for that matter anyone else—will be interested in the unbosomings of a thirteen-year-old schoolgirl. Still, what does that matter? I want to write, but more than that, I want to bring out all kinds of things that lie buried deep in my heart.

There is a saying that "paper is more patient than man"; it came back to me on one of my slightly melancholy days, while I sat chin in hand, feeling too bored and limp even to make up my mind whether to go out or stay at home. Yes, there is no doubt that paper is patient and as I don't intend to show this cardboard-covered notebook, bearing the proud name of "diary," to anyone, unless I find a real friend, boy or girl, probably nobody cares. And now I come to the root of the matter, the reason for my starting a diary: it is that I have no such real friend.

Let me put it more clearly, since no one will believe that a girl of thirteen feels herself quite alone in the world, nor is it so. I have darling parents and a sister of sixteen. I know about thirty people whom one might call friends—I have strings of boy friends, anxious to catch a glimpse of me and who, failing that, peep at me through mirrors in class. I have relations, aunts and uncles, who are darlings too, a good home, no—I don't seem to lack anything. But it's the same with all my friends, just fun and joking, nothing more. I can never bring myself to talk of anything outside the common round. We don't seem to be able to get any closer, that is the root of the trouble. Perhaps I lack confidence, but anyway, there it is, a stubborn fact and I don't seem to be able to do anything about it.

Hence, this diary. In order to enhance in my mind's eye the picture of the friend for whom I have waited so long, I don't want to set down a series of bald facts in a diary like most people do, but I want this diary itself to be my friend, and I shall call my friend Kitty. No one will grasp what I'm talking about if I begin my letters to Kitty just out of the blue, so albeit unwillingly, I will start by sketching in brief the story of my life.

My father was thirty-six when he married my mother, who was then twenty-five. My sister Margot was born in 1926 in Frankfort-on-Main, I followed on June 12, 1929, and, as we are Jewish, we emigrated to Holland in 1933, where my father was appointed Managing Director of Travies N.V. This firm is in close relationship with the firm of Kolen & Co. in the same building, of which my father is a partner.

The rest of our family, however, felt the full impact of Hitler's anti-Jewish laws, so life was filled with anxiety. In 1938 after the pogroms, my two uncles (my mother's brothers) escaped to the U.S.A. My old grandmother came to us, she was then seventy-three. After May 1940 good times rapidly fled: first the war, then the capitulation, followed by the arrival of the Germans, which is when the sufferings of us Jews really began. Anti-Jewish decrees followed each other in quick succession. Jews must wear a yellow star,[1] Jews must hand in their bicycles, Jews are banned from trains and are forbidden to drive. Jews are only allowed to do their shopping between three and five o'clock and then only in shops which bear the placard "Jewish shop." Jews

[1]To distinguish them from others, all Jews were forced by the Germans to wear, prominently displayed, a yellow six-pointed star.

must be indoors by eight o'clock and cannot even sit in their own gardens after that hour. Jews are forbidden to visit theaters, cinemas, and other places of entertainment. Jews may not take part in public sports. Swimming baths, tennis courts, hockey fields, and other sports grounds are all prohibited to them. Jews may not visit Christians. Jews must go to Jewish schools, and many more restrictions of a similar kind.

So we could not do this and were forbidden to do that. But life went on in spite of it all. Jopie used to say to me, "You're scared to do anything, because it may be forbidden." Our freedom was strictly limited. Yet things were still bearable.

Granny died in Jauary 1942; no one will ever know how much she is present in my thoughts and how much I love her still.

In 1934 I went to school at the Montessori Kindergarten and continued there. It was at the end of the school year, I was in form 6B, when I had to say good-by to Mrs. K. We both wept, it was very sad. In 1941 I went, with my sister Margot, to the Jewish Secondary School, she into the fourth form and I into the first.

So far everything is all right with the four of us and here I come to the present day.

. . . .

Wednesday, 8 July, 1942

Dear Kitty,

Years seem to have passed between Sunday and now. So much has happened, it is just as if the whole world had turned upside down. But I am still alive, Kitty, and that is the main thing, Daddy says.

Yes, I'm still alive, indeed, but don't ask where or how. You wouldn't understand a word, so I will begin by telling you what happened on Sunday afternoon.

At three o'clock (Harry had just gone, but was coming back later) someone rang the front doorbell. I was lying lazily reading a book on the veranda in the sunshine, so I didn't hear it. A bit later, Margot appeared at the kitchen door looking very excited. "The S.S. have sent a call-up notice for Daddy," she whispered. "Mummy has gone to see Mr. Van Daan already." (Van Daan is a friend who works with Daddy in the business.) It was a great shock to me, a call-up; everyone knows what that means. I picture concentration camps and lonely cells—should we allow him to be doomed to this? "Of course he won't go," declared Margot, while we waited together. "Mummy has gone to the Van Daans to discuss whether we should move into our hiding place tomorrow. The Van Daans are going with us, so we shall be seven in all." Silence. We couldn't talk any more, thinking about Daddy, who, little knowing what was going on, was visiting some old people in the Joodse Invalide; waiting for Mummy, the heat and suspense, all made us very overawed and silent.

Suddenly the bell rang again. "That is Harry," I said. "Don't open the door." Margot held me back, but it was not necessary as we heard Mummy and Mr. Van Daan downstairs, talking to Harry, then they came in and closed the door behind them. Each time the bell went, Margot or I had to creep softly down to see if it was Daddy, not opening the door to anyone else.

Margot and I were sent out of the room. Van Daan wanted to talk to Mummy alone. When we were alone together in our bedroom, Margot told me that the call-up was not for Daddy, but for her. I was more frightened than ever and began to cry. Margot is sixteen; would they really take girls of that age away alone? But thank goodness she won't go, Mummy said so herself; that must be what Daddy meant when he talked about us going into hiding.

Into hiding—where would we go, in a town or the country, in a house or a cottage, when, how, where . . . ?

These were questions I was not allowed to ask, but I couldn't get them out of my mind. Margot and I began to pack some of our most vital belongings into a school satchel. The first thing I put in was this diary, then hair curlers, handkerchiefs, schoolbooks, a comb, old letters; I put in the craziest things with the idea that we were going into hiding. But I'm not sorry, memories mean more to me than dresses.

At five o'clock Daddy finally arrived, and we phoned Mr. Koophuis to ask if he could come around in the evening. Van Daan went and fetched Miep. Miep has been in the business with Daddy since 1933 and has become a close friend, likewise her brand-new husband, Henk. Miep came and took some shoes, dresses, coats, underwear, and stockings away in her bag, promising to return in the evening. Then silence fell on the house; not one of us felt like eating anything, it was still hot and everything was very strange. We let our large upstairs room to a certain Mr. Goudsmit, a divorced man in his thirties, who appeared to have nothing to do on this particular evening; we simply could not get rid of him without being rude; he hung about until ten o'clock. At eleven o'clock Miep and Henk Van Santen arrived. Once again, shoes, stockings, books, and underclothes disappeared into Miep's bag and Henk's deep pockets, and at eleven-thirty they too disappeared. I was dog-tired and although I knew that it would be my last night in my own bed, I fell asleep immediately and didn't wake up until Mummy called me at five-thirty the next morning. Luckily it was not so hot as Sunday; warm rain fell steadily all day. We put on heaps of clothes as if we were going to the North Pole, the sole reason being to take clothes with us. No Jew in our situation would have dreamed of going out with a suitcase full of clothing. I had on two vests, three pairs of pants, a dress, on top of that a skirt, jacket, summer coat, two pairs of stockings, lace-up shoes, woolly cap, scarf, and still more; I was nearly stifled before we started, but no one inquired about that.

Margot filled her satchel with schoolbooks, fetched her bicycle, and rode off behind Miep into the unknown, as far as I was concerned. You see I still didn't know where our secret hiding place was to be. At seven-thirty the door closed behind us. Moortje, my little cat, was the only creature to whom I said farewell. She would have a good home with the neighbors. This was all written in a letter addressed to Mr. Goudsmit.

There was one pound of meat in the kitchen for the cat, breakfast things lying on the table, stripped beds, all giving the impression that we had left helter-skelter. But we didn't care about impressions, we only wanted to get away, only escape and arrive safely, nothing else. Continued tomorrow.

Yours, Anne

Thursday, 9 July, 1942

Dear Kitty,

So we walked in the pouring rain, Daddy, Mummy, and I, each with a school satchel and shopping bag filled to the brim with all kinds of things thrown together anyhow.

We got sympathetic looks from people on their way to work. You could see by their faces how sorry they were they couldn't offer us a lift; the gaudy yellow star spoke for itself.

Only when we were on the road did Mummy and Daddy begin to tell me bits and pieces about the plan. For months as many of our goods and chattels and necessities of life as possible had been sent away and they were sufficiently ready for us to have gone into hiding of our own accord on July 16. The plan had had to be speeded up ten days because of the call-up, so our quarters would not be so well organized, but we had to make the best of it. The hiding place itself would be in the building where Daddy has his office. It will be hard for outsiders to understand, but I shall explain that later on. Daddy didn't have many people working for him: Mr. Kraler, Koophuis, Miep, and Elli Vossen, a twenty-three-year-old typist who all knew of our arrival. Mr. Vossen, Elli's father, and two boys worked in the warehouse; they had not been told.

I will describe the building: there is a large warehouse on the ground floor which is used as a store. The front door to the house is next to the warehouse door, and inside the front door is a second doorway which leads to a staircase . . . .

The right-hand door leads to our "Secret Annexe." No one would ever guess that there would be so many rooms hidden behind that plain gray door. There's a little step in front of the door and then you are inside. . . .

If you go up the next flight of stairs and open the door, you are simply amazed that there could be such a big light room in such an old house by the canal. There is a gas stove in this room (thanks to the fact that it was used as a laboratory) and a sink. This is now the kitchen for the Van Daan couple, besides being general living room, dining room, and scullery.

A tiny little corridor room will become Peter Van Daan's apartment. Then, just as on the lower landing, there is a large attic. So there you are, I've introduced you to the whole of our beautiful "Secret Annexe."

Yours, Anne

. . . .

Friday, 21 August, 1942

Dear Kitty,

The entrance to our hiding place has now been properly concealed. Mr. Kraler thought it would be better to put a cupboard in front of our door (because a lot of houses are being searched for hidden bicycles), but of course it had to be a movable cupboard that can open like a door.

Mr. Vossen made the whole thing. We had already let him into the secret and he can't do enough to help. If we want to go downstairs, we have to first bend down and then jump, because the step has gone. The first three days we were all going about with masses of lumps on our foreheads, because we all knocked ourselves against the low doorway. Now we have nailed a cloth filled with wood wool against the top of the door. Let's see if that helps!

I'm not working much at present; I'm giving myself holidays until September. Then Daddy is going to give me lessons; it's shocking how much I've forgotten already. There is little change in our life here. Mr. Van Daan and I usually manage to upset each other, it's just the opposite with Margot whom he likes very much. Mummy sometimes treats me just like a baby, which I can't bear. Otherwise things are going better. I still don't like Peter any more, he is so boring; he flops lazily on his bed half the time, does a bit of carpentry, and then goes back for another snooze. What a fool!

It is lovely weather and in spite of everything we make the most we can of it by lying on a camp bed in the attic, where the sun shines through an open window.

Yours, Anne

. . . .

Friday, 24 December, 1943

Dear Kitty,

I have previously written about how much we are affected by atmospheres here, and I think that in my own case this trouble is getting much worse lately.

"Himmelhoch jauchzend und zum Tode betrübt"[1] certainly fits here. I am *"Himmelhoch jauchzend"* if I only think how lucky we are here compared with other Jewish children, and *"zum Tode betrübt"* comes over me when, as happened today, for example, Mrs. Koophuis comes and tells us about her daughter Corry's hockey club, canoe trips, theatrical performances, and friends. I don't think I'm jealous of Corry, but I couldn't help feeling a great longing to have lots of fun myself for once, and to laugh until my tummy ached. Especially at this time of the year with all the holidays for Christmas and the New Year, and we are stuck here like outcasts. Still, I really ought not to write this, because it seems ungrateful and I've certainly been exaggerating. But still, whatever you think of me, I can't keep everything to myself, so I'll remind you of my opening words—"Paper is patient."

When someone comes in from outside, with the wind in their clothes and the cold on their faces, then I could bury my head in the blankets to stop myself thinking: "When will we be granted the privilege of smelling fresh air?" And because I must not bury my head in the blankets, but the reverse—I must keep my head high and be brave, the thoughts will come, not once, but oh, countless times. Believe me, if you have been shut up for a year and a half, it can get too much for you some days. In spite of all justice and thankfulness, you can't crush your feelings. Cycling, dancing, whistling, looking out into the world, feeling

[1]A famous line from Goëthe: "On top of the world, or in the depths of despair."

young, to know that I'm free—that's what I long for; still, I musn't show it, because I sometimes think if all eight of us began to pity ourselves, or went about with discontented faces, where would it lead us? I sometimes ask myself, "Would anyone, either Jew or non-Jew, understand this about me, that I am simply a young girl badly in need of some rollicking fun? I don't know, and I couldn't talk about it to anyone, because then I know I should cry. Crying can bring such relief. . . .

Yours, Anne

. . . .

Sunday, 13 February, 1944

Dear Kitty,

Since Saturday a lot has changed for me. It came about like this. I longed—and am still longing—but . . . now something has happened, which has made it a little, just a little, less.

To my great joy—I will be quite honest about it—already this morning I noticed that Peter kept looking at me all the time. Not in the ordinary way, I don't know how, I just can't explain.

I used to think that Peter was in love with Margot, but yesterday I suddenly had the feeling that it is not so. I made a special effort not to look at him too much, because whenever I did, he kept on looking too and then—yes, then—it gave me a lovely feeling inside, but which I mustn't feel too often.

I desperately want to be alone. Daddy has noticed that I'm not quite my usual self, but I really can't tell him everything. "Leave me in peace, leave me alone," that's what I'd like to keep crying out all the time. Who knows, the day may come when I'm left alone more than I would wish!

Yours, Anne

Monday, 14 February, 1944

Dear Kitty,

On Sunday evening everyone except Pim and me was sitting beside the wireless in order to listen to the "Immortal Music of the German Masters." Dussel fiddled with the knobs continually. This annoyed Peter, and the others too. After restraining himself for half an hour, Peter asked somewhat irritably if the twisting and turning might stop. Dussel answered in his most hoity-toity manner, "I'm getting it all right." Peter became angry, was rude, Mr. Van Daan took his side, and Dussel had to give in. That was all.

The reason in itself was very unimportant, but Peter seems to have taken it very much to heart. In any case, when I was rummaging about in the bookcase in the attic, he came up to me and began telling me the whole story. I didn't know anything about it, but Peter soon saw that he had found an attentive ear and got fairly into his stride.

"Yes, and you see," he said. "I don't easily say anything, because I know beforehand that I'll only become tongue-tied. I begin to stutter, blush, and twist around what I want to say, until I have to break off because I simply can't find the words. That's what happened yesterday, I wanted to say something quite different, but once I had started, I got in a hopeless muddle and that's frightful. I used to have a bad habit; I wish I still had it now. If I was angry with anyone, rather than argue it out I would get to work on him with my fists. I quite realize that this method doesn't get me anywhere; and that is why I admire you. You are never at a loss for a word, you say exactly what you want to say to people and are never the least bit shy."

"I can tell you, you're making a big mistake," I answered. "I usually say things quite differently from the way I meant to say them, and then I talk too much and far too long, and that's just as bad."

I couldn't help laughing to myself over this last sentence. However, I wanted to let him go on talking about himself, so I kept my amusement to myself, went and sat on a cushion on the floor, put my arms around my bent knees, and looked at him attentively.

I am very glad that there is someone else in the house who can get into the same fits of rage as I get into. I could see it did Peter good to pull Dussel to pieces to his heart's content, without fear of my telling tales. And as for me, I was very pleased, because I sensed a real feeling of fellow-ship, such as I can only remember having had with my girl friends.

Yours, Anne

Wednesday, 16 February, 1944

Dear Kitty,

It's Margot's birthday. Peter came at half past twelve to look at the presents and stayed talking much longer than was strictly necessary—a thing he'd have never done otherwise. In the afternoon I went to get some coffee and, after that, potatoes, because I wanted to spoil Margot for just that one day in the year. I went through Peter's room; he took all his papers off the stairs at once and I asked whether I should close the trap door to the attic. "Yes," he replied, "knock when you come back, then I'll open it for you."

I thanked him, went upstairs, and searched at least ten

minutes in the large barrel for the smallest potatoes. Then my back began to ache and I got cold. Naturally I didn't knock, but opened the trap door myself, but still he came to meet me most obligingly, and took the pan from me.

"I've looked for a long time, these are the smallest I could find," I said.

"Did you look in the big barrel?"

"Yes, I've been over them all."

By this time I was standing at the bottom of the stairs and he looked searchingly in the pan which he was still holding. "Oh, but these are first-rate," he said, and added when I took the pan from him, "I congratulate you!" At the same time he gave me such a gentle warm look which made a tender glow within me. I could really see that he wanted to please me, and because he couldn't make a long complimentary speech he spoke with his eyes. I understood him, oh, so well, and was very grateful. It gives me pleasure even now when I recall those words and that look he gave me.

When I went downstairs, Mummy said that I must get some more potatoes, this time for supper. I willingly offered to go upstairs again.

When I came into Peter's room, I apologized at having to disturb him again. When I was already on the stairs he got up, and went and stood between the door and the wall, firmly took hold of my arm, and wanted to hold me back by force.

"I'll go," he said. I replied that it really wasn't necessary and that I didn't have to get particularly small ones this time. Then he was convinced and let my arm go. On the way down, he came and opened the trap door and took the pan again. When I reached the door, I asked, "What are you doing?" "French," he replied. I asked if I might glance through the exercises, washed my hands, and went and sat on the divan opposite him.

We soon began talking, after I'd explained some of the French to him. He told me that he wanted to go to the Dutch East Indies and live on a plantation later on. He talked about his home life, about the black market, and then he said that he felt so useless. I told him that he certainly had a very strong inferiority complex. He talked about the Jews. He would have found it much easier if he'd been a Christian and if he could be one after the war. I asked if he wanted to be baptized, but that wasn't the case either. Who was to know whether he was a Jew when the war was over? he said.

This gave me rather a pang; it seems such a pity that there's always just a tinge of dishonesty about him. For the rest we chatted very pleasantly about Daddy, and about judging people's characters and all kinds of things, I can't remember exactly what now.

It was half past four by the time I left.

In the evening he said something else that I thought was nice. We were talking about a picture of a film star that I'd given him once, which has now been hanging in his room for at least a year and a half. He liked it very much and I offered to give him a few more sometime. "No," he replied, "I'd rather leave it like this. I look at these every day and they have grown to be my friends."

Now I understand more why he always hugs Mouschi. He needs some affection, too, of course.

I'd forgotten something else that he talked about. He said, "I don't know what fear is, except when I think of my own shortcomings. But I'm getting over that too."

Peter has a terrible inferiority complex. For instance, he always thinks that he is so stupid and we are so clever. If I help him with his French he thanks me a thousand times. One day I shall turn around and say: "Oh, shut up, you're much better at English and geography!"

Yours, Anne

Friday, 18 February, 1944

Dear Kitty,

Whenever I go upstairs now I keep on hoping that I shall see "him." Because my life now has an object, and I have something to look forward to, everything has become more pleasant.

At least the object of my feelings is always there, and I needn't be afraid of rivals, except Margot. Don't think I'm in love, because I'm not, but I do have the feeling all the time that something fine can grow up between us, something that gives confidence and friendship. If I get half a chance, I go up to him now. It's not like it used to be when he didn't know how to begin. It's just the opposite—he's still talking when I'm half out of the room.

Mummy doesn't like it much, and always says I'll be a nuisance and that I must leave him in peace. Honestly, doesn't she realize that I've got some intuition? She looks at me so queerly every time I go into Peter's little room. If I come downstairs from there, she asks me where I've been. I simply can't bear it, and think it's horrible.

Yours, Anne

. . . .

Friday, 21 July, 1944

Dear Kitty,

Now I am getting really hopeful, now things are going well at last. Yes, really, they're going well! Super news! An attempt has been made on Hitler's life and not even by Jewish communists or English capitalists this time, but by a proud German general, and what's more, he's a count, and still quite young. The Führer's life was saved by Divine

Providence and, unfortunately, he managed to get off with just a few scratches and burns. A few officers and generals who were with him have been killed and wounded. The chief culprit was shot.

Anyway, it certainly shows that there are lots of officers and generals who are sick of the war and would like to see Hitler descend into a bottomless pit. When they've disposed of Hitler, their aim is to establish a military dictator, who will make peace with the Allies, then they intend to rearm and start another war in about twenty years' time. Perhaps the Divine Power tarried on purpose in getting him out of the way, because it would be much easier and more advantageous to the Allies if the impeccable Germans kill each other off; it'll make less work for the Russians and the English and they'll be able to begin rebuilding their own towns all the sooner.

But still, we're not that far yet, and I don't want to anticipate the glorious events too soon. Still, you must have noticed, this is all sober reality and that I'm in quite a matter-of-fact mood today; for once, I'm not jabbering about high ideals. And what's more, Hitler has even been so kind as to announce to his faithful, devoted people that from now on everyone in the armed forces must obey the Gestapo, and that any soldier who knows that one of his superiors was involved in this low, cowardly attempt upon his life may shoot the same on the spot, without court-martial.

What a perfect shambles it's going to be. Little Johnnie's feet begin hurting him during a long march, he's snapped at by his boss, the officer, Johnny grabs his rifle and cries out: "You wanted to murder the Führer, so there's your reward." One bang and the proud chief who dared to tick off little Johnnie has passed into eternal life (or is it eternal death?). In the end, whenever an officer finds himself up against a soldier, or having to take the lead, he'll be wetting his pants from anxiety, because the soldiers will dare to say more than they do. Do you gather a bit what I mean, or have I been skipping too much from one subject to another? I can't help it; the prospect that I may be sitting on school benches next October makes me feel far too cheerful to be logical! Oh, dearie me, hadn't I just told you that I didn't want to be too hopeful? Forgive me, they haven't given me the name "little bundle of contradictions" all for nothing!

Yours, Anne

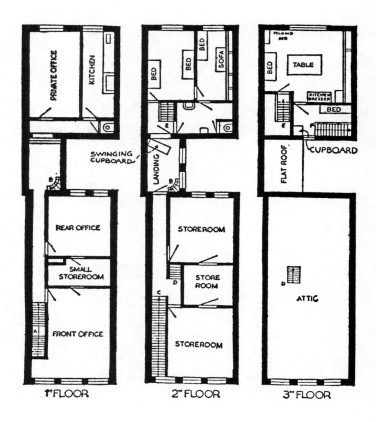

Autobiography and Biography

Bio- is a prefix that means "life," as you probably know from studying biology, the science of life. The word-part *-graph* means "something written." Combining the two gives *biography*, writing about life. And since *auto-* means "self," *autobiography* is writing about one's own life.

Biography is a very old form of writing. It is one of the oldest, in fact. Long before anyone thought of such things as novels, stone carvings were telling of the lives of real kings and heroes. Later, early books continued these stories and added the lives of saints and martyrs. Much of the Bible is biography.

These old biographies, however, were not at all like those written today. Stories of kings and heroes were usually exaggerated. Their purpose was to praise the king or make the hero larger than life. Often they were written to teach a lesson about the rewards for being good and heroic, and the punishment for being evil.

By contrast, modern biography looks at all sides of a person. It also takes a careful look at the times in which the subject lived. It exposes the bad along with the good, the failures as well as the successes. Even in autobiography the writer will confess to troubles and problems in an effort to present an honest and realistic picture.

A well-told story of a person's life is always interesting. It is like peeking through someone's window, or like living with the subject through some very personal moments. You share the person's most private thoughts and feelings. You really come to know what it must have been like to live in a different time and place under conditions different from those you are used to.

There are many values in autobiography that make it one of the most popular kinds of reading. In the lesson we will talk about four of those values:

1 Autobiographies give a view of setting, of life in a certain time and place.

2 Autobiographies give a view of the character of the writer.

3 Autobiographies tell anecdotes, small interesting stories from life.

4 Autobiographies give a sense of history beyond the simple facts.

Setting is as important in an autobiography as it is in fiction. In reading an autobiography, you must know
where and when the events of the
story occur. But besides the facts of
time and place, you must also understand the total environment.

1 Autobiography and Setting

The total environment consists of everything that is happening at a
certain place at a certain time. It includes the way the place looks and
the ways the people there behave. It also includes a more general feeling of what life is like. The total environment of Dallas, Texas in 1880
would be quite different from the total environment of Dallas today.
The total environment of New York's relaxed Greenwich Village is
different from that of its Upper East Side neighborhoods with their
plush apartments.

The total environment comes through to you as vividly in autobiography as it does in fiction. In autobiography, after all, you are reading
about real people who experienced a real place. If the writer is being
honest, you can feel for yourself what it was like to be alive in another
place at another time.

Notice how you begin to get a feeling for the total environment in the
following passage. Try to sense the environment—the air of the times—
as it was for Anne Frank on June 20, 1942.

> My father was thirty-six when he married my mother,
> who was then twenty-five. My sister Margot was born in
> 1926 in Frankfort-on-Main, I followed on June 12, 1929,
> and, as we are Jewish, we emigrated to Holland in 1933,
> where my father was appointed Managing Director of
> Travies N.V. . . .
> The rest of our family, however, felt the full impact of
> Hitler's anti-Jewish laws, so life was filled with anx-
> iety. . . . After May 1940 good times rapidly fled: first the
> war, then the capitulation, followed by the arrival of the
> Germans, which is when the sufferings of us Jews really
> began. Anti-Jewish decrees followed each other in quick

succession. Jews must wear a yellow star, Jews must hand in their bicycles, Jews are banned from trains and are forbidden to drive. . . . Jews must be indoors by eight o'clock and cannot even sit in their own gardens after that hour. . . .

So we could not do this and were forbidden to do that. But life went on in spite of it all. . . . Our freedom was strictly limited. Yet things were still bearable.

What is going on outside the home is of extreme importance in setting the scene. The Germans have arrived. They have put into effect the frightening "anti-Jewish decrees" from which the Frank family fled in Germany. "But," Anne says, "life went on in spite of it all." She finds her life "still bearable." She gives us details about her family and creates for us the feeling of a closely-knit family which provides comfort in a time of horrible political turmoil. Anne's words establish for us the total environment of her life.

Exercise A

The passage below is from the selection you have read. Answer the questions about this passage using what you have learned in this part of the lesson. Choose the best answer for each question. Put an x in the correct box or fill in the appropriate words.

We put on heaps of clothes as if we were going to the North Pole, the sole reason being to take clothes with us. No Jew in our situation would have dreamed of going out with a suitcase full of clothing. I had on two vests, three pairs of pants, a dress, on top of that a skirt, jacket, summer coat, two pairs of stockings, lace-up shoes, woolly cap, scarf, and still more; I was nearly stifled before we started, but no one inquired about that. . . .

So we walked in the pouring rain, Daddy, Mummy, and I, each with a school satchel and shopping bag filled to the brim with all kinds of things thrown together anyhow.

We got sympathetic looks from people on their way to work. You could see by their faces how sorry they were they couldn't offer us a lift; the gaudy yellow star spoke for itself.

The Diary of a Young Girl

1. People passing by are part of the setting here. What feeling do they add to the scene?

   ☐ a. Fear and anger

   ☐ b. Sorrow and sympathy

   ☐ c. Hatred and loathing

   ☐ d. Hustle and bustle

2. The fact of being Jewish makes the Franks self-conscious in this setting. A sentence near the beginning of the passage, and a short phrase at the end, point to this feeling. Copy either the sentence or the phrase in the space provided.

   _____

   _____

   _____

Now check your answers using the Answer Key on page 440. Correct any wrong answer and review this part of the lesson if you don't understand why your answer was wrong.

2 Autobiography and Character

The main purpose of a biography is to help readers know and understand its subject. In modern biography, the author looks at every side of a subject's character with just this in mind. In an honest autobiography, the writer tries to do the same thing. In fact, sometimes a person looks at himself or herself more carefully than at others.

It is not often that you get the chance to know a person as well as you do the subject of an autobiography. In an autobiography you learn of a character's ideals and goals. You see how those ideals and goals are pursued. You learn about the person's accomplishments and failures. And you come to know your subject's most secret needs and wishes.

Here, Anne Frank exposes one of her deepest feelings to readers.

> When someone comes in from outside, with the wind in their clothes and the cold on their faces, then I could bury my head in the blankets to stop myself thinking: "When will we be granted the privilege of smelling fresh air?" . . . Believe me, if you have been shut up for a year and a half, it can get too much for you some days. In spite of all justice and thankfulness, you can't crush your feelings. Cycling, dancing, whistling, looking out into the world, feeling young, to know that I'm free—that's what I long for. . . . I sometimes ask myself, "Would anyone, either Jew or non-Jew, understand this about me, that I am simply a young girl badly in need of some rollicking fun?" I don't know, and I couldn't talk about it to anyone, because then I know I should cry.

You have probably never known a young, active girl who has been cooped up in an apartment with seven other people for a year and a half. After reading this, you know one. You know what Anne thinks, how she feels, and what she longs for. This is one of the most moving passages in her book.

Anne emerges as a thoughtful, sensitive girl. She can express her feelings far better than most people her age. Readers are privileged to be able to share those feelings with her.

Exercise B

The passage below is from the selection you have read. Answer the questions about this passage using what you have learned in this part of the lesson. Choose the best answer for each question. Put an *x* in the correct box or fill in the appropriate words.

... *"zum Tode betrübt"* [the depths of despair] comes over me when, as happened today, for example, Mrs. Koophuis comes and tells us about her daughter Corry's hockey club, canoe trips, theatrical performances, and friends. I don't think I'm jealous of Corry, but I couldn't help feeling a great longing to have lots of fun myself for once, and to laugh until my tummy ached. Especially at this time of year with all the holidays for Christmas and the New Year, and we are stuck here like outcasts. Still, I really ought not to write this, because it seems ungrateful. ... But still, whatever you think of me, I can't keep everything to myself, so I'll remind you of my opening words—"Paper is patient."

1. At the beginning of the diary, Anne said, "Paper is more patient than man." She says it again here. What does she mean?

☐ a. People will die someday, but paper lasts forever.

☐ b. It takes a lot of patience to read a book.

☐ c. Paper waits patiently for someone to write upon it.

☐ d. People haven't the patience to listen to how you feel, but you can always write about your feelings.

2. Anne reveals many of her feelings in this passage. Write down two of them here using words from the passage. (Example: the depths of despair)

_____

_____

_____

Now check your answers using the Answer Key on page 440. Correct any wrong answer and review this part of the lesson if you don't understand why your answer was wrong.

An anecdote is a brief story. It's the kind of story you hear in everyday conversation. An anecdote from a friend might begin, "Wait till I tell you what happened when. . . ." And a story follows of some great or little adventure your friend had. Or some-

one in the family will say, "That reminds me of the time that. . . ." And you might be in for a story you've heard a dozen times before. But if you're lucky, it will be a story that is new and interesting.

Because autobiographies are about people's lives, they are filled with anecdotes. This is one of the things that makes them so interesting and easy to read when they are well-written. It's like listening to family gossip. One of the problems of writing autobiography, though, is deciding which anecdotes to include. There are many stories in everyone's life. Each anecdote must have a purpose for being included in an autobiography. The main purpose is to help readers understand the subject of the autobiography and his or her environment.

Consider this anecdote from Anne's diary. She tells you in her first sentence why she considers this anecdote important: "Since Saturday a lot has changed for me."

> Since Saturday a lot has changed for me. It came about like this. . . .
> To my great joy—I will be quite honest about it—already this morning I noticed that Peter kept looking at me all the time. Not in the ordinary way, I don't know how, I just can't explain.
> I used to think that Peter was in love with Margot, but yesterday I suddenly had the feeling that it is not so. I made a special effort not to look at him too much, because whenever I did, he kept on looking too and then—yes, then—it gave me a lovely feeling inside, but which I mustn't feel too often.

What Anne seems to be saying is that she is afraid she is falling in love with Peter. She's not sure if she wants that, or even if it's right. It gives her a feeling, she says, "which I mustn't feel too often."

The small anecdote is interesting for two reasons. It sheds more light on Anne, and it is the kind of experience everyone can relate to. Surely you have had this same feeling at one time or another about someone. And, like Anne, you probably weren't quite sure at the moment what to do about it.

Exercise C

The passage below is from the selection you have read. Answer the questions about this passage using what you have learned in this part of the lesson. Choose the best answer for each question. Put an *x* in the correct box or fill in the appropriate words.

In the evening he [Peter] said something else that I thought was nice. We were talking about a picture of a film star that I'd given him once, which has now been hanging in his room for at least a year and a half. He liked it very much and I offered to give him a few more sometime. "No," he replied. "I'd rather leave it like this. I look at these every day and they have grown to be my friends."

Now I understand more why he always hugs Mouschi. He needs some affection, too, of course.

1. What is the most important thing that both readers and Anne learn about Peter from this anecdote?

☐ a. He likes movie stars.

☐ b. He needs affection.

☐ c. He hugs Mouschi the cat.

☐ d. He won't accept gifts.

2. There is an expression near the end of the anecdote that tells readers Anne has learned a lesson. What is the expression? Write it here.

_____

_____

_____

Now check your answers using the Answer Key on page 440. Correct any wrong answer and review this part of the lesson if you don't understand why your answer was wrong.

Autobiography and Biography

4 Autobiography and the Sense of History

The difference between liking to read about history and not liking it lies in being able to imagine vividly the times and people you are reading about. History can sometimes seem like a boring series of events from a dead past. Another way to look at history, though, is to see that it is about people who were once alive and had thoughts and feelings much like the people you know. Being able to see the past this way is called having a sense of history. It means you have a feeling for the way events actually affected the people who lived through them.

It is true, unfortunately, that few history texts give the feeling of what it was like to be alive at a different time. They usually look at very large pictures: wars, laws, political activities, public events and trends. There is little room for the most interesting part of history—getting to know the people. Autobiography, however, does allow you to get to know how real people lived at a particular time. You learn how these people felt about what was happening around them. You get a sense of the moment because you live through it in your reading.

Here is Anne commenting on an historic event of her time—the attempted assassination of Adolf Hitler in 1944.

> Now I am getting really hopeful, now things are going well at last. Yes, really, they're going well! Super news! An attempt has been made on Hitler's life and not even by Jewish communists or English capitalists this time, but by a proud German general, and what's more, he's a count, and still quite young. The Führer's life was saved by Divine Providence and, unfortunately, he managed to get off with just a few scratches and burns. A few officers and generals who were with him have been killed and wounded. The chief culprit was shot.
>
> Anyway, it certainly shows that there are lots of officers and generals who are sick of the war and would like to see Hitler descend into a bottomless pit.

These two small paragraphs have taught you as much as a chapter from a history text. Hitler liked to blame all of Germany's problems on

Jewish Communists or English capitalists. The young people, he claimed, were his greatest supporters. But in this passage, Anne is overjoyed at evidence of how wrong these ideas have been. She has learned, from a newspaper story or a radio broadcast, of a plot to kill Hitler. Not only was the plot cooked up by his own officers, but it was a young man who tried to kill him. Quite naturally, Anne wishes Hitler in a "bottomless pit." Now it seems to her that some of his own people feel the same way. There are no dry facts here. Instead, the facts about the plot are made lively by Anne's intense feelings.

Exercise D

The passage below is from the selection you have read. Answer the questions about this passage using what you have learned in this part of the lesson. Choose the best answer for each question. Put an *x* in the correct box or fill in the appropriate words.

[Anne is summing up her feelings about the news of the attempt on Hitler's life.]

Do you gather a bit what I mean, or have I been skipping too much from one subject to another? I can't help it; the prospect that I may be sitting on school benches next October makes me feel far too cheerful to be logical! Oh, dearie me, hadn't I just told you that I didn't want to be too hopeful? Forgive me. . . .

1. What does Anne see as a prospect for October?
   - ☐ a. Her father is likely to buy real school benches for them.
   - ☐ b. The death of Hitler will surely occur.
   - ☐ c. There will be confusion.
   - ☐ d. She will be free.

2. What are the two feelings that Anne has at this moment in history? Write them here.

_____

_____

_____

Use the Answer Key on page 440 to check your answers. Correct any wrong answer and review this part of the lesson if you don't understand why your answer was wrong. Now go on to do the Comprehension Questions.

Comprehension Questions

Recognizing
Words in
Context

1. Anne says that on her *melancholy* days she sits with her chin in her hand. *Melancholy* is

   ☐ a. joy.

   ☐ b. patience.

   ☐ c. sadness.

   ☐ d. thoughtfulness.

Understanding
Main Ideas

2. Why did Anne name her diary Kitty?

   ☐ a. It was like a pet to her.

   ☐ b. It was just a wild idea she had.

   ☐ c. It was like talking to a friend for her.

   ☐ d. It was named for her pet cat Moortje.

Keeping
Events in
Order

3. Which one of the following is a correct statement?

   ☐ a. The Franks went into hiding after the German officer's attempt to kill Hitler.

   ☐ b. The Franks moved to Holland shortly after their marriage.

   ☐ c. The Franks lived in Frankfort-on-Main before they moved to Holland.

   ☐ d. The Franks went into hiding before Margot was called up.

4. When did hard times begin for the Jews in Holland?

   ☐ a. Just after the beginning of the war

   ☐ b. Just after the Franks went into hiding

   ☐ c. Just before Peter came to the annex

   ☐ d. Just before Anne was born

Understanding
Main Ideas

5. The Franks went into hiding when the Nazis sent a call-up notice for Margot. What did the call-up notice mean?

   ☐ a. Margot would have been sent to a concentration camp.

   ☐ b. Margot was called for military service against her will.

   ☐ c. Margot had violated some of the new decrees.

   ☐ d. Margot was probably a member of a resistance movement.

Recalling
Facts

6. How was the entrance to the secret annex hidden?

   ☐ a. With a trap door

   ☐ b. By a curtain

   ☐ c. By a cupboard

   ☐ d. With a false stairway

Making
Inferences

7. Anne quoted an old saying: "On top of the world or in the depths of despair." What else might she have said?

   ☐ a. Life is not worth living.

   ☐ b. I wish I were free again.

   ☐ c. The world is a crazy place to live.

   ☐ d. I have my ups and downs.

8. Anne said the family was stuck in the secret annex like *outcasts. Outcasts* are

☐ a. old, cast-off clothes.

☐ b. outlaws from justice.

☐ c. people who have been rejected.

☐ d. prisoners who have escaped.

9. When did Anne become close with Peter Van Daan?

☐ a. Just before they moved to the secret annex

☐ b. More than a year after going into hiding

☐ c. When they were small children in school

☐ d. Right after Peter moved into the secret annex

10. Probably the most important reason that Anne wrote to Kitty was that she was

☐ a. always happy.

☐ b. often lonely.

☐ c. afraid of people.

☐ d. angry with the world.

11. After *restraining* himself for half an hour, Peter told Mr. Dussel to stop turning the radio dial. What did Peter do for half an hour?

☐ a. He held back.

☐ b. He moved quickly.

☐ c. He argued.

☐ d. He complained.

12. What common need brought Peter and Anne together?

☐ a. A need to hear news from the outside

☐ b. A need to escape from harsh parents

☐ c. A need to share secrets in their diaries

☐ d. A need to tell their thoughts to someone

13. Where did Anne and Peter have their talks?

☐ a. In Anne's room

☐ b. In Peter's room

☐ c. In the private office

☐ d. In the kitchen

14. Who tried to kill Hitler?

☐ a. A German general

☐ b. A Jewish communist

☐ c. An English capitalist

☐ d. A German soldier

15. Why was Anne so excited about the attempt on Hitler's life?

☐ a. It seemed a good way to get even with him.

☐ b. It meant she would be able to marry Peter.

☐ c. She felt the war would soon be over.

☐ d. It meant there had been a revolution in Germany.

Now check your answers using the Answer Key on page 440. Correct any wrong answers you have by putting a check (✓) in the box next to the right answer. Count the number of questions you answered correctly and plot the total on the Comprehension Scores graph on page 444.

Next, look at the questions you answered incorrectly. What types of questions were they? Count the number of each type and enter the numbers in the spaces below:

Recognizing Words in Context   _____

Recalling Facts   _____

Keeping Events in Order   _____

Making Inferences   _____

Understanding Main Ideas   _____

Now use these numbers to fill in the Comprehension Skills Profile on page 445.

Discussion Guides

The questions below will help you to think about the selection and the lesson you have just read. If you don't discuss these questions in class, try to think about them or discuss them with your classmates.

Discussing Autobiography

1. An autobiography is supposed to explore human problems and values. How do the selections from Anne's diary do this?

2. It was pointed out in the lesson that history books look at large pictures. Autobiographies often look at very small pictures. The small picture here is Anne Frank in hiding in Amsterdam, Holland, between 1942 and 1944. After reading about Anne Frank, what questions would you like to ask about the larger picture? Some larger pictures would be: Europe, 1933-1945; World War II; the Netherlands in World War II.

3. Compare Anne Frank's diary with a biography you have read. How is it the same? How is it different?

Discussing the Selection

4. There are memorials to Anne Frank in many places around the world. Her book appears in thirty-three languages and in virtually every country. The play and movie about her experience are done over and over again. What, in your opinion, makes her such a well-known heroine?

5. What in these selections from Anne's diary makes you feel sad about her life? What gives you a good feeling?

6. Anne Frank has been called a symbol. How is she a symbol?

Discussing the Author's Work

7. Anne wrote in the Dutch language. What you have read is a translation. Are there ways you can tell that it wasn't written in English? Does it sound different from the way an American or English girl would write?

8. Most diaries are not written as if they were letters to an imaginary friend. How do you think writing to "Kitty" affected Anne's work?

9. Anne began writing her diary when she was thirteen. She was almost fifteen when she wrote the later entries. How are the first entries different from the later entries? How would you account for the differences?

Writing Exercise

Using Anne Frank's diary as a model, begin a diary of your own. Make entries in it for at least one week. Continue your diary as long as you wish. (Most famous people, and especially famous writers, keep diaries.)

Include anything you wish in your diary, but be sure to include:

- one event that occurred during the day
- your thoughts and feelings about the event

A word of caution: people often put very personal and revealing comments in secret diaries. If a teacher or someone else will read your diary, take this into consideration as you write.

Unit 9 The Historical Novel

Johnny Tremain
BY ESTHER FORBES

About the Illustration

How do you know that this scene takes place far in the past? Point out some details in the drawing to support your response.

Here are some questions to help you think:

☐ How does this street look different from streets that you see every day?

☐ If you were to find this same street and church today, how would it look different?

☐ How do you know that this boy lived long ago?

Unit 9

Introduction   What the Novel Is About/What the Lesson Is About

Selection   **Johnny Tremain**

Lesson   **The Historical Novel**

Activities   Comprehension Questions/Discussion Guides/Writing Exercise

Introduction

What the Novel Is About

Johnny Tremain begins in 1773. Johnny, age fourteen, is an apprentice silversmith who is learning the trade from old Mr. Lapham. He shows great promise at his work, drawing compliments from the best silversmith in Boston, Paul Revere. But in an unfortunate accident, Johnny's hand is badly burned. Though the burn finally heals, his hand remains crippled and deformed. Because of this, his days as a silversmith are over. There are very few trades, in fact, into which the master will accept him.

He befriends an older boy, Rab, who is an apprentice printer for a newspaper, *The Boston Observer*. The owner of the paper, Mr. Lorne, gives Johnny a job delivering papers. It's not a very good job, but it gives Johnny a living.

This newspaper is very loud in its opposition to English colonial policies. Because of this it attracts members of the Sons of Liberty to its offices. The Sons of Liberty is a radical political organization with such firebrand members as Paul Revere, John Hancock and Samuel Adams.

The novel follows Johnny and these famous men who become his friends through the important events in the years just before the American Revolution. After the Boston Tea Party, in which Johnny takes part, the British blockade Boston. Thousands of British troops are garrisoned in the town.

The chapter you will read begins on April 14, 1775. This is just five days before the start of the Revolution at Lexington and Concord. The British troops, after months of delay, are planning to go in search of arms and military stores that the colonists have been hiding. Paul Revere, Dr. Warren, Johnny and others must find out the British plans and get word to the Minute Men in the countryside.

Here is a list of some of the important names in the chapter:

General Thomas Gage—British commander in Boston.

Joseph Warren—A Boston doctor and hero of the Revolution. He fought and died at Bunker Hill a month after the events of this chapter.

Paul Revere—A silversmith. He was one of three men who rode to warn the Minute Men of the British plans.

Colonel Smith, Lieutenant Stranger, Major Pitcairn—British officers.

Dove—A boy about Johnny's age. He works as a stableboy for the British. He used to work with Johnny as an apprentice. He is stupid and lazy, and Johnny despises him.

Rab—Johnny's good friend from *The Boston Observer*. He is eighteen at the time of this chapter. Johnny is now sixteen.

Billy Dawes—Another of the three riders who went to warn the Minute Men.

The Afric Queen—A tavern in Boston.

What the Lesson Is About

The lesson that follows the reading selection is about the *historical novel*.

Historical novels are part history and part fiction. Imagined or fictional characters are placed in a setting from history. There they mingle with real characters from history and share their adventures. In *Johnny Tremain*, the setting is Boston in the years just before the Revolution. Many other settings have been used for other historical novels—the Civil War, the American frontier, the Napoleonic Wars, and so on.

There are certain basic rules, or guidelines, that most historical novels follow. These are discussed in the lesson.

The questions below will help you to focus on some characteristics of
the historical novel in *Johnny Tremain*. Read the chapter carefully and
try to answer these questions as you go along:

1 How does the author make you feel that the fictional character,
Johnny Tremain, knows and lives in the same world with the
actual historical characters?

2 What do details from history add to the story?

3 What part does the conflict between the British and the American colonists play in the story?

4 How does the farewell scene between Johnny and Rab give you
a personal or close-up view of history?

Johnny Tremain

Esther Forbes

X. 'Disperse, Ye Rebels!'

The fourteenth of April, 1775.

General Gage had sent out spies, dressed as Yankee men looking for work. The spies came back on this day. All the colonels were at the Province House with General Gage listening to their reports. Joseph Warren knew this, and so did Paul Revere, even Johnny Tremain. It was easy enough to find out that spies had returned, were reporting to the commanding officer—but what had they reported? This was not known.

The fifteenth of April.

This fell upon Saturday. At every regimental headquarters the same general orders were posted, signed by Gage himself. All the grenadier and light infantry companies were to be taken off duty until further orders. They were to be taught some new evolutions.

Johnny himself read these orders posted in the lower hall at the Afric Queen. One man was grumbling, 'New evolutions. What was Grandma Gage thinking about?' But Lieutenant Stranger as he read whistled and laughed. 'That,' he said, 'looks like something—at last.'

Each regiment had two companies picked and trained for special duty. The light infantry were the most active and cleverest men in each regiment. Lieutenant Stranger was a light infantry officer. These men were lightly armed and did scout and flanking work. In the grenadier companies you found tall, brisk, powerful fellows, hard-fighting men, always ready to attack.

If you have eleven regiments and pick off from each its two best companies, it adds up to about seven hundred men.

All day one could feel something was afoot. Johnny read it on Colonel Smith's florid face. He was stepping across the Queen's stable yard very briskly and remembering to pull in his paunch. There was ardor in his eye. Was it martial ardor?

Lieutenant Stranger was so happy over something he gave Dove threepence.

Spring had come unreasonably early this year. In the yard of the Afric Queen, peach trees were already in blossom. Stranger was so happy something was bound to happen. Over on the Common Johnny found Earl Percy's regiment unlimbering, polishing two cannons. The soldiers were forming a queue about a grindstone sharpening their bayonets. What of it? They were always doing things like that. Did all this mean something or nothing?

He went to Mr. Revere's, whose wife told him to look for him at Doctor Warren's. The two friends sat in the surgery making their plans and listening to reports that were coming from all directions. Seemingly the excitement among the officers, the preparations among the soldiers, had been noticed by at least a dozen others. But where were they going? Who would command them? No one knew. Possibly only Gage himself although before the start was actually made he would have to tell his officers.

All that day the British transports had been readying their landing boats. This might mean men would be taken aboard, move off down the coast (as Salem had been invaded two months before), or that they were standing by merely to ferry the men across the Charles River, land them in Charlestown or Cambridge. The work on the boats suggested that the men would not march out through the town gates. And yet . . . Gage might have ordered this work done merely to confuse the people of Boston. Blind them to his real direction. The talk at Doctor Warren's went on into the night.

Johnny Tremain

Johnny relaxed on a sofa in the surgery as the men talked. He was ready to run wherever sent, find out any fact for them. It was past midnight. He would not have known he had been asleep except that he had been dreaming. He had been hard at work down on Hancock's Wharf boiling lobsters—he and John Hancock and Sam Adams. The lobsters had men's eyes with long lashes and squirmed and looked up piteously. Hancock would avert his sensitive face to their distress, 'Go away, please' (but he kept pushing them under with his gold-headed cane). Sam Adams would rub his palms and chuckle.

Johnny woke up and realized that only Revere and Warren were still in the room and they were talking about Hancock and Adams. These two gentlemen had left Boston in March. They were representatives at the Provincial Congress at Concord. The British had forbidden the General Court to meet, but the Massachusetts men had merely changed the name of their legislative body and gone on sitting. But did the British know that both these firebrands were staying at the Clarks' out in Lexington?

'It will do no harm to warn them,' Revere was saying, getting to his feet. 'I'll row over to Charlestown tonight, go to Lexington, and tell them a sizable force may soon move. They had best hide themselves for the next few days.'

'And get word to Concord. The cannons and stores had best be hidden.'

'Of course.'

'Tell them we here in Boston have the situation well in hand. The second the troops move—either on foot or into those boats—we will send them warning in time to get the Minute Men into the field. I'd give a good deal to know which way they are going.'

'But suppose none of us can get out? Gage knows we'd send word—if we could. He may guard the town so well it will be impossible.'

Johnny was still half awake. He yawned and settled back to think of those lobsters. With eyes like men . . . long lashes . . . tears on their lashes. . .

Revere was pulling on his gloves.

' . . . Colonel Conant in Charlestown. I'll tell him to watch the spire of Christ's Church. You can see it well from Charlestown. If the British go out over the Neck, we will show one lantern. If in the boats—two. And come Hell or high water I'll do my best to get out and tell exactly what's acting. But I may get caught on my way over. Another man should also be ready to try to get out through the gates.'

They talked of various men and finally pitched upon Billy Dawes. He could impersonate anybody—from a British general to a drunken farmer. This might help him get through the gates.

As Paul Revere with Johnny at his heels left Warren's a man emerged from the darkness, laid a hand on Revere's arm. In the little light Johnny recognized the rolling black eye, poetic negligence of dress. It was Doctor Church.

'Paul,' he whispered, 'what's afoot?'

'Nothing,' said Revere shortly and went on walking.

'The British preparing to march?'

'Why don't you ask them?'

The queer man drifted away. Johnny was surprised that Revere would tell Church nothing, for he was in the very inner circle. Seemingly Revere himself was surprised by his sudden caution. 'But I can't trust that fellow . . . never have, never will.'

— 2 —

The sixteenth of April.

All over Boston bells were calling everyone to church. As though they had not a care in the world the British officers crowded into the Episcopal churches and army chaplains held services for the soldiers in the barracks. Paul Revere was over on the mainland carrying out his mission. Boston looked so usual and so unconcerned, Johnny began to wonder if they all had not made mountains of molehills, imagined an expedition when none was intended. But Rab was so certain the time was close at hand that he told Johnny that he himself was leaving Boston for good. There would be fighting before the week was out and he intended to be in it. Now he must report at Lexington.

Johnny took this news badly. He could not endure that Rab should leave him: desert him.

'But as soon as the first shot is fired, no man of military age can possibly get out of Boston. They'll see to it. It's now or never.'

He did not seem to feel any grief at abandoning Johnny, who sat disconsolately on his bed watching Rab. The older boy was cutting himself a final piece of bread and cheese. How many hundreds of times Johnny had seen those strong white teeth tearing at coarse bread. Rab had been eating bread and cheese all through their first meeting— and that was long ago. It seemed he'd be eating bread and cheese to the end. There was a sick qualm at the pit of Johnny's stomach. He couldn't eat bread and cheese, and it irritated him that Rab could.

The older boy was glowing with good health, good spirits.

He was eighteen, six feet tall and a grown man. He looked it as he moved about the low attic, stuffing his pockets with extra stockings. Rolling up a shirt in a checkered handkerchief. He is leaving me—and he doesn't care—thought Johnny.

'Perhaps I'll go too,' he offered, hoping Rab would say, 'I'd give everything I've got—even my musket—if you could come,' or merely, 'Fine, come along.'

'No, you can't,' said Rab. 'You've got your work to do right here in town. You stick around with your fat friend Dove. Gosh, I'm glad I'll never have to listen to Dove again. But you'll have a fine time with Dove, while I . . .'

'You know I cannot stomach Dove.'

'No? I thought he and you were getting on fine together.'

'And there's not one reason why I can't leave for Lexington too, except you don't want me.'

He knew this was not true, but he could not help badgering Rab, trying to make him say, 'I'll miss you as much as you'll miss me.'

Rab laughed at him. He was going to leave and he wasn't going to be 'slopped over.' Johnny was gazing at him sullenly. Rab took the extra stockings from his pocket, untied his handkerchief, and added them to his shirt and other necessities.

'You *want* to go,' Johnny accused him.

'Yes.'

'Well, then—*go!*'

'I'm going fast's I'm able.'

Oh, Rab, Rab! Have you ever seen those little eyes at the end of a musket? Rab, don't you go. Don't you go!

Rab was singing under his breath. It was the song of the Lincolnshire Poacher that Mr. Revere had taught Johnny and Johnny had taught Rab. There was something about Rab's singing, low, a little husky and not too accurate, that always moved Johnny. It was a part of that secret fire which came out in fighting, taking chances—and dancing with girls! The excitement glowed in Rab's eyes now. He was going into danger. He was going to fight—and the thought made some dark part of him happy.

Johnny wanted to tell him about those eyes, but instead he said, 'I guess you really want to get out to Lexington —and do some more dancing.'

'Here's hoping.'

From then on Johnny said nothing, sitting glumly on his bed, his head bowed. Then Rab came over to him and put a hand on his shoulder.

'Good-bye, Johnny. I'm off.'

Johnny did not look up.

'You're a bold fellow, Johnny Tremain.' He was laughing.

Johnny heard Rab's feet going down the ladder. The door of the shop closed after him. He ran to look out the window. Rab was standing outside the Lorne house shaking hands with his uncle, saying good-bye like a grown man. Now he was bending down to kiss Aunt Jenifer—not at all like a small boy kissing an aunt. He picked up Rabbit, who could toddle about, and kissed him, too. Then half-running, he passed lightly up Salt Lane and out of sight.

One moment too late, Johnny ran out into the alley. He couldn't let Rab go like that. He had not even said good luck, God be with you. Why . . . he might not ever see Rab again. He went back to his garret and flung himself on his bed. He half-wished he might cry and was half-glad he was too old for tears.

Today there was no sound from the shops and wharves. No cry of chimney sweep, oysterman, knife-grinder. The town was whist and still, for it was Sunday. As Johnny lay upon his bed, the church bells began to call for afternoon service. They babbled softly as one old friend to another.

Christ's Church and Cockerel, Old South, Old Meeting, Hollis, King's Chapel. He knew every one. He had heard them clanging furiously for fire, crying fiercely to call out the Sons of Liberty. He had heard them toll for the dead, rejoice when some unpopular act had been repealed, and shudder with bronze rage at tyranny. They had wakened him in the morning and sent him to bed at night, but he never loved them more than on Lord's Days when their golden clamor seemed to open the blue vaults of Heaven itself. You could almost see the angels bending down to earth—even to rowdy old Boston. 'Peace, peace,' the soft bells said. 'We are at peace . . .'

Suddenly close by, over at the Afric Queen, the British drumsticks fell. The fifes struck up 'too-too—tootlety-too.' Even on Sunday they were out drilling. So were other men —even on Sunday. For instance, over in Lexington.

The sixteenth of April drew to a close.

Monday was a quiet day. Lieutenant Stranger looked very solemn. Maybe there was not to be an expedition after all.

3

The eighteenth of April.

By afternoon the sergeants were going about the town, rounding up the grenadier and light infantry companies, telling them (in whispers) to report at moonrise at the bottom of the Common 'equipped for an expedition.'

The sergeants would tap their red noses with their fingers and bid the men be 'whist,' but it was common knowledge in the barracks and on the streets that seven hundred men would march that night.

This very night—come darkness—the men would move, but in what direction? And who would be in charge of the expedition? Surely not more than one of the colonels would be sent.

Johnny, who had his own colonel to watch, Colonel Smith, hardly left the Afric Queen all day and helped the pot-boy serve drinks to the officers in the dining room. A young officer sitting with Stranger did say, as he stirred his brandy-and-water with his thumb, that he hoped before long thus to stir Yankee blood—and what of that? Colonel Smith did have an army chaplain to dine with him that day. Did that mean he was suddenly getting religious, as people are said to before they go into danger?

Of one thing Johnny was sure. Dove knew much less than he did. Dove was so thick-witted he had no idea anything unusual was afoot. He honestly believed that the grenadiers and light infantry were merely going to be taught 'new evolutions.' As usual, Dove was too wrapped in his own woes to think much of what was happening about him.

By five Johnny thought he would leave the Queen and report to Paul Revere that he had discovered nothing new. First one more glance at Dove.

For once he found him hard at work, his lower lip stuck out, his whitish pig-lashes wet. He was polishing a saddle.

'That guy,' he complained, 'hit me for nothing. He said I was to get to work on his campaign saddle.'

'Who's he?'

'Colonel Smith, of course.'

'Did you do as he told you?'

'I tried. I didn't know he had two saddles. So I went to work on the usual one. I shined it until you can see your face in it. And he takes it out of my hands and hit me on the head with it. Says I'm a stupid lout not to know the difference between a parade saddle and a campaign saddle. How'd I know? Why, he's been over here about a year and that campaign saddle hasn't ever been unpacked. I had to get it from Lieutenant Stranger. How'd I know?'

Johnny said nothing. He realized he had heard something which conceivably might be important. Careful . . . careful . . . don't you say anything to scare him.

'Where's your polish? I'll help with the stirrups.'

The instant Johnny went to work, Dove as usual lay back on the hay.

'One of the stirrups wrapped 'round my head. Cut my ear. It bled something fierce.'

Johnny was studying the saddle on his knees. It was of heavy black leather, brass (not silver) mountings. Three girths instead of two. All sorts of hooks and straps for attaching map cases, spyglasses, flasks, kits of all sorts.

Colonel Smith is going on a campaign. But perhaps not. He might merely be riding down to New York.

He leaned back on his heels. 'Say, what if you and I took time out to eat supper? The Queen's cook has promised me a good dinner, because I helped them at table this afternoon.

Roast goose. I'll fix it so you can get in on it, too.'

'Oh, for goodness' sake—no.'

'It's past five o'clock. Colonel can't be going anywhere tonight.'

'Oh, for land's sake, Johnny, he says I'm to show him that saddle by six sharp, and if he don't like its looks he's going to cut me to mincemeat. He's always saying things like that. He's the . . .'

Johnny did not listen to what Colonel Smith was. He was thinking.

'Well, after that—when Colonel Smith has settled down to play whist. Can you get off?'

'Tonight isn't like any other night. He told me to bring Sandy around for him, fed and clean and saddled with this old campaign saddle by eight o'clock tonight . . .'

Colonel Smith is going on a long journey. Starting tonight at eight. It might be a campaign. He had an idea.

'I should think if the Colonel was making a long trip he'd take Nan, she's so light and easy to ride . . . if he has far to go.'

'He does like her better—she don't jounce his fat so. He always rides her 'round Boston. But only yesterday he had Lieutenant Stranger take her over to the Common when the men were drilling. Stranger says she still is squirmy when she hears drums and shooting. I heard him say so.'

'Oh.' Drums and shooting. This was not to be a peaceful ride to, say, New York. His cloth whipped over the black saddle leather. He spat on it and rubbed even harder. The one thing he must not say was the wrong thing. Nothing was better than the wrong thing. So for a while he said nothing.

'Sandy's good as gold, but he's an old horse and a little stiff. His front left leg won't last forever.'

'Colonel Smith didn't say he was going off on him forever.'

This did not help much. But Dove went on:

'He and the horse doctor and Lieutenant Stranger were all looking at him just this morning. The horse doctor said old Sandy could do thirty miles easy. And Stranger said, no, he wouldn't swear you could get Nan on and off a boat without her fussing.'

So . . . the campaign would start around eight that night. The Colonel's horse would be put on and off a boat. There would be a risk at least of drums and shooting. They were not going farther than thirty miles. Those men who thought the target of the expedition was going to be Lexington and Concord were right. And it would be Colonel Smith who would go in command.

All Johnny's hidden excitement went into his polishing. The brass mountings turned to gold. The black leather to satin.

'There! You take that in and show your Colonel!'

But he would wait one moment more, Dove might have something more to say when he came back after he had seen the Colonel.

Johnny went into Goblin's stall, but the horse pretended not to know him, and put back his ears and nipped at him.

Sandy next. The big yellow horse carefully moved over to give him room in the stall, nickered a little. He fondled the broad white-striped face, pulled gently at the ears—little furry ears, lost in mane like a pony's.

'I guess,' Johnny said, 'it looks like you'll be seeing that Rab before I do. May be Lexington. You tell that Rab he'd best look sharp. Take good care of himself. Tell that Rab . . . oh, anything.'

Dove came back in a jubilee.

'Colonel says I've done a fine job and so quick he's going to give me tomorrow as a holiday. He don't expect to get back before night.' Certainly this campaign was going to be a short one—if everything went as the British expected.

4

'It is tonight all right,' Johnny said to Doctor Warren, 'and Colonel Smith will command.' He went on to tell what he had found out from Dove. That the expedition would start tonight and that Lexington and Concord were the likely objects, the men sitting about in Warren's surgery had already guessed. But they were interested to learn that the Colonel and presumably his troops, expected to return to Boston the day after they set out and that he was to command them. Seemingly Gage, a punctilious man, had chosen Francis Smith because he had been in service longer than any of the other (and smarter) colonels.

'Hark.'

Outside the closed window on Tremont Street a small group of soldiers were marching stealthily toward the Common. These were the first they heard. But soon another group marched past, then another. A man whose duty it was to watch the British boats at the foot of the Common came in to say he had actually seen the men getting into the boats, heading for Cambridge.

Doctor Warren turned to Johnny, 'Run to Ann Street. Bid Billy Dawes come to me here, ready to ride. Then go to North Square. I've got to talk to Paul Revere before he starts. Both he and Dawes will be expecting a messenger.'

Billy Dawes was in his kitchen. He was a homely, lanky, young fellow with close-set eyes, and a wide, expressive mouth. He and his wife had dressed him for the part he would play—a drunken farmer. His wife, who looked more like a schoolgirl than a serious matron, could not look at him without going from one giggling fit to another. She laughed even more, and Billy joined her, when Johnny came in and said the time had come. The young man stuck a dilapidated hat with a broken feather on his head and his wife picked up a bottle of rum and poured it over the front of his torn jacket. Then she kissed him and they both laughed. As he stood before them, his expression changed.

His eyes went out of focus. His grin became foolish. He hiccoughed and swayed. He both looked and smelled like a drunken farmer. But he did have money in his pocket which no country blade would have had after a big toot in town. He knew one of the soldiers guarding the Neck that night. He believed he'd get out all right.

The scene in the Dawes kitchen was so light-hearted and so comical—and Johnny as well as little Mrs. Dawes laughed so hard—he wondered if she had any idea of the risk her husband was running. For by any law of any land a man caught exciting to armed rebellion might be shot. The second the door closed after the young man, Johnny knew. Mrs. Dawes stood where her husband had left her, all laughter wiped from her face. Billy Dawes was not the only gifted actor in his family.

From Ann Street Johnny ran toward North Square. This he found crowded with light infantry and grenadier companies, all in full battle dress. They got in his way and he in theirs. One of the men swore and struck at him with his gun butt. The regulars were getting ugly. He could not get to the Reveres' front door, but by climbing a few fences he reached their kitchen door, and knocked softly. Paul Revere was instantly outside in the dark with him.

'Johnny,' he whispered, 'the *Somerset* has been moved into the mouth of the Charles. Will you run to Copp's Hill and tell me if they have moved in any of the other warships? I think I can row around one, but three or four might make me trouble.'

'I'll go look.'

'Wait. Then go to Robert Newman—you know, the Christ's Church sexton. He lives with his mother opposite the church.'

'I know.'

'They have British officers billeted on them. *Don't rap at that door.* Take this stick. Walk by the house slowly, limping, tapping with the stick until the light in an upper window goes out. Then go 'round to the alley behind the house. Tell Newman the lanterns are to be hung now. Two of them. He knows what to do.'

As Johnny stood among the graves of lonely Copp's Hill looking across the broad mouth of the Charles, he could see lights in the houses of Charlestown. And over there he knew men were watching Boston, watching Christ's lofty spire—waiting for the signal. And as soon as they saw it, the best and fastest horse in Charlestown would be saddled and made ready for Paul Revere, who had himself promised to get over—if possible. Ride and spread the alarm. Summon the Minute Men. He watched the riding lights on the powerful sixty-four-gun *Somerset.* The British had evidently thought her sufficient to prevent boats crossing the river that night. She was alone.

The moon had risen. The tide was rising. The *Somerset* was winding at her anchor. The night was unearthly sweet. It smelled of land and of the sea, but most of all it smelled of spring.

Salem Street, where the Newmans lived, like North Square, was filled with soldiers. The redcoats were assembling here, getting ready to march down to the Common —and they would be a little late. Their orders were to be ready by moonrise. A sergeant yelled at Johnny as he started to limp past them, but when he explained in a piteous whine that his foot had been squashed by a blow from a soldier's musket and all he wanted was to get home to his mama, an officer said the men were to let 'the child' pass. Johnny was sixteen, but he could pull himself together and play at being a little boy still.

Downstairs in the Newman house he could look in and see a group of officers as usual, almost as always, playing at cards. Their jackets were unbuttoned, their faces flushed. They were laughing and drinking. There was on the second floor one light. Johnny couldn't believe anyone up there could hear him tapping in the street below. Instantly the light went out. He had been heard.

Newman, a sad-faced young man, got out at a second-story window in back, ran across a shed roof, and was in the alley waiting for Johnny.

'One or two?' he whispered.

'Two.'

That was all. Robert Newman seemed to melt away in the dark. Johnny guessed what the little tinkle was he heard. Newman had the keys to Christ's Church in his hand.

The two friends, Paul Revere and Joseph Warren, were standing in the Doctor's surgery. They were alone. Revere was urging Warren to cross with him that very night to Charlestown. If there was fighting tomorrow, Gage would not hesitate to hang him—at last—for high treason. But Warren said no. He would stay and keep track of the British plans until the very last moment.

'The second a shot has been fired, I'll send a messenger to you,' Revere promised.

'I'll wait until then. Why, Revere, I never saw you worry about anything before. I'll be a lot safer tonight than you'll be—catching crabs out on that river. Being shot at by the *Somerset*. And falling off horses—I'll not forget you and Parson Tomley's ambling jade.'

Johnny Tremain

He was always ragging Revere about falling off horses. It was some old joke between them which Johnny did not know, and both the men suddenly began to laugh. The mood between them had been heavy when Johnny came in, but now it lightened. They parted as casually as any friends who believe they will meet in a few days. But each knew the other was in deadly peril of his life. It was ten o'clock.

Doctor Warren told his colored man to make up a bed for Johnny in the surgery. The boy could not think of bed. He stole down to the Common to see the 'secret' embarkation. It was almost over, and was no secret. Hundreds of towns-folk stood about silently watching the boats returning from Cambridge shore and taking on yet another scarlet-coated cargo. But where these men were heading and who com-manded them, scarce a man in the crowd knew except Johnny. Farther down the river he knew the *Somerset* was on guard. By now Paul Revere was in his boat, trying to steal around her. In Charlestown the horse waited for him.

He saw Sandy step into a boat with never a quiver. He recognized Lieutenant Stranger's own horse and for a moment saw the young man's dark face in the moonlight. Being a horse-minded boy, he noticed that there was a little trouble with a showy white horse built like Sandy, but much younger. This was Major Pitcairn's. Were the marines being sent as well as the grenadiers and light infantry companies? Or was the rough, genial, stout-hearted old major merely going along for the fun of it?

At least, he thought this observation important enough to report to Warren. Other spies had been bringing news of the embarkation. It had been noticed that Pitcairn was not in his usual tavern. He had been seen with a civilian cape wrapped about him heading for the Common. Doubtless he was going. Gage had sent him either because he knew he was a better officer than Colonel Smith or because he had a way with Yankees. Everyone liked the pious, hard-swearing, good-tempered Major Pitcairn.

A barmaid from Hull Street came in to say she had been watching the *Somerset* at just the time Bentley and Richardson were rowing Paul Revere to Charlestown. Not a shot had been fired. It was also known that Billy Dawes had woven and bribed his inebriated way past the guards on the Neck. And the horse he was leading and pretending to try to sell had not looked like much—a thin bony beast in a bridle patched with rope. It was one of the fastest horses in Boston.

Then Doctor Warren told Johnny to lie down and get some sleep. It was almost midnight.

Johnny took off his jacket and boots, rolled up in a blanket on the bed the black man had made for him. The night before and the night before that he had been much upset over Rab's leaving. His thoughts had turned to the empty bed beside him. He had slept badly. Although people were still about the surgery, exchanging ideas, trying to guess what the future might be, he immediately fell asleep.

It was dawn. He was alone in the surgery and still sleeping. But out in Lexington on the Village Green the first shot was fired. One shot and then a volley. And Major Pitcairn was saying, 'Disperse, ye rebels, ye villains, disperse! Why don't ye lay down your arms?'

The war had begun.

It was the dawn of the Nineteenth of April. But Johnny Tremain still slept.

The Historical Novel

Historical novels combine the facts of history with the make-believe of a novel. Imagined events occur in the midst of things you have probably read about in your history books. Fictional characters move side by side with real people from history. In *Johnny Tremain*, Johnny and many of the other characters were created by author Esther Forbes. But actual historical figures from the time of the American Revolution, like Paul Revere, John Hancock and General Gage, also appear in the story. Like a biography, then, an historical novel presents history in personal terms. It lets a reader experience history through the eyes and feelings of people.

To be an historical novel, however, a novel needs more than a setting in a bygone time. It needs more than a cast of actual characters. Many novels use settings in the past to provide background or atmosphere. These are not historical novels at all; they are romances or adventures. For example, a love story set in France during the French Revolution is not necessarily an historical novel.

In an historical novel, the setting—the time, the place and the events —must play an important role in the story. And the conflict in the novel must involve a real conflict from history. This is what, later on in the lesson, we will call a social conflict. It goes almost without saying that the facts of an historical novel must be well researched and accurate. The story itself must give an honest and accurate picture of the times and the true feelings of the people who lived through them.

In *Johnny Tremain*, the conflict is the American Revolution. Other historical novels have used other wars. *The Red Badge of Courage* is one you may know; it uses the Civil War as its social conflict. James Fenimore Cooper uses the conflicts of the Americam Frontier in his historical novels. He wrote *The Leatherstocking Tales*, a series that included *The Last of the Mohicans*.

In this lesson we will look at four features that make *Johnny Tremain* a true historical novel:

1 Imagined characters are mixed with actual historical figures.

2 Real events and details play an important role in the story.

3 The central conflict focuses on a change in society.

4 Historical events are seen through the eyes of individuals.

The main character of an historical novel is always one created by the author. In addition, this character has to have friends and family who are also imagined. Other characters—townspeople, soldiers, acquaintances are created by the author as they are needed.

1 Mixing Real and Imagined Characters

These characters share the events of history with real characters. Real and fictional characters are made to know one another and inter-act in the story. But the real character is never made to do anything that can't be supported by facts from history.

Chapter 10 is a record of a very important week in the life of Johnny Tremain. It is also a very important week in American history. The chapter opens with a barrelful of real characters. How many of them do you recognize?

> The fourteenth of April, 1775.
> General Gage had sent out spies, dressed as Yankee men looking for work. The spies came back on this day. All the colonels were at the Province House with General Gage listening to their reports. Joseph Warren knew this, and so did Paul Revere, even Johnny Tremain. It was easy enough to find out that spies had returned, were reporting to the commanding officer—but what had they reported? This was not known.

General Thomas Gage was the commander of English troops in Boston in 1775. Joseph Warren was a young Boston doctor and patriot. He was a firebrand radical and one of the leading revolutionaries. In another month he would become one of the heroes of the Battle of Bunker Hill, where he died.

Everyone knows Paul Revere for his famous ride. William Dawes, who also rode out to alert the Minute Men, appears later in the chapter. He is called Billy Dawes in the story. You also hear of British Major Pitcairn who led the fateful expedition to Lexington and Concord.

Johnny Tremain mingles freely with all these famous people. Other fictional characters in the chapter are Johnny's friend Rab, Dove the stableboy, soldiers, barmaids and merchants.

Exercise A

He [Johnny] went to Mr. Revere's, whose wife told him to look for him at Doctor Warren's. The two friends sat in the surgery making their plans and listening to reports that were coming from all directions. Seemingly the excitement among the officers, the preparations among the soldiers, had been noticed by at least a dozen others. But where were they going? Who would command them? No one knew. Possibly only Gage himself although before the start was actually made he would have to tell his officers. . . . The talk at Dr. Warren's went on into the night.

Johnny relaxed on a sofa in the surgery as the men talked. He was ready to run wherever sent, find out any fact for them.

1. How does the author make you feel that Johnny knows the historical characters well?

   ☐ a. Johnny knows their names.

   ☐ b. Johnny visits at their homes.

   ☐ c. Johnny helps them to make plans.

   ☐ d. The men say they know Johnny well.

2. A sentence in the last part of the passage shows that Johnny participates in the action with these real people. Copy the sentence here.

_____

_____

_____

Now check your answers using the Answer Key on page 441. Correct any wrong answer and review this part of the lesson if you don't understand why your answer was wrong.

The Historical Novel

2 Real Facts and Events of History

One of the basic rules for historical novels is that the background used be historically correct. First of all, the history-book facts must be exactly right. This includes names, dates and major events. But more than this, the author must get details of setting right. What did the town look like then? How did the people dress? How did they speak? Transportation, businesses and buildings must all be described accurately.

Many novels set in the past give very little attention to details like these. Their descriptions may be accurate or they may not. Accuracy isn't that important when the details don't play a major role in the novel. But they do play a major role in an historical novel. The facts must be correct and drawn in fine detail. This takes considerable library research. Authors of historical novels must have the same love of history that historians do. Some authors of historical novels, like Esther Forbes, are professional historians as well.

In the following scene, Paul Revere is preparing for his famous mission. Watch for historical details that give you a feeling for how people really spoke and acted.

> Revere was pulling on his gloves.
> '. . . Colonel Conant in Charlestown. I'll tell him to watch the spire of Christ's Church. You can see it well from Charlestown. If the British go out over the Neck, we will show one lantern. If in the boats—two. And come Hell or high water I'll do my best to get out and tell exactly what's acting. But I may get caught on my way over. Another man should also be ready to try to get out through the gates.'
> They talked of various men and finally pitched upon Billy Dawes.

The usual picture we get of this famous ride is of Paul jumping on his horse and shouting "The British are coming!" But many more men are involved, the author tells us. Revere is joined by at least Billy Dawes and Colonel Conant. We see that people leaving the city are being watched. Revere will have to sneak out to Charlestown by boat. Dawes will try a land route.

Johnny Tremain

Notice how the author tries to duplicate expressions Paul Revere might have used in 1775. She can't reproduce his speech exactly, but she can seize on some expressions. We usually talk about the Old North Church where the signal lanterns were hung. Revere would probably have used the church's name, Christ's Church. And so he does here. He calls the land route out of Boston "The Neck," as it would have been called then. You probably notice other expressions we don't use today: "tell what's acting," and "pitched upon Billy Dawes." These are added to the speech to give a sense of historical reality.

Exercise B

The passage below is from the selection you have read. Answer the questions about this passage using what you have learned in this part of the lesson. Choose the best answer for each question. Put an x in the correct box or fill in the appropriate words.

Today there was no sound from the shops and wharves. No cry of chimney sweep, oysterman, knife-grinder. The town was whist and still, for it was Sunday. As Johnny lay upon his bed, the church bells began to call for afternoon service. They babbled softly as one old friend to another. Christ's Church and Cockerel, Old South, Old Meeting, Hollis, King's Chapel. He knew every one. He had heard them clanging furiously for fire, crying fiercely to call out the Sons of Liberty. He had heard them toll for the dead, rejoice when some unpopular act had been repealed, and shudder with bronze rage at tyranny.

1. The details in this passage are used mainly to

    ☐ a. provide a feeling for church bells.

    ☐ b. tell how lovely Sundays are.

    ☐ c. lead into the next part of the story.

    ☐ d. provide a picture and feeling of old Boston.

2. In the spaces provided, list these historic details which you learn from reading the passage:

a. the names of two old trades:

_____

_____

b. the name of an historic political group:

_____

c. at least two uses of church bells in those days:

_____

_____

Now check your answers using the Answer Key on page 441. Correct any wrong answer and review this part of the lesson if you don't understand why your answer was wrong.

Conflict is at the center of every novel. A conflict happens when opposing forces create a struggle or problem of some sort. How the characters react to the conflict produces the action of the story.

The Historical Novel

3 Society in Conflict

In an historical novel, the most important conflict is always a social one. Historical novels always take place at the time of an important conflict going on in society. Most often, a new form of society is coming into being as an old one dies. The conflict is between the new and the old order of things.

The death of a social order based on slavery is frequently the source of conflict in novels about Civil War. The new social order is represented by the industrial North. In novels about the American Revolution, the old social order is the British colonial system. The new social order is American democracy. The conflict between these last two is the main conflict in *Johnny Tremain*.

This sort of conflict may also be included in historical romance or adventure. But in an historical novel, it is one of the main issues. The following passage is based on the social conflict of the time.

> Johnny woke up and realized that only Revere and Warren were still in the room and they were talking about Hancock and Adams. These two gentleman had left Boston in March. They were representatives at the Provincial Congress at Concord. The British had forbidden the General Court to meet, but the Massachusetts men had merely changed the name of their legislative body and gone on sitting. But did the British know that both these firebrands were staying at the Clarks' out in Lexington?
>
> 'It will do no harm to warn them,' Revere was saying, getting to his feet.

The author calls Hancock and Adams "firebrands." They were the young, radical leaders of their time. People like them and Paul Revere and Dr. Warren were leading the country toward revolution. But at that time there were as many people in the American colonies who were against the revolutionaries as were for them. There was indeed a social conflict between new and old orders.

The British forbade the rebellious colonists to form a legislature. The colonists met anyway. The leaders, Hancock and Adams, were in hiding. Paul Revere and Dr. Warren could have been arrested at any time the British wished. Johnny Tremain has joined the conflict on the side of the radicals. What he does during this social conflict makes the storyline of the novel.

Exercise C

The passage below is from the selection you have read. Answer the questions about this passage using what you have learned in this part of the lesson. Choose the best answer for each question. Put an *x* in the correct box or fill in the appropriate words.

Johnny took off his jacket and boots, rolled up in a blanket on the bed the black man had made for him. The night before and the night before that he had been much upset over Rab's leaving. His thoughts had turned to the empty bed beside him. He had slept badly. Although people were still about the surgery, exchanging ideas, trying to guess what the future might be, he immediately fell asleep.

It was dawn. He was alone in the surgery and still sleeping. But out in Lexington on the Village Green the first shot was fired. One shot and then a volley. And Major Pitcairn was saying, 'Disperse, ye rebels, ye villains, disperse! Why don't ye lay down your arms?'

1. What is it about the coming conflict, the revolution, that troubles the people in Dr. Warren's surgery?

   ☐ a. The future is uncertain.

   ☐ b. Major Pitcairn's attitude is frightening.

   ☐ c. Their ideas are muddled.

   ☐ d. The coming of dawn alarms them.

2. Major Pitcairn is part of the old social order. How does he think of the people of the new social order with which he is in conflict? A word he speaks shows what he thinks of these people. Write that word here.

_____

Now check your answers using the Answer Key on page 441. Correct any wrong answer and review this part of the lesson if you don't understand why your answer was wrong.

The Historical Novel

4 History on Personal Terms

The lesson about autobiography (Unit 8, *Anne Frank: The Diary of a Young Girl*) points out that history has more meaning when it is seen through the eyes of real people. This point applies to historical novels, too.

If you read all of *Johnny Tremain*, you will learn a great deal about American history in the years just before the Revolution. The book does not describe the causes of the Revolution as a history book does. But it does give you an honest feeling for what it was like to live in Boston during those years. It is a personal view of history seen through Johnny's eyes.

Historical novels tell you about very ordinary things. In *Johnny Tremain*, you learn what it is like to get up on a Sunday in Boston. You see what it is like to work and learn a trade under the old apprentice system. You are shown what businesses there are around town. Most importantly, the historical novel describes how people feel. All these things let you feel the spirit of the times, a feeling it is very hard to get from a history book.

For example, one thing you surely wouldn't learn in studying the American Revolution is how an English soldier may have felt on the eve of battle. Author Esther Forbes provides that experience for you in this passage.

All day one could feel something was afoot. Johnny read it on Colonel Smith's florid face. He was stepping across the Queen's stable yard very briskly and remembering to pull in his paunch. There was ardor in his eye. Was it martial ardor?

Lieutenant Stranger was so happy over something he gave Dove threepence.

Spring had come unreasonably early this year. In the yard of the Afric Queen, peach trees were already in blossom. Stranger was so happy something was bound to happen. Over on the Common Johnny found Earl Percy's regiment unlimbering, polishing two cannons. The soldiers were forming a queue about a grindstone sharpening their bayonets. What of it? They were always doing things like that. Did all this mean something or nothing?

The British have been occupying Boston for a lone time. They are bored stiff. They think the colonists are a real nuisance. Now they have a chance to show those colonists a thing or two. The time is coming for doing a real job of soldiering.

"All day one could feel something was afoot." You are asked to feel what is happening along with the people in the story. You watch small things going on and you sense the tension. Officers are strutting. They are trying to act like soldiers again. The troops are sharpening bayonets and polishing cannons.

"Did all this mean something or nothing?" the author asks. The reader, who has experienced this scene through the eyes of the British soldier, knows the answer to this question. Esther Forbes has drawn us, along with the characters of the story, into history in the making.

Exercise D

The passage below is from the selection you have read. Answer the questions about this passage using what you have learned in this part of the lesson. Choose the best answer for each question. Put an *x* in the correct box or fill in the appropriate words.

[Johnny's friend Rab is going off to fight in the coming conflict.]

'You *want* to go,' Johnny accused him.
'Yes.'
'Well, then—*go!*'
'I'm going fast's I'm able.'
Oh, Rab, Rab! Have you ever seen those little eyes at the end of a musket? Rab, don't you go. Don't you go!

Rab was singing under his breath. . . . There was something about Rab's singing, low, a little husky and not too accurate, that always moved Johnny. It was part of that secret fire which came out in fighting, taking chances—and dancing with girls! The excitement glowed in Rab's eyes now. He was going into danger. He was going to fight—and the thought made some dark part of him happy.

1. How does Rab feel as he goes off to war?

   ☐ a. He is excited by the sense of danger.

   ☐ b. He is probably frightened.

   ☐ c. He is disgusted with Johnny.

   ☐ d. He feels very doubtful about the whole thing.

2. What are the lines in the passage that show Johnny's feelings at this point in history—that he is afraid for his friend's life? Write those lines here.

_____

_____

_____

Use the Answer Key on page 441 to check your answers. Correct any wrong answer and review this part of the lesson if you don't understand why your answer was wrong. Now go on to do the Comprehension Questions.

Johnny Tremain

Comprehension Questions

Answer these questions without looking back at the selection. Choose the best answer to each question and put an *x* in the box beside it.

Recognizing Words in Context

1. "He was . . . remembering to pull in his *paunch*." A *paunch* is a

   ☐ a. sword.

   ☐ b. handkerchief.

   ☐ c. horse.

   ☐ d. stomach.

Understanding Main Ideas

2. During most of the chapter, what is it that the patriots are trying to figure out?

   ☐ a. Whether or not to start a revolution

   ☐ b. What the British soldiers were going to do

   ☐ c. Whether they should warn Hancock and Adams

   ☐ d. If the British officers were for or against them

Keeping Events in Order

3. When were the British troops taken off regular duty?

   ☐ a. After Paul Revere left for Charlestown

   ☐ b. Before the first meeting of the Provincial Congress

   ☐ c. Just after the return to Boston of the British spies

   ☐ d. Just before Hancock and Adams went into hiding

4. "Johnny recognized . . . the poetic *negligence* of dress." *Negligence* means

☐ a. bravery.

☐ b. carelessness.

☐ c. formality.

☐ d. patriotism.

5. Dove was a stableboy for British officers. How did he feel about his employers?

☐ a. He respected them.

☐ b. He adored them.

☐ c. He was afraid of them.

☐ d. He had no feeling for them.

6. While Johnny spoke to Dove, he

☐ a. sharpened a bayonet.

☐ b. watched for spies.

☐ c. polished a saddle.

☐ d. tended to a horse.

7. The British troops left Boston at night. This probably meant they had planned

☐ a. a surprise mission.

☐ b. to start a war.

☐ c. a retreat.

☐ d. to surround Boston.

8. ". . . Soldiers were marching *stealthily* toward the Common." In other words they were marching

☐ a. rather noisily.

☐ b. bravely and boldly.

☐ c. with display and pomp.

☐ d. with some secrecy.

9. Billy Dawes and his wife both laughed over his mission. This was because they

☐ a. didn't realize the danger in Billy's mission.

☐ b. knew Billy could get away with anything.

☐ c. wanted to keep each other from worrying.

☐ d. were enjoying the chance to fool the British.

10. What was the *Somerset,* and what was it doing?

☐ a. It was a naval ship patrolling the harbor.

☐ b. It was a fort defending the harbor.

☐ c. It was the Massachusetts legislature in meeting.

☐ d. It was a British regiment getting ready for battle.

11. How did the British troops leave Boston?

☐ a. By marching over the Neck

☐ b. By passing through the gates

☐ c. By taking boats

☐ d. By passing Christ's Church

12. Which of the following is a correct statement?

☐ a. Rab left Boston before shots were fired at Lexington.

☐ b. Dove was hit with a saddle after Paul Revere left for Charlestown.

☐ c. War broke out before Johnny fell asleep in the surgery.

☐ d. Johnny spoke to Dove after troops left for Lexington.

13. When were the lights hung in Christ's Church?

☐ a. Just before Johnny visited the Dawes's home

☐ b. Before Johnny saw the orders for new evolutions

☐ c. Just after Johnny saw Major Pitcairn's horse on a boat

☐ d. After Johnny spoke to Robert Newton

14. Johnny was sleeping when the first shot was fired at Lexington. This shot meant that

☐ a. Boston was under attack.

☐ b. Paul Revere had not gotten through in time.

☐ c. Rab had been killed.

☐ d. the Revolution had begun.

15. Johnny's task throughout this chapter was

☐ a. gathering information for Revere and Warren.

☐ b. caring for officers' horses.

☐ c. to get messages to Concord.

☐ d. acting as servant for Dr. Warren.

Now check your answers using the Answer Key on page 441. Correct any wrong answers you have by putting a check (√) in the box next to the right answer. Count the number of questions you answered correctly and plot the total on the Comprehension Scores graph on page 444.

Next, look at the questions you answered incorrectly. What types of questions were they? Count the number of each type and enter the numbers in the spaces below:

Recognizing Words in Context   _____

Recalling Facts   _____

Keeping Events in Order   _____

Making Inferences   _____

Understanding Main Ideas   _____

Now use these numbers to fill in the Comprehension Skills Profile on page 445.

Discussion Guides

The questions below will help you to think about the selection and the lesson you have just read. If you don't discuss these questions in class, try to think about them or discuss them with your classmates.

Discussing Historical Novels

1. If you read about the beginning of the American Revolution in a history book just before you read *Johnny Tremain,* what could you learn that would help you understand the novel?

2. If you read about the beginning of the Revolution in a history book after you read *Johnny Tremain,* why should you be able to understand the history better?

3. You could not know most of the places mentioned in the story without having lived in Boston. Still, they add to the story. How?

Discussing the Story

4. Do you ever feel as though you are making history? That is, do you ever feel that history is being made in your time? Do you think Paul Revere felt that way? How is history made? Who makes it?

5. Rab was eighteen and anxious to go and fight in a war. Why do you think he wanted to go? Would you feel the same way?

6. In Chapter 9, Johnny had seen a man shot by a firing squad. He found it very upsetting to watch. He felt that the holes at the ends of the muskets looked like little cruel eyes. When Rab was leaving, Johnny thought to himself, "Oh Rab, have you ever seen those little eyes at the end of a musket?" What did Johnny mean?

Discussing the Author's Work

7. Esther Forbes spent her life in Massachusetts, in and near Boston. How does this show in her novel?

8. The author seems to know quite a bit about the English army as it was in 1775. How would she know this?

9. Esther Forbes also wrote a book called *Paul Revere and the World He Lived In.* Find it in the library. How is it different from *Johnny Tremain?*

Johnny Tremain

Writing Exercise

Read about a famous person from history in a biography, a history book or an encyclopedia. Imagine an adventure you "shared" with that person and write a short account of it. Here are some suggestions:

You are a messenger for General Grant during the Civil War.

You are in the Montgomery bus boycott with Martin Luther King, Jr.

You join a march with Susan B. Anthony to get voting rights for women.

You join Robert Peary on his trip to the North Pole.

You explore the St. Lawrence River with Samuel de Champlain.

Unit 10   Fantasy

The Hobbit
BY J.R.R. TOLKIEN

About the Illustration

How would you describe the world where this scene takes place? Point out some details in the drawing to support your response.

Here are some questions to help you think:

☐ How do you know that this scene couldn't be happening in the world of your everyday experience? What details make it seem like a fantasy world?

☐ What details in this picture make it seem realistic? What things in the drawing might you see in your everyday experience?

Unit 10

Introduction	What the Novel Is About/What the Lesson Is About
Selection	**The Hobbit**
Lesson	**Fantasy**
Activities	Comprehension Questions/Discussion Guides/Writing Exercise

Introduction

What the Novel Is About

Hobbits are little people about half our size. They tend to be fat in the stomach, which is not surprising since they eat six meals a day. They dress in brightly colored clothes but wear no shoes on their furry, thick-soled feet. They live in a land called the Shire, which might be anywhere. They're a peaceful people who would prefer to let the rest of the world pass them by. They like nothing better than to have a neighbor in for tea (or to be invited out to tea).

But there's more to a hobbit than meets the eye. They are fiercely loyal to their friends. They are clever and quick-witted. They will fight to the death if they have to.

Bilbo Baggins would rather not have to. He's 50 years old (that's younger than it sounds; hobbits live to be about 120) and perfectly content with his life, which revolves around the preparation of meals. An adventure is about the last thing Bilbo wants.

But adventure comes knocking on his door in the form of thirteen dwarves. They are looking for a fourteenth member (thirteen is an unlucky number) to help them reclaim their ancestors' gold. It is presently guarded by a dragon, who sleeps on it. The dwarves are looking for a "burglar"—an "expert treasure hunter," if you wish—to make up their party. Bilbo, as one dwarf notes, looks more like a grocer than a burglar. But Gandalf the wizard thinks differently: "There is a lot more in him than you guess, and a deal more than he has any idea of himself."

So Bilbo sets out on a quest for gold. Along the way, he meets many dangers (and misses a great many meals). And he wins a game of riddles with a slimy, pale creature called Gollum. The prize is a gold ring that makes its wearer invisible.

The ring has other powers, too, though Bilbo doesn't realize it. The ring plays a small part in *The Hobbit*. But the ring is the focus of the author's great series, *The Lord of the Rings*, which you will want to read after *The Hobbit*.

The Hobbit and its sequel, *The Lord of the Rings,* were written by an

Englishman, J.R.R. Tolkien. He wrote the stories in his spare time to entertain his small son. Over the years, the stories grew. They became more detailed until, together, they tell of an entire fantasy world with a history and culture all its own. The appeal of the stories is enormous. Their many fans have created a "hobbit market" of calendars, games, T-shirts and the like. The world of the hobbits can seem very real and very appealing. It is probably the best and most ambitious example of what fantasy is.

What the Lesson Is About

The lesson that follows the reading selection is about fantasy.

A fantasy is a story in which an author "breaks free" from the real world. It will, therefore, take place in an unreal world—a fairyland, an unknown planet, a time in the future, a city beneath the sea. In a fantasy there are unreal characters, too. Here we have hobbits, dwarves, elves, dragons, a wizard and many other strange creatures. In other fantasies there may be talking rabbits or lovable robots.

Everyone grows up with fantasy. And no one ever grows too old to enjoy this story form. Fairy tales are fantasies. Most of Walt Disney's stories are set in fantasy lands with fantastic characters. Millions enjoy the living fantasies of Disneyland and Disney World year after year. Science fiction, folk tales and myths are all examples of fantasy.

Fantasy as a story form has certain basic characteristics. We will discuss some of them in this lesson.

The questions below will help you to focus on some characteristics of fantasy in the chapter from *The Hobbit*. Read the chapter and try to answer these questions as you go along:

1. The author describes a fantasy world where hobbits live, but there are still familiar things in it. What are they?

2. Everyone knows that hobbits and dwarves are unreal creatures. How does the author make them seem real and believable within the fantasy world?

3. Magic is a part of fantasy. How are readers told early in the chapter that there will be magic in the story?

4. How is Bilbo Baggins like you and other people you know? Who or what in the real world is like Smaug the dragon?

The Hobbit

J.R.R. Tolkien

Chapter 1
An Unexpected Party

In a hole in the ground there lived a hobbit. Not a nasty, dirty, wet hole, filled with the ends of worms and an oozy smell, nor yet a dry, bare, sandy hole with nothing in it to sit down on or to eat: it was a hobbit-hole, and that means comfort.

It had a perfectly round door like a porthole, painted green, with a shiny yellow brass knob in the exact middle. The door opened on to a tube-shaped hall like a tunnel: a very comfortable tunnel without smoke, with panelled walls, and floors tiled and carpeted, provided with polished chairs, and lots and lots of pegs for hats and coats—the hobbit was fond of visitors. The tunnel wound on and on, going fairly but not quite straight into the side of the hill— The Hill, as all the people for many miles round called it—and many little round doors opened out of it, first on one side and then on another. No going upstairs for the hobbit: bedrooms, bathrooms, cellars, pantries (lots of these), wardrobes (he had whole rooms devoted to clothes), kitchens, dining-rooms, all were on the same floor, and indeed on the same passage. The best rooms were all on the lefthand side (going in), for these were the only ones to have windows, deep-set round windows looking over his garden and meadows beyond, sloping down to the river.

This hobbit was a very well-to-do hobbit, and his name was Baggins. The Bagginses had lived in the neighbourhood of The Hill for time out of mind, and people considered them very respectable, not only because most of them were rich, but also because they never had any adventures or did anything unexpected: you could tell what a Baggins would say on any question without the bother of asking him. This is a story of how a Baggins had an adventure, and found himself doing and saying things altogether unexpected. He may have lost the neighbours' respect, but he gained—well, you will see whether he gained anything in the end.

The mother of our particular hobbit—what is a hobbit? I suppose hobbits need some description nowadays, since they have become rare and shy of the Big People, as they call us. They are (or were) a little people, about half our height, and smaller than the bearded Dwarves. Hobbits have no beards. There is little or no magic about them, except the ordinary everyday sort which helps them to disappear quietly and quickly when large stupid folk like you and me come blundering along, making a noise like elephants which they can hear a mile off. They are inclined to be fat in the stomach; they dress in bright colours (chiefly green and yellow); wear no shoes, because their feet grow natural leathery soles and thick warm brown hair like the stuff on their heads (which is curly); have long clever brown fingers, good-natured faces, and laugh deep fruity laughs (especially after dinner, which they have twice a day when they can get it). Now you know enough to go on with. As I was saying, the mother of this hobbit—of Bilbo Baggins, that is—was the fabulous Belladonna Took, one of the three remarkable daughters of the Old Took, head of the hobbits who lived across The Water, the small river that ran at the foot of The Hill. It was often said (in other families) that long ago one of the Took ancestors must have taken a fairy wife. That was, of course, absurd, but certainly there was still something not entirely hobbit-like about them, and once in a while members of the Took-clan would go and have adventures. They discreetly disappeared, and the family hushed it up; but the fact remained

The Hobbit

that the Tooks were not as respectable as the Bagginses, though they were undoubtedly richer.

Not that Belladonna Took ever had any adventures after she became Mrs. Bungo Baggins. Bungo, that was Bilbo's father, built the most luxurious hobbit-hole for her (and partly with her money) that was to be found either under The Hill or over The Hill or across The Water, and there they remained to the end of their days. Still it is probable that Bilbo, her only son, although he looked and behaved exactly like a second edition of his solid and comfortable father, got something a bit queer in his makeup from the Took side, something that only waited for a chance to come out. The chance never arrived, until Bilbo Baggins was grown up, being about fifty years old or so, and living in the beautiful hobbit-hole built by his father, which I have just described for you, until he had in fact apparently settled down immovably.

By some curious chance one morning long ago in the quiet of the world, when there was less noise and more green, and the hobbits were still numerous and prosperous, and Bilbo Baggins was standing at his door after breakfast smoking an enormous long wooden pipe that reached nearly down to his woolly toes (neatly brushed)—Gandalf came by. Gandalf! If you had heard only a quarter of what I have heard about him, and I have only heard very little of all there is to hear, you would be prepared for any sort of remarkable tale. Tales and adventures sprouted up all over the place wherever he went, in the most extraordinary fashion. He had not been down that way under The Hill for ages and ages, not since his friend the Old Took died, in fact, and the hobbits had almost forgotten what he looked like. He had been away over The Hill and across The Water on business of his own since they were all small hobbit-boys and hobbit-girls.

All that the unsuspecting Bilbo saw that morning was an old man with a staff. He had a tall pointed blue hat, a long grey cloak, a silver scarf over which a white beard hung down below his waist, and immense black boots.

"Good morning!" said Bilbo, and he meant it. The sun was shining, and the grass was very green. But Gandalf looked at him from under long bushy eyebrows that stuck out further than the brim of his shady hat.

"What do you mean?" he said. "Do you wish me a good morning, or mean that it is a good morning whether I want it or not; or that you feel good this morning; or that it is a morning to be good on?"

"All of them at once," said Bilbo. "And a very fine morning for a pipe of tobacco out of doors, into the bargain. If you have a pipe about you, sit down and have a fill of mine! There's no hurry, we have all the day before us!" Then Bilbo sat down on a seat by his door, crossed his legs, and blew out a beautiful grey ring of smoke that sailed up into the air without breaking and floated away over The Hill.

"Very pretty!" said Gandalf. "But I have no time to blow smoke-rings this morning. I am looking for someone to share in an adventure that I am arranging, and it's very difficult to find anyone."

"I should think so—in these parts! We are plain quiet folk and have no use for adventures. Nasty disturbing uncomfortable things! Make you late for dinner! I can't think what anybody sees in them," said our Mr. Baggins, and stuck one thumb behind his braces, and blew out another even bigger smoke-ring. Then he took out his morning letters, and began to read, pretending to take no more notice of the old man. He had decided that he was not quite his sort, and wanted him to go away. But the old man did not move. He stood leaning on his stick and gazing at the hobbit without saying anything, till Bilbo got quite uncomfortable and even a little cross.

The Hobbit

"Good morning!" he said at last. "We don't want any adventures here, thank you! You might try over The Hill or across The Water." By this he meant that the conversation was at an end.

"What a lot of things you do use *Good morning* for!" said Gandalf. "Now you mean that you want to get rid of me, and that it won't be good till I move off."

"Not at all, not at all, my dear sir! Let me see, I don't think I know your name?"

"Yes, yes, my dear sir—and I do know your name, Mr. Bilbo Baggins. And you do know my name, though you don't remember that I belong to it. I am Gandalf, and Gandalf means me! To think that I should have lived to be good-morninged by Belladonna Took's son, as if I was selling buttons at the door!"

"Gandalf, Gandalf! Good gracious me! Not the wandering wizard that gave Old Took a pair of magic diamond studs that fastened themselves and never came undone till ordered? Not the fellow who used to tell such wonderful tales at parties, about dragons and goblins and giants and the rescue of princesses and the unexpected luck of widows' sons? Not the man that used to make such particularly excellent fireworks! I remember those! Old Took used to have them on Midsummer's Eve. Splendid! They used to go up like great lilies and snapdragons and laburnums of fire and hang in the twilight all evening!" You will notice already that Mr. Baggins was not quite so prosy as he liked to believe, also that he was very fond of flowers. "Dear me!" he went on. "Not the Gandalf who was responsible for so many quiet lads and lasses going off into the Blue for mad adventures. Anything from climbing trees to visiting Elves —or sailing in ships, sailing to other shores! Bless me, life used to be quite inter—I mean, you used to upset things badly in these parts once upon a time. I beg your pardon, but I had no idea you were still in business."

"Where else should I be?" said the wizard. "All the same I am pleased to find you remember something about me. You seem to remember my fireworks kindly, at any rate, and that is not without hope. Indeed for your old grandfather Took's sake, and for the sake of poor Belladonna, I will give you what you asked for."

"I beg your pardon, I haven't asked for anything!"

"Yes, you have! Twice now. My pardon. I give it you. In fact I will go so far as to send you on this adventure. Very amusing for me, very good for you—and profitable too, very likely, if you ever get over it."

"Sorry! I don't want any adventures, thank you. Not today. Good morning! But please come to tea—any time you like! Why not tomorrow? Come tomorrow! Good-bye!" With that the hobbit turned and scuttled inside his round green door, and shut it as quickly as he dared, not to seem rude. Wizards after all are wizards.

"What on earth did I ask him to tea for!" he said to himself, as he went to the pantry. He had only just had breakfast, but he thought a cake or two and a drink of something would do him good after his fright.

Gandalf in the meantime was still standing outside the door, and laughing long but quietly. After a while he stepped up, and with the spike of his staff scratched a queer sign on the hobbit's beautiful green front-door. Then he strode away, just about the time when Bilbo was finishing his second cake and beginning to think that he had escaped adventures very well.

The next day he had almost forgotten about Gandalf. He did not remember things very well, unless he put them down on his Engagement Tablet: like this: *Gandalf Tea Wednesday*. Yesterday he had been too flustered to do anything of the kind.

Just before tea-time there came a tremendous ring on the front-door bell, and then he remembered! He rushed and put on the kettle, and put out another cup and saucer, and an extra cake or two, and ran to the door.

"I am so sorry to keep you waiting!" he was going to say, when he saw that it was not Gandalf at all. It was a dwarf with a blue beard tucked into a golden belt, and very bright eyes under his dark-green hood. As soon as the door was opened, he pushed inside, just as if he had been expected.

He hung his hooded cloak on the nearest peg, and "Dwalin at your service!" he said with a low bow.

"Bilbo Baggins at yours!" said the hobbit, too surprised to ask any questions for the moment. When the silence that followed had become uncomfortable, he added: "I am just about to take tea; pray come and have some with me." A little stiff perhaps, but he meant it kindly. And what would you do, if an uninvited dwarf came and hung his things up in your hall without a word of explanation?

They had not been at table long, in fact they had hardly reached the third cake, when there came another even louder ring at the bell.

"Excuse me!" said the hobbit, and off he went to the door.

"So you have got here at last!" was what he was going to say to Gandalf this time. But it was not Gandalf. Instead there was a very old-looking dwarf on the step with a white beard and a scarlet hood; and he too hopped inside as soon as the door was open, just as if he had been invited.

"I see they have begun to arrive already," he said when he caught sight of Dwalin's green hood hanging up. He hung his red one next to it, and "Balin at your service!" he said with his hand on his breast.

"Thank you!" said Bilbo with a gasp. It was not the correct thing to say, but *they have begun to arrive* had flustered him badly. He liked visitors, but he liked to know them before they arrived, and he preferred to ask them himself. He had a horrible thought that the cakes might run short, and then he—as the host: he knew his duty and stuck to it however painful—he might have to go without.

"Come along in, and have some tea!" he managed to say after taking a deep breath.

"A little beer would suit me better, if it is all the same to you, my good sir," said Balin with the white beard. "But I don't mind some cake—seed-cake, if you have any."

"Lots!" Bilbo found himself answering, to his own surprise; and he found himself scuttling off, too, to the cellar to fill a pint beer-mug, and to the pantry to fetch two beautiful round seed-cakes which he had baked that afternoon for his after-supper morsel.

When he got back Balin and Dwalin were talking at the table like old friends (as a matter of fact they were brothers). Bilbo plumped down the beer and the cake in front of them, when loud came a ring at the bell again, and then another ring.

"Gandalf for certain this time," he thought as he puffed along the passage. But it was not. It was two more dwarves, both with blue hoods, silver belts, and yellow beards; and each of them carried a bag of tools and a spade. In they hopped, as soon as the door began to open—Bilbo was hardly surprised at all.

"What can I do for you, my dwarves?" he said.

"Kili at your service!" said the one. "And Fili!" added the other; and they both swept off their blue hoods and bowed.

"At yours and your family's!" replied Bilbo, remembering his manners this time.

"Dwalin and Balin here already, I see," said Kili. "Let us join the throng!"

"Throng!" thought Mr. Baggins. "I don't like the sound of that. I really must sit down for a minute and collect my wits, and have a drink." He had only just had a sip—in the corner, while the four dwarves sat around the table, and talked about mines and gold and troubles with the goblins, and the depredations of dragons, and lots of other things which he did not understand, and did not want to, for they sounded much too adventurous—when, *ding-dong-a-ling-dang,* his bell rang again, as if some naughty little hobbit-boy was trying to pull the handle off.

"Someone at the door!" he said, blinking.

"Some four, I should say by the sound," said Fili. "Besides, we saw them coming along behind us in the distance."

The poor little hobbit sat down in the hall and put his head in his hands, and wondered what had happened, and what was going to happen, and whether they would all stay to supper. Then the bell rang again louder than ever, and he had to run to the door. It was not four after all, it was FIVE. Another dwarf had come along while he was wondering in the hall. He had hardly turned the knob, before they were all inside, bowing and saying "at your service" one after another. Dori, Nori, Ori, Oin, and Gloin were their names; and very soon two purple hoods, a grey hood, a brown hood, and a white hood were hanging on the pegs, and off they marched with their broad hands stuck in their gold and silver belts to join the others. Already it had almost become a throng. Some called for ale, and some for porter, and one for coffee, and all of them for cakes; so the hobbit was kept very busy for a while.

A big jug of coffee had just been set in the hearth, the seed-cakes were gone, and the dwarves were starting on a round of buttered scones, when there came—a loud knock. Not a ring, but a hard rat-tat on the hobbit's beautiful green door. Somebody was banging with a stick!

Bilbo rushed along the passage, very angry, and altogether bewildered and bewuthered—this was the most

Fantasy   **401**

awkward Wednesday he ever remembered. He pulled open the door with a jerk, and they all fell in, one on top of the other. More dwarves, four more! And there was Gandalf behind, leaning on his staff and laughing. He had made quite a dent on the beautiful door; he had also, by the way, knocked out the secret mark that he had put there the morning before.

"Carefully! Carefully!" he said. "It is not like you, Bilbo, to keep friends waiting on the mat, and then open the door like a pop-gun! Let me introduce Bifur, Bofur, Bombur, and especially Thorin!"

"At your service!" said Bifur, Bofur, and Bombur standing in a row. Then they hung up two yellow hoods and a pale green one; and also a sky-blue one with a long silver tassel. This last belong to Thorin, an enormously important dwarf, in fact no other than the great Thorin Oakenshield himself, who was not at all pleased at falling flat on Bilbo's mat with Bifur, Bofur, and Bombur on top of him. For one thing Bombur was immensely fat and heavy. Thorin indeed was very haughty, and said nothing about *service;* but poor Mr. Baggins said he was sorry so many times, that at last he grunted "pray don't mention it," and stopped frowning.

"Now we are all here!" said Gandalf, looking at the row of thirteen hoods—the best detachable party hoods—and his own hat hanging on the pegs. "Quite a merry gathering! I hope there is something left for the late-comers to eat and drink! What's that? Tea! No thank you! A little red wine, I think, for me."

"And for me," said Thorin.

"And raspberry jam and apple-tart," said Bifur.

"And mince-pies and cheese," said Bofur.

"And pork-pie and salad," said Bombur.

"And more cakes—and ale—and coffee, if you don't mind," called the other dwarves through the door.

"Put on a few eggs, there's a good fellow!" Gandalf called after him, as the hobbit stumped off to the pantries. "And just bring out the cold chicken and pickles!"

"Seems to know as much about the inside of my larders as I do myself!" thought Mr. Baggins, who was feeling positively flummoxed, and was beginning to wonder whether a most wretched adventure had not come right into his house. By the time he had got all the bottles and dishes and knives and forks and glasses and plates and spoons and things piled up on big trays, he was getting very hot, and red in the face, and annoyed.

"Confusticate and bebother these dwarves!" he said aloud. "Why don't they come and lend a hand?" Lo and behold! there stood Balin and Dwalin at the door of the kitchen, and Fili and Kili behind them, and before he could say *knife* they had whisked the trays and a couple of small tables into the parlour and set out everything afresh.

Gandalf sat at the head of the party with the thirteen dwarves all round: and Bilbo sat on a stool at the fireside, nibbling at a biscuit (his appetite was quite taken away), and trying to look as if this was all perfectly ordinary and not in the least an adventure. The dwarves ate and ate, and talked and talked, and time got on. At last they pushed their chairs back, and Bilbo made a move to collect the plates and glasses.

"I suppose you will all stay to supper?" he said in his politest unpressing tones.

"Of course!" said Thorin. "And after. We shan't get through the business till late, and we must have some music first. Now to clear up!"

. . . .

That evening the dwarves sing a song of "long forgotten gold . . . in dungeons deep and caverns old." This is gold and other treasure that had belonged to their ancestors. It is treasure their ancestors died for when Smaug the dragon attacked. Only a few dwarves escaped to tell the story. One of those who escaped the dragon was Thorin's grandfather, who left a map and a key. Armed with the map and key, the thirteen dwarves hope to reclaim their treasure. That's where Bilbo comes in. Gandalf has told the dwarves that Bilbo is a "burglar." That is to say, he is an expert treasure hunter. Or at least he "will be when the time comes," Gandalf insists.

Bilbo has never thought of himself as either a burglar or a treasure hunter. At first, the very idea of a dangerous mission sends him into a fit and a faint. But then the Tookish side of his nature takes hold of him. His ancestor Bull-roarer Took had been a great fighter. And besides, Bilbo overhears the dwarves doubting his courage and ability. "He looks more like a grocer than a burglar!" they say.

That does it. "You think I am no good," says the injured Bilbo. "I will show you. Tell me what you want done and I will try it." And as Gandalf has known he would all along, Bilbo agrees to join the dwarves in their adventure.

"First I should like to know a bit more about things," said he, feeling all confused and a bit shaky inside, but so far still Tookishly determined to go on with things. "I mean about the gold and the dragon, and all that, and how it got there, and who it belongs to, and so on and further."

"Bless me!" said Thorin, "haven't you got a map? and didn't you hear our song? and haven't we been talking about all this for hours?"

"All the same, I should like it all plain and clear," said he obstinately, putting on his business manner (usually reserved for people who tried to borrow money off him), and doing his best to appear wise and prudent and professional and live up to Gandalf's recommendation. "Also I should like to know about risks, out-of-pocket expenses, time required and remuneration, and so forth"—by which he meant: "What am I going to get out of it? and am I going to come back alive?"

"O very well," said Thorin. "Long ago in my grandfather Thror's time our family was driven out of the far North, and came back with all their wealth and their tools to this Mountain on the map. It had been discovered by my far ancestor, Thrain the Old, but now they mined and they tunnelled and they made huger halls and greater work-shops—and in addition I believe they found a good deal of gold and a great many jewels too. Anyway they grew immensely rich and famous, and my grandfather was King under the Mountain again and treated with great reverence by the mortal men, who lived to the South, and were gradu-ally spreading up the Running River as far as the valley overshadowed by the Mountain. They built the merry town of Dale there in those days. Kings used to send for our smiths, and reward even the least skillful most richly. Fathers would beg us to take their sons as apprentices, and pay us handsomely, especially in food-supplies, which we never bothered to grow or find for ourselves. Altogether those were good days for us, and the poorest of us had money to spend and to lend, and leisure to make beautiful things just for the fun of it, not to speak of the most marvellous and magical toys, the like of which is not to be found in the world now-a-days. So my grandfather's halls became full of armour and jewels and carvings and cups, and the toymarket of Dale was the wonder of the North.

"Undoubtedly that was what brought the dragon. Dragons steal gold and jewels, you know, from men and elves and dwarves, wherever they can find them; and they guard their plunder as long as they live (which is practically forever, unless they are killed), and never enjoy a brass ring of it. Indeed they hardly know a good bit of work from a bad, though they usually have a good notion of the current market value; and they can't make a thing for themselves, not even mend a little loose scale of their armour. There were lots of dragons in the North in those days, and gold was probably getting scarce up there, with the dwarves flying south or getting killed, and all the general waste and destruction that dragons make going from bad to worse. There was a most specially greedy, strong and wicked worm called Smaug. One day he flew up into the air and came south. The first we heard of it was a noise like a hurricane coming from the North, and the pine-trees on the Mountain creaking and cracking in the wind. Some of the dwarves who happened to be outside (I was one luckily—a fine adventurous lad in those days, always wandering about, and it saved my life that day)—well, from a good way off we saw the dragon settle on our mountain in a spout of flame. Then he came down the slopes and when he reached the woods they all went up in fire. By that time all the bells were ringing in Dale and the warriors were arming. The dwarves rushed out of their great gate; but there was the dragon waiting for them. None escaped that way. The river rushed up in steam and a fog fell on Dale, and in the fog the dragon came on them and destroyed most of the

The Hobbit

warriors—the usual unhappy story, it was only too common in those days. Then he went back and crept in through the Front Gate and routed out all the halls, and lanes, and tunnels, alleys, cellars, mansions and passages. After that there were no dwarves left alive inside, and he took all their wealth for himself. Probably, for that is the dragons' way, he has piled it all up in a great heap far inside, and sleeps on it for a bed. Later he used to crawl out of the great gate and come by night to Dale, and carry away people, especially maidens, to eat, until Dale was ruined, and all the people dead or gone. What goes on there now I don't know for certain, but I don't suppose anyone lives nearer to the Mountain than the far edge of the Long Lake now-a-days.

"The few of us that were well outside sat and wept in hiding, and cursed Smaug; and there we were unexpectedly joined by my father and my grandfather with singed beards. They looked very grim but they said very little. When I asked how they had got away, they told me to hold my tongue, and said that one day in the proper time I should know. After that we went away, and we have had to earn our livings as best we could up and down the lands, often enough sinking as low as blacksmith-work or even coal-mining. But we have never forgotten our stolen treasure. And even now, when I will allow we have a good bit laid by and are not so badly off"—here Thorin stroked the gold chain round his neck—"we still mean to get it back, and to bring our curses home to Smaug—if we can.

"I have often wondered about my father's and my grandfather's escape. I see now they must have had a private Side-door which only they knew about. But apparently they made a map, and I should like to know how Gandalf got hold of it, and why it did not come down to me, the rightful heir."

"I did not 'get hold of it,' I was given it," said the wizard.

"Your grandfather Thror was killed, you remember, in the mines of Moria by Azog the Goblin—"

"Curse his name, yes," said Thorin.

"And Thrain your father went away on the twenty-first of April, a hundred years ago last Thursday, and has never been seen by you since—"

"True, true," said Thorin.

"Well, your father gave me this to give to you; and if I have chosen my own time and way of handing it over, you can hardly blame me, considering the trouble I had to find you. Your father could not remember his own name when he gave me the paper, and he never told me yours; so on the whole I think I ought to be praised and thanked. Here it is," said he handing the map to Thorin.

"I don't understand," said Thorin, and Bilbo felt he would have liked to say the same. The explanation did not seem to explain.

"Your grandfather," said the wizard slowly and grimly, "gave the map to his son for safety before he went to the mines of Moria. Your father went away to try his luck with the map after your grandfather was killed; and lots of adventures of a most unpleasant sort he had, but he never got near the Mountain. How he got there I don't know, but I found him a prisoner in the dungeons of the Necromancer."

"Whatever were you doing there?" asked Thorin with a shudder, and all the dwarves shivered.

"Never you mind. I was finding things out, as usual; and a nasty dangerous business it was. Even I, Gandalf, only just escaped. I tried to save your father, but it was too late. He was witless and wandering, and had forgotten almost everything except the map and the key."

"We have long ago paid the goblins of Moria," said Thorin; "we must give a thought to the Necromancer."

"Don't be absurd! He is an enemy quite beyond the powers of all the dwarves put together, if they could all be collected again from the four corners of the world. The one thing your father wished was for his son to read the map and use the key. The dragon and the Mountain are more than big enough tasks for you!"

"Hear, hear!" said Bilbo, and accidentally said it aloud.

"Hear what?" they all said turning suddenly towards him, and he was so flustered that he answered "Hear what I have got to say!"

"What's that?" they asked.

"Well, I should say that you ought to go East and have a look round. After all there is the Side-door, and dragons must sleep sometimes, I suppose. If you sit on the door-step long enough, I daresay you will think of something. And well, don't you know, I think we have talked long enough for one night, if you see what I mean. What about bed, and an early start, and all that? I will give you a good breakfast before you go."

"Before *we* go, I suppose you mean," said Thorin. "Aren't you the burglar? And isn't sitting on the door-step your job, not to speak of getting inside the door? But I agree about bed and breakfast. I like eggs with my ham, when starting on a journey: fried not poached, and mind you don't break 'em."

After all the others had ordered their breakfasts without so much as a please (which annoyed Bilbo very much), they all got up. The hobbit had to find room for them all, and filled all his spare-rooms and made beds on chairs and sofas, before he got them all stowed and went to his own little bed very tired and not altogether happy. One thing he did make his mind up about was not to bother to get up very early and cook everybody else's wretched breakfast. The Tookishness was wearing off, and he was not now quite so sure that he was going on any journey in the morning.

As he lay in bed he could hear Thorin still humming to himself in the best bedroom next to him:

> *Far over the misty mountains cold*
> *To dungeons deep and caverns old*
> *We must away, ere break of day,*
> *To find our long-forgotten gold.*

Bilbo went to sleep with that in his ears, and it gave him very uncomfortable dreams. It was long after the break of day, when he woke up.

Fantasy

"Ridiculous," you might say to yourself as you begin reading a fantasy. "Utterly fantastic." And so it is, in a way. A fantasy does not pretend to be real. In fact, it is aimed at being just the opposite. It may be full of characters who, though they may act like people, aren't people at all. It could be placed in a setting that is out of this world. It is like a daydream or a fairy tale where things happen that couldn't possibly occur outside the book.

Yet fantasy has a way of taking hold of your mind. What seems at first to be silly turns out to be interesting. As you read on, the fantasy grows on you little by little. You begin to take it seriously. You become involved with the fantastic characters and their problems. If the fantasy is well done, the fantasy world becomes as real to you as your own world. In the end you find yourself wanting to believe that the fantasy world in the story really exists—somewhere—if only you could find it. There is no Wonderland down a rabbit hole like the one that Alice found. Still, people have been talking about this fantasy world for more than a hundred years. And people so want to believe in the fantasy world of Walt Disney characters that they flock to Disneyland and Disney World by the millions year after year to see it come alive.

You are not likely to stumble upon the Shire where Bilbo Baggins lives. But that doesn't make the place any less real while you are reading the book or while you are thinking about it. A good fantasy persuades you to forget for a moment what is real and what is not. You stop worrying whether something is possible or impossible. Anything is possible within the world of the story. You just settle back and enjoy it.

J.R.R. Tolkien is one of the great masters of fantasy. His famous novel *The Hobbit* contains all the elements of a fantasy world. Most fantasies have four things in common:

1 They take place in an unreal world.

2 They present incredible or unreal characters.

3 They involve magic and the impossible.

4 They reflect or mirror some important aspect of our own world.

If there are going to be strange creatures or strange characters in a story,
they cannot be placed in the everyday
world. You know your backyard too
well to ever believe there could be dragons there. You would never be comfortable with the idea of a small man
with furry feet in your local supermarket.

But imagine the setting is another planet. Or perhaps it is your home-
town, but in the far distant future—or the far distant past. Or suppose it
is just "sometime" and "somewhere" and you are left to imagine when
and where it might be.

You could believe in little green men, for example, if they lived on
Mars. Or you could say, yes, there might have been dragons—somewhere at sometime. In cases like these, you believe in strange creatures
and strange places for the sake of the story. You believe because you
want to.

In *The Hobbit*, J.R.R. Tolkien created an entire fantasy world so that
his story would be believable. He made the creation of this world his first
order of business. Before you meet any of the characters or find out what
they are up to, you are introduced to their world.

> In a hole in the ground there lived a hobbit. Not a nasty,
> dirty, wet hole, filled with ends of worms and an oozy smell,
> nor yet a dry, bare, sandy hole with nothing in it to sit down
> on or to eat: it was a hobbit-hole, and that means comfort.
> It had a perfectly round door like a porthole, painted
> green, with a shiny yellow brass knob in the exact middle.
> The door opened on to a tube-shaped hall like a tunnel: a
> very comfortable tunnel without smoke, with panelled
> walls, and floors tiled and carpeted, provided with polished
> chairs, and lots of pegs for hats and coats—the hobbit was
> fond of visitors.

From reading the very first sentence, you can tell you are entering a
fantasy world. Something strange, a hobbit, lives in a hole in the
ground. But this is no ordinary animal's hole. Notice how the author
takes great pains to furnish this hole with familiar things. It is tiled and
panelled just as your home might be. It has furniture and coat pegs

because the hobbit likes visitors. He seems a likable middle-class gentle-man in a neat home. But you are still a little puzzled. What, after all, is a hobbit, and what is he doing in a hole in the ground?

The author's desire to help you imagine his fantasy world is very important here. He has helped you over your first disbelief by setting a scene that is not completely foreign to you. You believe in the fantasy world because the author makes it easy and fun to imagine it. You want to see what goes on in this strange place.

Exercise A

The passage below is from the selection you have read. Answer the questions about this passage using what you have learned in this part of the lesson. Choose the best answer for each question. Put an *x* in the correct box or fill in the appropriate words.

[Thorin is telling the story of lost gold.]

"Long ago in my grandfather Thror's time our family was driven out of the far North, and came back with all their wealth and their tools to this Mountain on the map. It had been discovered by my far ancestor, Thrain the Old, but now they mined and they tunnelled and they made huger halls and greater workshops—and in addition I believe they found a good deal of gold and a great many jewels too. Anyway they grew immensely rich and famous, and my grandfather was King under the Mountain again and treated with great reverence by the mortal men, who lived to the South. . . ."

    1. What makes the world described here fantastic?

        ☐ a. It has a king who is a grandfather.

        ☐ b. It is a rich underground kingdom.

        ☐ c. It is inhabited by ancestors.

        ☐ d. It is immensely rich and famous.

The Hobbit

2. The author provides details about the time and the place where this fantastic kingdom was. But these are details that leave much to your imagination. The time, for example, was "long ago." But when, exactly? In the space below, list two similarly vague details about the kingdom's location. (Use words from the passage.)

_____

_____

Now check your answers using the Answer Key on page 442. Correct any wrong answer and review this part of the lesson if you don't understand why your answer was wrong.

2 Fantasy — The Unreal Characters of Fantasy

Most of the characters in a fantasy are unreal. There are frequently ordinary humans about, but they are rarely as interesting as the fantasy characters. Alice in her famous Wonderland is a human character, but she is not nearly as much fun as the talking rabbits, the Cheshire Cat and the playing cards. R2-D2 and Darth Vader of *Star Wars* are much more popular than the ordinary human Luke Skywalker. There are mortals in *The Hobbit*, but they, too, play minor roles.

But in fantasy, even unusual or unreal characters are given some human traits to make them believable for you. The White Rabbit of *Alice in Wonderland* is always late. The Queen of hearts is a jealous old woman. And R2-D2 is a lovable, clever little fellow.

See how carefully Tolkien describes his hobbits.

> They are (or were) a little people, about half our height. . . .
> There is little or no magic about them, except the ordinary
> everyday sort which helps them to disappear quietly and
> quickly when large stupid folk like you and me come blun-
> dering along. . . . They are inclined to be fat in the stom-
> ach; they dress in bright colours . . . wear no shoes,
> because their feet grow natural leathery soles and thick
> warm brown hair like the stuff on their heads (which is
> curly); have long clever brown fingers, good-natured faces,
> and laugh deep fruity laughs (especially after dinner,
> which they have twice a day when they can get it).

Now you can easily imagine a hobbit even though one has never existed. Hobbits are paunchy because they eat too much. They have long, nimble fingers. And they have a distinctive sort of personality. They are good-natured and have a pleasant laugh. Perhaps you have an Uncle Julius who could be a hobbit—if he had leathery, hair-covered feet, that is. The author has described characters you can believe in, ones with a variety of human traits.

Notice one other way that the author tricks you into believing in the possibility of hobbits. For a moment, he places you in the world of his story. He says that hobbits have only the "ordinary everyday sort" of

The Hobbit

magic that lets them disappear when you come along. Briefly, you almost believe that there is an "ordinary everyday sort" of magic, and that the only reason you've never seen a hobbit is that they disappear—not because they don't exist.

Readers want to believe in a fantasy world and its fantasy characters. But the author still has to work hard to make these seem possible to you. Little by little, he brings your world and the fantasy world closer together.

Exercise B

The passage below is from the selection you have read. Answer the questions about this passage using what you have learned in this part of the lesson. Choose the best answer for each question. Put an *x* in the correct box or fill in the appropriate words.

Just before tea-time there came a tremendous ring on the front-door bell. . . . It was a dwarf with a blue beard tucked into a golden belt, and very bright eyes under his dark-green hood. As soon as the door was opened, he pushed inside, just as if he had been expected.

He hung his hooded cloak on the nearest peg, and "Dwalin at your service!" he said with a low bow.

"Bilbo Baggins at yours!" said the hobbit, too surprised to ask any questions for the moment. When the silence that followed had become uncomfortable, he added: "I am just about to take tea; pray come and have some with me." A little stiff perhaps, but he meant it kindly. And what would you do, if an uninvited dwarf came and hung his things up in your hall without a word of explanation?

1. Dwalin is a fantasy character. But what about him makes him seem human?

    ☐ a. His outfit

    ☐ b. His blue beard

    ☐ c. His name

    ☐ d. His pushy behavior

2. The author uses another trick here. He talks directly to readers and suggests you might have a dwarf drop in on you sometime. Write the sentence in which he does this.

_____

_____

_____

Now check your answers using the Answer Key on page 442. Correct any wrong answer and review this part of the lesson if you don't understand why your answer was wrong.

The world we live in behaves in a predictable way. Objects fall down, not up. People grow older, not younger. The wind blows and the sun shines. We are used to these things, and their occurrence does not surprise us.

By contrast, strange things may happen in a fantasy world. As you have seen, there may be strange creatures. People may have strange powers. Almost anything can happen. But before readers will accept something strange, they must be prepared for it. The ground rules must be laid down, so to speak. And once the author establishes the rules, they cannot be changed in the middle of the story.

Readers love magic in stories. But the author first has to set this up as a "rule" of the book. You have already noticed Tolkien's observation of the hobbits' "ordinary everyday" magical powers. Just this casual mention is enough to tell you that magic is part of this story.

Later in the story a magic ring will play a very important part. When it does, you are not at all disbelieving because passages like this early in the story tell you about other pieces of magic jewelry.

> "Gandalf ! Good gracious me! Not the wandering wizard that gave Old Took a pair of magic diamond studs that fastened themselves and never came undone till ordered? . . . Not the man that used to make such particularly excellent fireworks! I remember those! Old Took used to have them on Midsummer's Eve. Splendid! They used to go up like great lilies and snapdragons and laburnums of fire and hang in the twilight all evening! Dear me!" he went on. "Not the Gandalf who was responsible for so many quiet lads and lasses going off into the Blue for mad adventures. . . ."

In this excited conversation with Gandalf, many "rules" for this fantasy are laid down. You are shown that wizards are part of this world. Later, when a sorcerer is mentioned, you will be ready to accept that, too. The wizard, you are told, can make fireworks. When he does that later, you will accept it as natural in this world. And there are magic cuff links, why not a magic ring? These are the rules of the game you are playing with the author. And it's the author's job to let you know what they are.

Exercise C

". . . Dragons steal gold and jewels, you know, from men and elves and dwarves, wherever they can find them; and they guard their plunder as long as they live (which is practically forever, unless they are killed). . . . There was a most specially greedy, strong and wicked worm named Smaug. One day he flew up into the air and came south. The first we heard of it was a noise like a hurricane coming from the North. . . . we saw the dragon settle on our mountain in a spout of flame. Then he came down the slopes and when he reached the woods they all went up in fire. . . ."

1. Which of the unreal things below does the existence of an evil, flying dragon prepare you to accept?

   ☐ a. Eagles friendly to Bilbo and the dwarves

   ☐ b. The arrival of a spaceship

   ☐ c. A world where objects fall up

   ☐ d. Stones with magical powers

2. There is a fierce battle with the dragon later in the novel. The dragon will fight like an airborne flamethrower. Write down two of the clues in this passage which prepare you for this. (Use words from the passage.)

   _____

   _____

So far you have seen how fantasy is different from other kinds of stories. The setting is unreal, the characters are strange and the action is impossible or magical. But one more quality separates excellent fantasies, those that last many generations, from

those that are not so enduring. The best fantasies speak to you about your own life. Even though they are set in fantasy worlds, they tell you about the world we all inhabit. To put it another way, our own world is mirrored or reflected in the fantasy world. This is what author Lewis Carroll had in mind when, in naming the sequel to *Alice in Wonderland*, he chose the title *Through the Looking Glass*.

Fantasy does not, however, mirror our world in the usual way. The fantasy world and the real world do not seem exactly alike. Rather, like a mirror in a fun house, fantasy reflects a distorted image of our world. But when you look twice in the strange looking glass of fantasy, you can see a situation that could occur in real life. At first *The Hobbit* seems nothing more than a fantastic entertainment. But look again. The author is using his fantasy world to say something about real life.

An injustice has been done. An evil and greedy individual has seized wealth that is not his own. He doesn't use the wealth for any good purpose. He just sits on it and enjoys the greedy pleasure of having it. What is worse, he destroys the country around him. No doubt you can name a few greedy and evil powers in the real world who do much the same thing.

A group bands together to try to recover what has been taken from it. On the sidelines is Bilbo Baggins. He is very self-satisfied and content to let the evil of the world alone as long as it doesn't bother him. He won't do anything that makes him late for dinner. But along comes a wizard who shakes Bilbo from his unconcern. Bilbo decides to join the crusade against the evil in the world.

Knowing what you do about the dwarves and their problem with the dragon, can you see something of what was just described "mirrored" in this passage?

> Then Bilbo sat down on a seat by his door, crossed his legs, and blew out a beautiful grey ring of smoke that sailed up

into the air without breaking and floated away over The Hill.

"Very pretty!" said Gandalf. "But I have no time to blow smoke-rings this morning. I am looking for someone to share in an adventure that I am arranging, and it's very difficult to find anyone."

"I should think so—in these parts! We are plain quiet folk and have no use for adventures. Nasty disturbing uncomfortable things! Make you late for dinner! I can't think what anybody sees in them," said our Mr. Baggins, and stuck one thumb behind his braces [suspenders], and blew out another even bigger smoke-ring.

Bilbo is complacent and self-satisfied. He enjoys his comfortable home and his easy life a great deal—perhaps too much. He has no use for "nasty disturbing uncomfortable things," especially if they "make you late for dinner." You probably laughed at Bilbo here. He seems stuffy.

For all Bilbo knows, there may be great evil in the world. But he is content to let someone else tend to such matters. He doesn't want even to hear about it. And, says this mirror in the fantasy world, that's just the way most of you out there are. You would rather blow smoke rings (or sit home and watch TV) than get out and do some good in the world. The wizards of the world have a very difficult time finding anyone willing to share in an adventure.

Exercise D

The passage below is from the selection you have read. Answer the questions about this passage using what you have learned in this part of the lesson. Choose the best answer for each question. Put an *x* in the correct box or fill in the appropriate words.

"All the same, I should like it all plain and clear," said he [Bilbo] obstinately, putting on his business manner (usually reserved for people who tried to borrow money off him), and doing his best to appear wise and prudent and professional and live up to Gandalf's recommendation. "Also, I should like to know about risks, out-of-pocket expenses, time required and remuneration, and so forth"—by which he meant: "What am I going to get out of it? and am I going to come back alive?"

1. When we have mixed feelings about doing something, we often behave as Bilbo does. How does he act?

   ☐ a. Eager

   ☐ b. Hostile

   ☐ c. Frightened

   ☐ d. Businesslike

2. When we think selfishly about doing work for a good cause, we may privately ask ourselves selfish questions. What is the selfish question that Bilbo asks?

   _____

   _____

Use the Answer Key on page 442 to check your answers. Correct any wrong answer and review this part of the lesson if you don't understand why your answer was wrong. Now go on to do the Comprehension Questions.

Comprehension Questions

Answer these questions without looking back at the selection. Choose the best answer to each question and put an *x* in the box beside it.

Recalling
Facts

1. Which of these are hobbits fond of?

   ☐ a. Food and visitors

   ☐ b. Mystery and adventure

   ☐ c. Work and exercise

   ☐ d. Business and profits

Making
Inferences

2. The author says hobbits disappear quietly and quickly when large, stupid folk like you and me come along. When he says this, the author is explaining why

   ☐ a. hobbits hate humans.

   ☐ b. we will never see a hobbit.

   ☐ c. Gandalf will have a hard time finding a hobbit.

   ☐ d. hobbits never make much noise.

Understanding
Main Ideas

3. Which one of the following titles hints at what the story is about?

   ☐ a. *A Tale of a Lonesome Dragon*

   ☐ b. *The Fourteen Wizards*

   ☐ c. *The Unenthusiastic Adventurer*

   ☐ d. *A Hobbit in Search of Battle*

4. When did the dwarves begin to arrive at Bilbo's home?

□ a. Six days after Gandalf's visit

□ b. Just before tea-time on Wednesday

□ c. During breakfast on Tuesday

□ d. Right after Gandalf's visit

5. When did Gandalf get possession of the map?

□ a. After Thrain had been captured by the Necromancer

□ b. During Smaug's raid on the mountain

□ c. After he spoke with Bilbo the first time

□ d. Before Thror went to the mines of Moria

6. To what kind of person in our society could you compare Gandalf?

□ a. A social leader who makes things happen.

□ b. A troublemaker who should know better.

□ c. A soldier of fortune who goes looking for wars.

□ d. An old busybody who can't leave well enough alone.

7. Gandalf scratched a sign on the hobbit's door. What was it for?

□ a. It was a good luck symbol.

□ b. It had something to do with magic.

□ c. It was to remind Gandalf where Bilbo Baggins lived.

□ d. It was probably a signal for the dwarves.

8. When Gandalf left, Bilbo Baggins was too *flustered* to make a note on his engagement tablet. In other words, he was

☐ a. happy and excited.

☐ b. quite frightened by what had happened.

☐ c. in a state of nervous confusion.

☐ d. anxiously awaiting coming events.

9. Dwalin and Balin arrived and said, "Let us join the *throng*!" A *throng* is a

☐ a. crowd.

☐ b. party.

☐ c. meeting.

☐ d. celebration.

10. Who was the leader of the group of dwarves?

☐ a. Dwalin

☐ b. Balin

☐ c. Thorin

☐ d. Bombur

11. The King under the Mountain was "treated with great *reverence* by the mortal men." This means they treated him with great

☐ a. fear and suspicion.

☐ b. respect.

☐ c. hostility.

☐ d. good cheer and affection.

The Hobbit

12. What did the dwarves do for a living?

☐ a. They were millers and bakers.

☐ b. They were smiths and miners.

☐ c. They were wizards and magicians.

☐ d. They were traders and shopkeepers.

13. Both the dwarves and the dragons were wealthy. What was the difference in their attitudes towards wealth?

☐ a. The dragons were thrifty; the dwarves spent freely.

☐ b. The dragons earned their wealth; the dwarves inherited theirs.

☐ c. The dwarves used their wealth; the dragons hoarded theirs.

☐ d. The dwarves kept trying to increase their wealth; the dragons were careless about theirs.

14. Which happened first?

☐ a. Smaug flew down from the North.

☐ b. The dwarves became very rich.

☐ c. Gandalf was given the map.

☐ d. Thrain the Old discovered the Mountain.

15. One of the events told about in the chapter gives a clue to how old Gandalf and Thorin are. They are both

☐ a. about seventy.

☐ b. fifty years old.

☐ c. more than a hundred.

☐ d. quite young, actually.

Now check your answers using the Answer Key on page 442. Correct any wrong answers you have by putting a check (✓) in the box next to the right answer. Count the number of questions you answered correctly and plot the total on the Comprehension Scores graph on page 444.

Next, look at the questions you answered incorrectly. What types of questions were they? Count the number of each type and enter the numbers in the spaces below:

Recognizing Words in Context   _____

Recalling Facts   _____

Keeping Events in Order   _____

Making Inferences   _____

Understanding Main Ideas   _____

Now use these numbers to fill in the Comprehension Skills Profile on page 445.

Discussion Guides

The questions below will help you to think about the selection and the lesson you have just read. If you don't discuss these questions in class, try to think about them or discuss them with your classmates.

Discussing Fantasy

1. Review the names of characters in the story. How do these names add to the sense of fantasy? Why didn't Tolkien call some of them Bob, David or Michael?

2. A story has to happen at a particular time and place. How does the author seem to tell you the time and place without really giving any details? (Reread the beginning of the chapter to find examples.)

3. Things in fantasy are often a mixture of what is real and what is unreal. What is real and what is unreal about: the hobbit's house; Gandalf's clothing; the dwarves; Smaug and the mountain where he lives?

Discussing the Story

4. Who can you name from real life who is like Gandalf? Give reasons for your ideas.

5. Who or what in real society might be like Smaug? (What familiar word sounds the same as Smaug?)

6. In what ways do you consider yourself like Bilbo Baggins? How are you not like him?

Discussing the Author's Work

7. This is an adventure story, but Tolkien has mixed in a good bit of humor. What did you find humorous in the chapter?

8. The dwarves could all have arrived together at one time. What did the author accomplish by having them come in small groups of two and three?

9. If you had to pick somewhere in the world where the story takes place, you would have to say England. J.R.R. Tolkien was English. What in the story makes it sound more English than American?

Writing Exercise

Characters in a fantasy are often based on real people. Think of some-one you know—from your family, your neighborhood or your school—who is like one of the characters in *The Hobbit*. Write a 150-word essay describing that person and explaining why he or she is like the charac-ter in *The Hobbit*.

Answer Key

Answer Key

Unit 1: **Julie of the Wolves**

Setting

Exercise A
1. b
2.a. cliffs; a rock
  b. parka

Exercise B
1. c
2. shaman (priestess or "bent woman"); a fiery spirit

Exercise C
1. a
2. He would hail the blue sky and shout out his praise for the grasses and bushes.

Exercise D
1. d
2. from Aunt Martha's house to the beach by the sea (Remember that Aunt Martha's house represents the new Eskimo ways and the world of white people, while the beach and the sea represent the world Miyax shared with Kapugen.)

Comprehension Questions

1. a
2. c
3. a
4. b
5. d

6. b
7. c
8. a
9. d
10. c

11. a
12. b
13. c
14. d
15. b

Unit 2: **Summer of My German Soldier**

Character ———————————————————

Exercise A
1. b
2. Fearless Freddy, brave hunter of crawdads.

Exercise B
1. d
2. "You may not know this, but you and Anton are all the friends I've got."

Exercise C
1. d
2. The words seemed to dash out.

Exercise D
1. a
2. cruelty

Comprehension Questions ———————————————————

1. a
2. a
3. b
4. d
5. c

6. b
7. a
8. d
9. d
10. b

11. c
12. a
13. c
14. c
15. d

Unit 3: A Day No Pigs Would Die

How Authors Use Language

Exercise A
1. c
2. "I don't cotton to raise a fool."

Exercise C
1. c
2. like a big clean apron;
   like a cork in a bottle;
   as wrong as sin on Sunday

Exercise B
1. b
2. like stale death;
   like the big brown bar of soap;
   like hard work

Exercise D
1. a
2. we tore up a good part of Vermont

Comprehension Questions

1. b
2. c
3. a
4. d
5. c

6. a
7. b
8. c
9. a
10. b

11. a
12. c
13. c
14. a
15. c

Unit 4: **To Kill a Mockingbird**

Tone and Mood

Exercise A
1. a
2. "What is it, Heck?"

Exercise B
1. b
2. the scurrying going on; teeming with people; crowded around; Mrs. Merriweather galloped to me

Exercise C
1. d
2. he had never lost our friendship

Exercise D
1. a
2. the wind rustling in the trees; shuffled and dragged his feet; the soft swish of cotton on cotton; wheek, wheek; his trousers swished softly

Comprehension Questions

1. a
2. c
3. b
4. c
5. a

6. b
7. b
8. a
9. b
10. c

11. b
12. d
13. d
14. c
15. a

Unit 5: **Of Mice and Men**

Conflict

Exercise A

1. c

2. "I could get along so easy and so nice . . ."

Exercise B

1. b

2. "Nuts! . . . I ain't got time for no more."

Exercise C

1. d

2. "Aw, Lennie!"

Exercise D

1. b

2. "First chance I get I'll give you a pup."

Comprehension Questions

1. b
2. a
3. c
4. b
5. a

6. c
7. d
8. c
9. a
10. b

11. a
12. d
13. b
14. c
15. a

Unit 6: **Mom, the Wolf Man and Me**

Theme _____

Exercise A
1. b
2. The doorman asks everyone who comes up who they are and that makes a lot of people nervous. He even asks people who've been there before.

Exercise B
1. a
2. I felt funny then. I guess I wanted her to be like Andrew's mother

Exercise C
1. c
2. Unlike me, she really cares if she's the only one doing something a certain way.

Exercise D
1. a
2. She'd give anything to have a father.

Comprehension Questions _____

1. c
2. d
3. a
4. d
5. b

6. b
7. a
8. c
9. b
10. c

11. c
12. d
13. b
14. a
15. a

Unit 7: **A Separate Peace**

Symbolism

Exercise A
1. b

2. fear

Exercise B

1. d
2. "It's you, pal," Finny said to me at last, "just you and me."

Exercise C

1. c

2. We struggled in some equality for a while . . . .

Exercise D
1. a

2. thankful

Comprehension Questions

1. b	6. a	11. d
2. c	7. d	12. a
3. c	8. c	13. b
4. b	9. b	14. d
5. a	10. d	15. a

Unit 8: **Anne Frank: The Diary of a Young Girl**

Autobiography and Biography

Exercise A
1. b
2. No Jew in our situation would have dreamed of going out with a suitcase full of clothing; the gaudy yellow star spoke for itself

Exercise B
1. d
2. jealous; great longing; ungrateful

Exercise C
1. b
2. Now I understand more

Exercise D
1. d
2. cheerful; hopeful

Comprehension Questions

1. c
2. c
3. c
4. a
5. a
6. c
7. d
8. c
9. b
10. b
11. a
12. d
13. b
14. a
15. c

Best-Selling Chapters

Unit 9: **Johnny Tremain**

The Historical Novel

Exercise A
1. b
2. He was ready to run wherever sent, find out any fact for them.

Exercise B
1. d
2.a. chimney sweep; oysterman; knife-grinder
   b. Sons of Liberty
   c. fire alarm; call to meeting; announce deaths; celebrate good news; tell of bad news

Exercise C
1. a
2. Rebels. ("Villains" is also an acceptable answer.)

Exercise D
1. a
2. Oh, Rab, Rab! Have you ever seen those little eyes at the end of a musket? Rab, don't you go.

Comprehension Questions

1. d
2. b
3. c
4. b
5. c
6. c
7. a
8. d
9. c
10. a
11. c
12. a
13. d
14. d
15. a

Unit 10: **The Hobbit**

Fantasy

Exercise A
1. b
2. "The far North"; "this Mountain on the map"; "King under the Mountain"; "mortal men . . . to the South"

Exercise B
1. d
2. And what would you do, if an uninvited dwarf came and hung his things up in your hall without a word of explanation?

Exercise C
1. a
2. "he flew up into the air"; "settle . . . in a spout of flame"; "the woods . . . all went up in fire"

Exercise D
1. d
2. "What am I going to get out of it?"

Comprehension Questions

1. a	6. a	11. b
2. b	7. d	12. b
3. c	8. c	13. c
4. b	9. a	14. d
5. a	10. c	15. c

Comprehension Scores Graph
&
Comprehension Skills Profile

Comprehension Scores

Use this graph to plot your comprehension scores. At the top of the graph, find the name of the chapter you just read. Follow the line beneath it down until it crosses the line for the number of questions you got right. Put an *x* where the lines cross. Connect the *x*'s to form a graph of your comprehension. The numbers on the right side of the graph show your comprehension score.

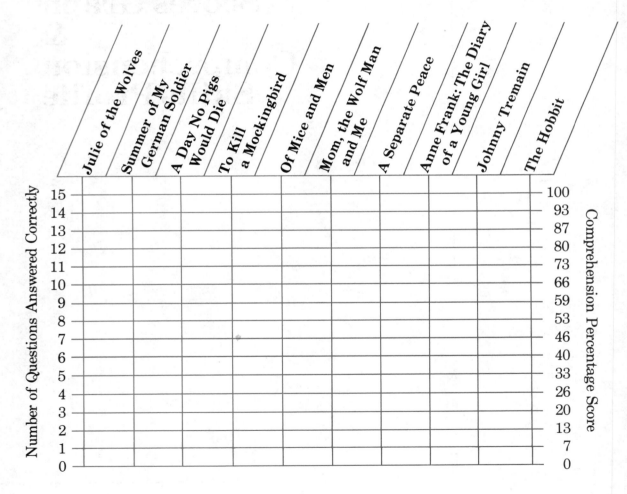

Best-Selling Chapters

Comprehension Skills Profile

Use this profile to see which comprehension skills you need to work on. Moving from left to right, fill in one block for each question of a particular type you get wrong. When you have finished all ten units in this book, look for the rows that have the most blocks filled in. This will show you which kinds of questions give you trouble. Your teacher may want to give you extra help with these skills.

Recognizing Words in Context																											

Recalling Facts																											

Keeping Events in Order																											

Making Inferences																											

Understanding Main Ideas																											

Bibliography

Forbes, Esther. *Johnny Tremain.* Boston: Houghton Mifflin Company, 1943.

Frank, Anne. *Anne Frank: The Diary of a Young Girl,* ed. Otto Frank. New York: Doubleday & Company, 1967. First published in Amsterdam, Holland, 1947.

George, Jean Craighead. *Julie of the Wolves.* New York: Harper and Row, 1972.

Greene, Bette. *Summer of My German Soldier.* New York: The Dial Press, 1973.

Klein, Norma. *Mom, the Wolf Man and Me.* New York: Pantheon Books, 1972.

Knowles, John. *A Separate Peace.* New York: Macmillan Publishing Company, 1959.

Lee, Harper. *To Kill a Mockingbird.* New York: J.B. Lippincott Company, 1960.

Peck, Robert Newton. *A Day No Pigs Would Die.* New York: Alfred A. Knopf, Inc., 1972.

Steinbeck, John. *Of Mice and Men.* New York: Viking Penguin, Inc., 1937.

Tolkien, J.R.R. *The Hobbit.* Houghton Mifflin Company, 1966.